THE TRANSFORMATION OF MANAGEMENT

The Transformation of Management

Mike Davidson

Butterworth-Heinemann
Boston Oxford Melbourne Singapore Toronto Munich New Delhi Tokyo

Butterworth-Heinemann

 A member of the Reed Elsevier group

Copyright © 1996 by Mike Davidson

Library of Congress Cataloging-in-Publication Data

Davidson, Mike
    The transformation of management / Mike Davidson.
        p.   cm.
    Includes bibliographical references and index.
    ISBN 0-7506-9774-1
    1. Management.   2. Strategic planning.   I. Title.
    HD31.T247   1995
    658.4—dc20   95-25906
                                        CIP

British Library Cataloguing-in-Publication Data
A catalogue record for this book is available from the British Library.

The publisher offers discounts on bulk orders of this book.
For information, please write:

Manager of Special Sales
Butterworth–Heinemann
313 Washington Street
Newton, MA 02158–1626

10 9 8 7 6 5 4 3 2 1

Printed in the United States of America

To Carol, Claire, Simon, Gail and James

Contents

List of Figures

List of Tables

Acknowledgements

The author and publishers wish to thank the following for permission to reproduce the following material:

Simon & Schuster Inc., for Figure 1.3, from Richard Tanner Pascale, *Managing on the Edge* (1991). © 1990 by Richard Pacale.

The Free Press, a Division of Simon & Schuster Inc., for Figure 3.3, from Michael Porter, *Competitive Advantage: Creating and Sustaining Superior Performance*. © 1985 by Michael Porter.

Fortune, for Figure 3.6, the cover story graphic from the December 27, 1982 issue.

Johnson & Johnson, for the Credo quoted in Figure 3.8.

McGraw-Hill, for Figure 3.11, the cover story graphic from the November 5, 1984 issue of *BusinessWeek*. © 1994 by The McGraw-Hill Companies.

Kathy Hudson, for the extract from the Eastman Kodak documentation on future planning (1989).

Villard Books, New York, for Figure 8.8, from Daryl Connor, *Managing at the Speed of Change* (1993). © 1993 by Daryl R. Connor. Reprinted by permission of Villard Books, a Division of Random House, Inc.

Every effort has been made to contact all the copyright-holders, but if any have been inadvertently omitted the publishers will be pleased to make the necessary arrangement at the earliest opportunity.

Introduction

"I firmly believe that any organization in order to survive and achieve success, must have a sound set of beliefs on which it premises all its policies and actions. Next, I believe that the most important single factor in corporate success is faithful adherence to those beliefs. And, finally, I believe if an organization is to meet the challenge of a changing world, it must be prepared to change everything about itself except those beliefs as it moves through corporate life."

(Thomas Watson, Jr.)

"Fools say they learn by experience. I prefer to learn from others' experience."

(Bismarck)

"Fortune favors the brave." (Terence)

There *are* some rules that govern the interaction of competitors, the evolution of complex systems and the behavior of human beings in organizations.

That they are sometimes soft, often derived through observation, usually followed more by instinct than conscious design, and never wholly deterministic for any given situation does not mean we cannot base our actions on them. Indeed it means the opposite. The whole purpose of strategic management is to have the courage so to do, and thereby to beat not just competition but evolution itself.

However to do so means using our heads as well as our hearts, pitting others' experience against our hope, and dealing with reality as it is, not as we wish it were. Such is life for those who would lead.

This book is for leaders – busy leaders. Busy because they are having to deal with the pace of change and intensity of competition that has been thrust upon us in the last ten years. Busy because they are trying to transform their organizations so as to win in this new, hyperactive world. And, all too many of them, busy because they are frantically searching for ways to maintain the competitive health of their organizations.

1

So this is not a long book. The anecdotes are brief and there to illustrate, not just to entertain. The histories, except one, are left out. And lengthy justification of its ideas is left to others. But it should help. For its lessons are not from theory, but from practice. Its insights are from the school of hard knocks. It invites you to learn, like Bismarck, from others' experience. And thereby, in due course, learn more from a whole new set of mistakes, so that eventually we can tame this beast of change, and harness it to our purposes of building an ever newer and better world. Let's start by defining the concept that is the heart of this book and, I hope to persuade you, the key to sustained competitive success – grand strategy.

We live in difficult times. For most of the working lives of most people who pick up this book most large organizations haven't worked very well. Moreover, in most of those organizations, most of the people haven't been very happy much of the time. Yet, by way of contrast, it is a common observation that the opposite – successful organizations and happy people – tend to go together most of the time. Many of us would sadly claim that there were considerably more of those successful organizations run by happy people when we started working than there are today. So what's gone wrong? What are the reasons? Are we worse managers than our parents? Have organizations changed? Or people? Or both? Has the task somehow become more difficult, and the techniques not kept up?

Most important of all, is there any reason to hope for a renaissance of management that can create a better world? That is a situation where the rule, and not the exception, is successful organizations run by happy people; where the goals of organizations inspire passion and not cynicism; where management is more about exploiting opportunities than solving problems; where leaders coach and counsel rather than command and control; and where we know how to sustain these characteristics in the face of intensive competition and wrenching change, so that future generations do not have to repeat the pain and suffering being experienced throughout the world of organizations today.

The thesis of this book is that there *are* reasons why we live in difficult times, that there *is* hope of a management renaissance, and, more than hope, that there is a discipline – grand strategy – to bring it about. Grand strategy is therefore about the transformation of management itself. Its purpose is to find a superior way of managing – the ultimate competitive advantage, and the only competitive advantage that can survive the kind of unpredictable and accelerating change of the era in which we live. In this introduction we will explore the scope of grand strategy and some of the themes of this book as a way of introducing the more detailed exploration of where it comes from, what it is and how to use it that follows. We begin with its ultimate aim – successful organizations and happy people.

What are successful organizations? I suggest that, in the business world, they have three characteristics:

- they are more profitable than their competitors
- they are growing faster than their competitors, and
- they are recognized as leaders of at least some part of their industries.

And, in a workplace context, what are happy people? I suggest they too have three main characteristics:

- they feel they have significant control over their own lives
- they feel they are respected for the contribution they make, and
- they feel they are contributing to something worth doing.

My personal mission, these last ten years, has been to help organizations try to bring these conditions about, in the belief that these things do indeed go together, for some very good, mutually supporting reasons. What I have tried to do is help leaders and the leadership teams of organizations find ways of managing, suited to their specific, strategic circumstances, that create what the system engineers call a positive feedback loop between these two sets of conditions – more of the one leading to more of the other, and so on – a mutually reinforcing relationship that leads to more successful organizations, and happier people, at one and the same time. This I have come to believe is as good a way of defining the challenge of leadership as there is. And it is the challenge of leadership – or more precisely competitive leadership – that has always fascinated me, and that in the final analysis this book is about. Let me use a little bit of personal history to introduce the subject.

In the Spring of 1984, just before I established my consulting practice, I was attending an executive conference in Boston. One evening we had dinner at the Kennedy Library. My wife and I watched the extraordinary film about his life that they show there. In fact it so transported us back to that earlier era that when we emerged from the darkness of the auditorium both of us momentarily forgot where we were and why. Then we wandered the halls reading some of the notes he had made himself during the Cuban missile crisis, and they took me back 22 years to the crisis itself.

In the Fall of 1962 the Cuban missile crisis had come along at just the right moment to save my hide! I was in my last term at Clifton – what the British call a Public School, and the Americans a Private, or Prep School – due to make a presentation to my history class about a major twentieth century event. Two days before the class I hadn't even thought of anything to talk about, nor had I any interest in doing the research, or preparing a presentation. My mind was totally absorbed by the scholarship examination in mathematics I was to take a month later.

Then out of the blue came the missile crisis. All I had to do was put up a map, make some vague comments about the unacceptability to the US of having some missiles pointed at it from an island a few miles south of Miami, observe that the US was already doing much the same thing to the USSR from its bases in Turkey, and open the floor to debate. My history teacher knew exactly what I'd done, or rather hadn't done, but there wasn't much he could do about it. It was the liveliest debate of the term! Another bullet dodged, back to mathematics, roll on Cambridge.

But I remember that, as the discussion heated up all those years ago, I found myself thinking not so much about the crisis as about President Kennedy:

What was it like to be in the job where the proverbial buck stops?
What goes on in your mind when you are considering the decisions only you can make?
What kind of decisions are those?
Which are the most difficult ones? And, why?
Which are the ones that matter most? and . . .
How do you make sure they get implemented as you intended?

I then went up to Cambridge to read Mathematics and attended the courses, and took the examinations on that subject. But, before long, I found myself spending most of my time reading history books, in particular ones about the struggle between nations since, as I said, it was the challenge of leadership in the presence of competition that really intrigued me, and war seemed to me the most intensive form of competition I could imagine.

Twenty-two years later, in 1984, I was still fascinated by the same topic – the lonely job of the guy, or gal, at the top, behind the desk where the buck has just stopped; the challenge of the leader at his or her loneliest, when the chips are down and it is time for the hard choices. So I started a business with a brochure that said on the front "A cure for top management loneliness", to help leaders of organizations deal with their unique jobs, as they tried to make their organizations more successful and happier places to work.

Now, what is this job? And, what are its distinctive challenges? It turns out they are quite timeless. They've always been the same. And they are the same for every organization. Let's go back to the very first, human organizations of all, several million years ago. What were they? Family groupings, and hunting parties, which formed the hunter/gatherer societies that were the birthplace of human civilization. The modern business organization is in direct line of descent from those hunting parties – co-operative ventures trying to ensure that they and the people who depend on them enjoy a greater share of the world's resources than rival enterprises. So let's use the hunting party, within an early human society, to explore the roots of the timeless challenges of leadership.

The primitive hunting party, like every team and organization ever since, faced two immediate challenges:

1. How was it going to deal with a hostile environment of animals and rival hunting parties so as to provide a superior source of food for itself and its dependents, and . . .
2. How was it going to organize its members to do that, and then to share the results in such a way they would be happy to continue the partnership?

The first challenge deals with competition in the world external to an organization, and poses the problem of strategy. The second deals with performance in its internal world, and poses the problem of integration. The hunting parties that thrived were those best able to devise solutions to these two problems. Then, over time, as conditions changed, as the most successful combinations of hunting parties and family groups grew in size because of their very success, as new tools were invented and new, more sophisticated methods of hunting and fending off rival groupings were developed, those burgeoning mini-civilizations faced a third challenge – how to cope with change. Evolution had done it for them in the past, but evolution itself implied a huge advantage to a group whose members were able to take advantage of or, even more advantageous, shape change better than their rivals. So was added a third challenge to the list that all organizations share:

3. How was it going to deal with changes in either or both of its external or internal environments, and so cope with the need to change its methods of strategy and/or its means of integration?

In reality every organization also faces a fourth, common challenge, which we didn't stop to notice because it was self-evident in the very name of these earliest and simplest examples – families and hunting parties. Why does an organization exist? What are its purposes? What is it in business for at all? And this we call the challenge of mission.

So the four, fundamental challenges faced by all organizations are

Mission   Competition   Performance   Change

These four words are the 'what' of grand strategy and so introduce the chapter headings of Part II of this book – Prescription. Now what about the leaders of those early, human organizations – first the hunting parties, and then the tribes that naturally followed them into existence as the advantages of combining them with their associated family groupings made such 'societies' the most successful? Where did they come from? How did they emerge?

Initially I imagine it was just brute strength – the strongest took charge of both the hunting and the dividing of the spoils thereafter. But, gradually, as those hunting parties and their associated societies grew, the cloak of leadership must have shifted to those who could best provide answers to the increasingly more complicated problems the groups faced. And just like it works in the modern equivalent of a new hunting party – the entrepreneurially led, start-up venture – the answers that worked conferred great prestige on their sources. Then, if they went on working, these answers became the conventional wisdom of the group, and so the foundation of the cultures of those primitive, little civilizations.

The leaders were the source of that wisdom, the providers of answers to the major problems the groups faced: How to deal with competition, whether animal or human, how to get the desired results, and how to cope with change. Finally the leaders personified the purpose, or mission of the group in their very being, because they had been the initiators of the actions that had led to survival and success. So the match between the group's most urgent needs and the primary skills of potential leaders determined who rose to the fore – the great hunters when the primary mission was hunting, the great warriors when the main threat was from other tribes, the elders when the need was for solutions to the problems of living together, and the witch-doctors when they had to deal with things beyond their understanding altogether – and, if they were successful for long enough, the kind of society that then evolved was built in their image. In the light of which, the reasons why early societies often regarded their leaders as gods is perhaps not so hard to understand.

Organizational leadership then is about finding the wisdom and courage to make the choices that are entailed in answering these four, great questions:

1. Mission: what are we trying to accomplish?
2. Competition: how do we get a competitive edge?
3. Performance: how do we deliver the results?
4. Change: how do we cope with change?

Grand strategy is simply the name that we give to the all-encompassing discipline that it entails. So grand strategy is an agenda for leadership, not a recipe for management. It is an agenda with four components but only one aim; and that aim is to find and keep vital the ultimate competitive advantage – a superior way of running the organization that ensures mutually supporting solutions to all four challenges, all of the time, so that everything is done, and every operating decision is made in a pre-eminently strategic frame of mind. Thus, as shall see, 'strategic management', that much overused and abused term, is simply operational management driven by a deliberately chosen, explicitly articulated and comprehensively institutionalized grand strategy, as opposed to being a collection of responses to the tactical exigencies of the moment.

Grand strategy thus ensures that we not only win today by beating our current competitors, but also that we go on winning tomorrow by beating evolution itself. It finally brings to the world of organizations what man has long struggled to bring to nature – the ability to manage change instead of change managing us. It has almost become a cliché that the central managerial task of our times is the management of change. Grand strategy is the discipline we need to bring about the transformation of management that will enable us to do so. In Part II we will explore each of its components in depth, and suggest some ways to use them.

But before we get to prescription we need to tackle diagnosis, which we will do in Part I. After all, why should you care? Why does this matter? What does it have to do with the malaise that seems to have affected so many of our once mighty organizations? And even if it can help, why isn't this just a subject for the tiny number of people who lead the major institutions of our society? What relevance does it have to anybody below the very top? Well, I think you should care very deeply, first as an individual, second as a member of whatever kind of team you play on, and third as a world citizen struggling to make sense of the times in which we live.

First, there is a part of every job where the buck stops right there. And in that piece of your job you need the insights of grand strategy. All of us face these four great questions. They are inherent certainly to every management position, and increasingly to every other job in the decentralized, task-oriented, knowledge-worker world that is emerging as the twentieth century draws to a close. Without a clear, integrating, grand strategy your actions are bound to be fragmented at best, and at odds with each other at worst. In less competitive, more stable times maybe it didn't matter as much, but today it has become a condition for survival, let alone success.

Second, in the complex, interdependent system that is the modern organization we all need to be aware of our organization's grand strategy, so that we can play our role and help others play theirs. Even if we don't make the ultimate decisions, we certainly play a part in getting them made for our immediate unit and increasingly, as various forms of participative management are more and more widely adopted, for our whole organizations.

Finally, in every age man wants to believe that there is something special about this particular time, that it is an important moment in history, and that there is an opportunity to be part of some great event or movement which will leave its imprint on the history of the human race. For at least the last two thousand years you can make a good argument that pretty much everyone has been able to say that. Something important, something special has been going on in every age. Maybe that's true by definition – being man's response to, or attempt at exploiting the change that never ceases in our world, in our ideas about it and in our capabilities for dealing with it. Maybe the real challenge is not so much to try to figure out how to make our time special, but to find what's special about our time, so that we can contribute to it, gain the most from it and above all learn to manage it so that it doesn't manage us.

What's special about our age is, I think, becoming pretty clear and, economically, there are two parts to it. First we are moving into a genuinely new economic era. This is a discontinuous change that has taken place three times since the beginning of the industrial revolution near the end of the eighteenth century. One more time we are seeing it happen. This is not to say that there is some inevitable cycle that we are bound to repeat. But by common observation the industries that have driven the post-war economy are by and large mature, and are being displaced as the engines of growth by a whole new set, based on the emerging technologies of, for example, microelectronics, robotics, biotech, material science, computer science and telecommunications.

Second, we are moving into a genuinely global economy coupled with a convergence of attention by all the major economies on this new set of industries. This is going to mean a gigantic clash between global, corporate entities as well as between them and governments, at the same time as there is more and more interdependence between nations, and more and more of a common, global market-place.

Compounding these economic forces we are also facing major cultural clashes between and within society after society, large and small. At the national economic level, Western Individualistic Capitalism faces its next huge challenge, after seeing off socialism, with the rise of Communitarian Capitalism as it is practiced in the fastest-growing countries in the world along the Pacific Rim. Will this next attempt to put the group before the individual fare better than socialism? Or will those cultures become more like the West's? This ancient struggle between man as an individual and man as a member of a group is also going on within nation after nation, whether it be the multiple diversities of modern America versus the notion of an overriding, common nationhood, the religious divisions in Northern Ireland, the ethnic hostilities in Bosnia, or the tribal ones in Rwanda.

The claim of a few years ago that history had come to an end with the collapse of Communism, and the apparent vindication of Western Democratic Capitalism has proved very premature indeed. The competition between different cultures, different ways to run economies and different modes of governance is still very much alive, and growing more, not less intensive as the world becomes a smaller place.

The transformation that is taking place in the global economy means that all the assumptions of grand strategy are being thrown up in the air. It is truly time for 'back to basics', but not in the sense of 'back to what we were doing' in easier times. That is the one thing we *know* won't work! There will be new industries, new ways of working, new ways of organizing enterprises and new ways of managing and, even more important, leading the people who work in them. Those organizations from the old economy who gain from this cataclysmic change will do so not because they go back to what they were doing before things began to go wrong, but because they find superior, new answers to the four, great questions of grand strategy suited to their new situation in a new world. The winners in the new industries will be those who find superior answers to the same four questions, best suited to the nature of the businesses spawned by the new technologies.

But most of us won't work for the relatively small number of glamour companies that will become the icons of the new economy. What's more important for most of us, than that there will be some spectacular winners that we will all wish we had joined or bought stock in, is that *every* kind of organization will have to be run in new ways in this new economy if it is to survive, let alone be successful. These new ways of working, of managing, and of leading will be very varied, far more so than in the previous era, because one of the features of the new economy will be extraordinary diversity, as the strategic value of focus in a huge global market provides the opportunity for myriad specializations. The scale of the economy is now the scale of nature. The enormous richness of species that evolution brought to nature, competition is now bringing to the massive, global economy.

But there is also a dark side, for the historical lot of species has been extinction. The evolutionary law that no two species can make their living in the same way in the same environment now also comes into play with all its full force. The question is: are we just going to await our evolutionary fate, hope that we have the skills that will be valued and that the organizations that we are in have the capabilities to survive and succeed? Or are we going to take control of our own destinies? The promise of grand strategy is that it provides a way of understanding the task, and a set of tools for tackling it that will enable those who dare to transform the way they manage, and by so doing build their piece of one of the winning organizations of the new economy.

Part I
Diagnosis

Introduction

'The ultimate goal of the corporation is survival.' So wrote Peter Drucker long years before the truth of his insight was made unavoidably evident by the turbulence of the Nineties. Return on investment, cashflow, market share, product leadership, technological renewal, all these and many more are important goals of the corporation; but, at the highest level of strategy, they are no more than means to the supreme, institutional imperative – to secure its continuing existence as a viable, independent, economic entity.

The arrival of unprecedented competitive intensity and accelerating change, the twin strategic constants of our age, has turned the pursuit of this goal into a competitive struggle involving all the resources of the corporation. Grand strategy deals with the connections between that competition and the performance of these resources. A simple idea, but not an easy one. Simple because it is rather obvious that to compete successfully *externally* requires people to perform appropriately *internally*. But far from easy, as company after company has discovered at bitter cost.

In practice organizations have found it extraordinarily difficult to change what they actually do – their business processes and the behaviour of their people – to keep pace with what is needed to win in the market-place. Time after time over the last two decades industry leader after industry leader has been displaced by upstarts with no name or reputation, no breakthrough technological advance and a seemingly insurmountable shortage of resources. They have invariably done it by adopting a way of managing themselves which proved to translate into an irresistible advantage in the value they could provide the customers of the old leaders.

This connection – between external competition and internal performance – has always been there, and has always been the underlying basis for continued survival and success. But in more stable times, before wrenching change and untraditional competitors had respectively created and made obvious the chasm between what exists and what is needed, it was easy to forget it. By the end of the Eighties the extremities faced by so many corporations finally exposed the fundamental problem that underlay their lack of competitive health. It became unavoidably clear that new customer demands, new technologies, new ways of competing and a new kind of worker – the knowledge-worker – required an equally new way of managing to turn them all into a new, winning combination. That is why grand strategy is a subject which can most easily be studied when change and competition are straining organizations to the full.

In more comfortable times success, steady growth, good profits, ample job opportunities and the ability of the corporation to provide well for all on whom it depends cover over the essential sinews of existence. Good times help us forget the fundamentals. Warm flesh conceals the bone underneath. But today, when the intensity of competition is forcing us to cut to that bone, we are made brutally re-aware of the profounder realities. Lost markets, lost jobs and huge destruction of shareholder wealth have uncovered what prosperity had hidden. It is the way we run our companies that ultimately determines how well they compete. The deepest connections between what we do and what happens to us are laid bare for all to see.

The first part of this book offers a diagnosis of what it is that has led to the situation where grand strategy is once again the primary challenge facing the leaders of our organizations, and just what this challenge is. Part II will then suggest a prescription for using grand strategy to maintain the competitive health of those who still have it, and to return to competitive health for those who have lost it.

In Part I we will first put our current period of economic turbulence into its proper historical context, to establish the pervasive nature of the challenge we face. Then we will see what happened when one great company lost sight of the foundation of its success and allowed its original grand strategy to be corrupted by the completeness of that success. Next we will explore how the evolving competitive environment determines the priorities of the leaders of organizations. Finally we will turn these priorities into an agenda for these leaders which makes grand strategy the explicit guide for operational management, and so provides the basis for maintaining the organization's competitive health at the same time as dealing with the everyday challenges of running the business. We will begin Part I by trying to make some sense of the chaos of competition and change that seems to be overwhelming us from all sides.

1 The Fifth Wave: An Ending and a Beginning

"It is impossible to step in the same river twice."   (Heraclitus)

"Mankind has discovered more in the last ten years than in the whole history of mankind before that . . . and we're going to do the same in the next ten years."   (Bruce Merrifield, 1984)

"Of the forty-three 'excellent' companies only fourteen could be considered excellent five years later.
Of the corporations in the Fortune 500 rankings five years ago, 143 are missing today."   (Richard Tanner Pascale, 1990)

Beginning in 1945, for about twenty-five years, we had a macro, business environment which was essentially stable, where change was mostly predictable and competition was moderate. There were, of course, business cycles, but the underlying characteristics of the nature of the market, the major technologies and the primary sources of competition did not change very much, or at least not in ways where there wasn't ample notice of what was going on. The main industrial drivers of the economy were automobiles, electrical appliances, aircraft and aviation, chemicals, synthetic fibers, pharmaceuticals, and radio and television.

The next twenty-five years were very different. Starting with the oil crisis, and then the other commodity shocks, resources, including money, became for the first time, at least in America's history, scarce and expensive. Accompanying this we have experienced a rising intensity of competition as transportation and communication advances have broken down walls between countries, while deregulation did the same for industries, new technologies began to make obsolete great tracts of manufacturing assets, and the widespread, rapid availability of information and training in the latest techniques equalized the capabilities of competitors.

In the most recent period even business cycles appear to have had a different complexion, with the up parts being shorter and weaker, and the down parts longer and more severe. This has led to all sorts of iconoclastic forecasts of economic doom, and permanent changes in our economic fortunes to a lower-growth, lower-prosperity future.

However, there is another view, a view which says that what we have experienced in these two, approximately twenty-five year periods, are the two parts of a long wave – the first from the end of the Second World War until the early Seventies, the expansionary, or inflationary "A" phase; the second from the early Seventies until now, the recessionary, or deflationary "B" phase – driven by the latest in the bursts of technological innovation, and waves of population growth that have characterized the economic history of the United States, and other western countries, for the last two hundred years. In fact the pattern of economic growth since the beginning of the nineteenth century with a lot of smoothing looks as in Fig. 1.1.

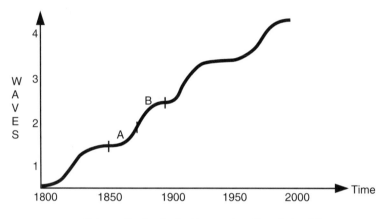

Drivers: Technological Innovation, Population Waves

Fig. 1.1 *Economic growth patterns in the United States, 1980–2000*

There have been four long waves, each about fifty years in length. The first began just before the end of the eighteenth century, and the last is just about at its end in the middle of the last decade of the twentieth century. A chronology of these waves along with their principal industrial drivers is shown in Table 1.1.

We can see how the depressions of the 1840s, 1890s and 1930s in the United States marked the end of the recessionary, "B" periods of the first, second and third waves. In each case the industrial drivers of the ending wave had lost all their ability to propagate economic growth, and the new industries had not yet reached the size where they could take over. Much of the early Nineties "doom-predicting"

Table 1.1   Mandel's chronology of long waves

Wave	Phase	Length (years)	Dates	Drivers
First	A	33	1792–1825	Coal, Canals, Textiles,
	B	22	1825–1847	Wrought Iron
Second	A	27	1847–1874	Railways, Steam Power,
	B	19	1874–1893	Gaslighting, Smelting Technology
Third	A	20	1893–1913	Steel, Petroleum,
	B	26	1913–1939	Telephone, Automobiles I, Electric Power
Fourth	A	35	1939–1974	Automobiles II,
	B		1974–	Electrical Appliances, Aircraft and Aviation, Chemicals, Synthetic Fibers, Pharmaceuticals, Radio and Television

has been driven by the simple expectation that history will repeat itself at the end of the fourth wave, resulting in another depression. Whether one accepts this pessimistic view of our short-term prospects or not, the data certainly suggests that we are fast approaching another inflection point where a "B" phase ends, and, if the long wave phenomenon repeats itself, an "A" phase begins. This would accord with what we have recently experienced in the shake-outs and shifts in the companies and industries making up our economy.

It would also explain the changing nature of the business cycle. During growth periods the short-term business cycles, which are oscillations around the long wave, are inherently more benign (shorter, and less severe) than in slower times, because of the influence of the underlying direction and performance of the economy. The long "hangover" suffered by the US and, with it, the rest of the world's economy after the end of the Reagan boom of the mid-Eighties – first the drawn-out recession under Bush, and then the anaemic recovery under Clinton – can now be seen for what it really was, as Fig. 1.2 illustrates. The "boom" was the first half of an oscillation around the underlying, fourth wave which came to an end just as that wave was reaching its flattest point – the second half of a

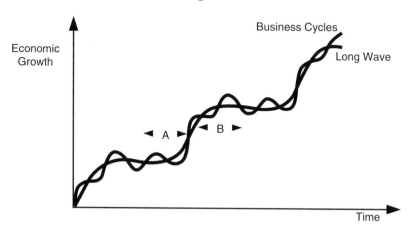

Fig. 1.2 *Impact of the long wave on business cycles*

"B" period. The recession and rather weak recovery were further oscillations around that flattest part. The drivers of the fourth wave had finally run out of steam, and the new industries, which will drive future growth, were not powerful or large enough to take up the slack.

The well documented, recent innovation in new industries gives us more than a good guess at some at least of the drivers of future growth – telecommunications, biotechnology, material sciences, microcomputers and software, and robotics. Following the pattern of previous long waves, there has been a major cluster of innovations toward the end of the current "B" period. The companies and industries created by these innovations are now poised to be the next sources of economic growth. At the same time the largest (baby boom) generation in the history of the United States will reach its peak buying period – mid-to-late forties in age – in the last years of this century and first years of the next.

The good news is that, if the pattern of long waves does hold, we are approaching a sustained period of prosperity and growth, which may prove to be of a previously unequalled nature. The bad news is that we are in the middle of a very painful shakeout whose predecessors were the depressions of the 1930s and 1890s. The worse news is that we don't really know what's going to happen, or how to manage in the world that's coming. Lester Thurow, dean of the MIT Sloan School of Management, has said that we are experiencing six economic revolutions (comments in parentheses are mine).

1. Aftermath of the Financial Crash in the world's money centers (New York, London and Tokyo in particular)
2. Slowdown in Growth (until the next "A" phase really gets going, if it does)
3. Collapse of Communism (but maybe the re-emergence of Fascism)
4. Importance of Education (as knowledge becomes the source of value-added, rather than merely labor)
5. Rise of Communitarian Capitalism (in Germany, Japan and maybe the rest of the Pacific Rim)
6. Competitive Convergence (of the major economies on the drivers of future growth).

This presages a world far more complex than the waves experienced by the relatively more separate, national economies of the past two hundred years. On top of these "revolutions" is the emergence of the Newly Industrialized Economies (NIEs), such as "the little tigers" – South Korea, Hong Kong, Taiwan and Singapore – and China, which are making the new, global economy more than just the world of the Triad – America, Europe and Japan. One of the reasons we are not experiencing the depression which has characterized the ending of previous long waves may be that the NIEs' strong growth is at least in part making up for the recessionary tendencies in the developed economies. In this context it is interesting and important to remember, as *The Economist* recently pointed out, that for most of recorded history China has had the largest national economy in the world. The last 150 or so years have been a temporary exception, not the historical rule. In a newly interdependent, genuinely global economy the re-emergence of China as an economic world power surely has the potential to be the single most important force of all.

Working in the other direction, a reason why we may not experience the rapid growth of the "A" phase of a "fifth wave" is that the Baby Boom Generation is the first in American history which is not uniformly more prosperous than its parents, leading to potentially more cautious purchasing behavior during its peak buying period than in previous waves.

It would be a brave forecaster who claimed to be able to predict how all that will shake down into a genuine global economy. Even if the pattern of the long wave holds at some foundational level, so that the underlying economic environment improves, the huge changes in the forces driving global business are going to lead to national economies very different to the ones we have experienced in either the good, or bad, phases of the last cycle.

However, regardless of whether there is a recognizable "fifth wave" or not, the discontinuity in what has been called the "techno-economic paradigm" is really not very different to what has happened in the previous shifts from one wave to the next. Nor is the recent ferment of activity in the area of management technique. We can now see that the last twenty years have formed most of the "B", or deflationary, phase of the fourth long wave of the American economy beginning, according to Mandel's Chronology, in 1974. All four of the "A" phases of previous waves have been relatively simple (from a management perspective) periods of rapid growth, driven by the technological innovations clustered toward the end of the preceding "B" phases. An illustration of this clustering of innovation is shown by the period 1876 to 1903, spanning the end of the second wave, which Mandel put at 1893. In this twenty-seven year period there were twelve basic inventions which were a major part of what drove the third wave:

		Date
1.	The telephone, by Alexander Graham Bell	1876
2.	The talking machine, by Thomas A. Edison	1877
3.	The electric light, by Edison	1879
4.	The gasoline automobile (although the first practical model did not come until 1905)	1889
5.	The trolley car, by Van Depoele and Sprague	1884–7
6.	Photographic film and roll-holder by George Eastman and William H. Walker (followed by transparent film in 1889)	1884
7.	The linotype, by Mergenthaler	1885
8.	The electric reduction furnace, by Cowles	1885
9.	The recording adding machine, by Burroughs	1888
10.	The motion-picture machine, by Edison	1889
11.	High frequency wireless, by Marconi	1896
12.	The airplane, by Orville and Wilbur Wright	1903

The first challenge after such a cluster of breakthroughs is one of technical and manufacturing innovation – to turn the new technologies into practical products and processes. Then follows the entrepreneurial race to build the capacity of these just-invented processes, needed to meet the demand for those just-invented products. Only later, when the first rush to create new supply to meet new demand is over, does the real, new, managerial challenge appear.

The "B" phases, beginning when the growth of the new industries has begun to slow, have therefore been typified by advances in management technique, driven by the need to manage the new technologies and organizations thrown up by the preceding "A" phases. In periods where growth had slowed and competition increased, attention has naturally turned to the challenge of managing the new enterprises more efficiently and effectively to meet the new pressures on profitability. The last twenty years have been just like previous "B" phases, characterized by a search for new management techniques to manage the enterprises created by the industries that drove the growth of the post-Second World War economy. We will explore this period, indeed the whole of the fourth wave's evolution of management technique, in depth in Chapter 3. Here we will look across the first three waves, at some of the more significant things each of those previous "B" phases led us to invent in the area of management, and thus, very broadly, at how the modern enterprise has evolved over the period since the industrial revolution.

In the "B" phase of the first wave (1825–1847) we had to learn how to manage the very first, specialized enterprises of manufacturing, transportation, distribution and financing. The corporate form itself came into being, and with it the beginning of the separation of ownership and management. It was also in this period that the truly revolutionary "American system of manufacture" (the fabrication and assembly of interchangeable parts) was introduced. Invented in the small arms industry to lower costs, driven by the price-based bidding for large contracts for the US Army, it rapidly spread to other metal goods and then to the machinery to make them.

In the "B" phase of the second wave (1874–1893), it could almost be said that management itself was invented as the size of the typical industrial firm rose rapidly, facilitated by the new, manufacturing technology and transportation infrastructure. Beginning with the railroads the whole concept of formal organization, with its attending elements of functional specialization, co-ordinating, planning and control processes, and layers of middle management, was developed to manage the first, really large, industrial enterprises the world had ever seen.

The modern corporation as we know it came into being in the third "B" phase (1913–1939). It encompassed the delineation of centralized and decentralized roles, the development of line and staff concepts of authority and, what has been described as the greatest of all American inventions, training. This was the time when Alfred P. Sloan, perhaps the leading organizational architect of this third "B" phase, was using his administrative genius to turn General Motors into the largest industrial enterprise of its time. The ideas of the product and production genius Henry Ford built the automotive industry in its first, innovation-driven growth period. Sloan brought order and market focus to the gigantic new firms it created, and thereby overtook Ford in the industry's second, consolidation-dominated phase.

The profusion, confusion and disillusion of management techniques we have seen in the last decade-and-a-half is no different in character to what was going on in earlier "B" phases. In the very first *Harvard Business Review*, in October 1922, nine years into the "B" phase of the third wave (and thereby corresponding approximately to the stage we were at in the fourth wave in the mid-Eighties), we find:

> It is surprising to observe to what extent able, intelligent business men have turned, and are still turning, to the methods and counsel of the quack with his boasted, ready-made, dogmatic and infallible methods of dissecting the mental and moral qualities of persons in relation to a given task.

The problems may have changed, but the way we grope for the answers, stumbling from one guru's nostrum to the next in a continually rising triumph of hope over experience, clearly hasn't. Fig. 1.3 shows what it has looked like during the fourth, long wave; no doubt similar graphs could have been drawn for the earlier ones. The illustration is taken from Richard Tanner Pascale's marvellous book *Managing on the Edge*. He uses it to demonstrate the faddishness with which American business has treated new management ideas in recent years. In support he quotes business journalist, John Byrne: "Business fads have always been with us. What's different – and alarming – today is the sudden rise and fall of so many conflicting fads and fashions". Pascale then goes on, "Interestingly, fads are largely an American phenomenon. While faddish books sell abroad, they are taken as grist for thought, not as prescriptions to be acted upon. In the rare instances in which ideas such as Deming's notions of 'statistical quality control' and 'quality circles' stimulate

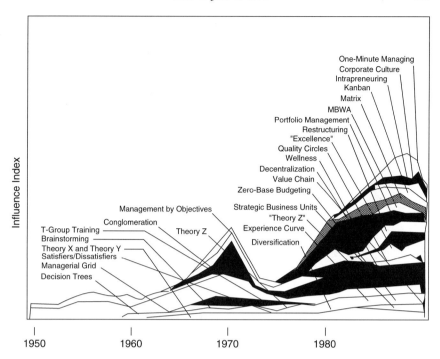

Influence Index

One-Minute Managing
Corporate Culture
Intrapreneuring
Kanban
Matrix
MBWA
Portfolio Management
Restructuring
"Excellence"
Quality Circles
Wellness
Decentralization
Value Chain
Zero-Base Budgeting
Strategic Business Units
"Theory Z"
Experience Curve
Diversification

Management by Objectives
Conglomeration
Theory Z
T-Group Training
Brainstorming
Theory X and Theory Y
Satisfiers/Dissatisfiers
Managerial Grid
Decision Trees

1950   1960   1970   1980

* Curves shown are for illustrative purposes. Empirical foundation of chart based upon frequency of citations in the literature. However, increased interest in business topics in the past decade tends to exaggerate amplitude of recent fads when compared to earlier decades. As a result, the author has modified curves to best reflect relative significance of trends over entire period.

Source: Pascale (1991).

Fig. 1.3 *Ebbs, flows, and residual impact of business fads, 1950–1988**

serious consideration, as has been the case in Japan, they are adopted as an enduring way of doing business. Meanwhile, in the United States, 75 percent of all quality circles begun with enthusiasm in 1982 had been discontinued by 1986".

Anyone who has experienced the superficiality and lack of resolve with which much of corporate America has toyed with management techniques these last two decades knows there is considerable truth in these observations. However, there is also another, healthier interpretation. First, notice the last two sentences under the exhibit. The amplitude of these curves, in the later years, has been modified downward because of "increased interest in business topics in the past decade". This "increased interest" is exactly what this chapter's interpretation of the long wave predicts. The fact that there are so many ideas is also what one would expect from the world's largest, most free and most diverse economy. Finally, their ebb and flow is simply the result of experimentation and its inevitable outcome, varied success and failure.

These are all signs of health, not sickness, at a more fundamental level than the overeagerness of the American manager to grasp for the quick fix of the latest fad. We have been searching for new answers to new management challenges. As in previous cycles, this searching has had two quite different kinds of needs to meet, and if there is a real complaint to be made about the way this search has been conducted, it is not so much its sometimes misdirected enthusiasm but that we have not been very good at first separating these two kinds of needs, and then seeking the right remedies for each. The first need is the problem of managing the giant corporations spawned by the 1939–1974 expansionary era as they face the daunting challenge of adapting themselves to a world where they are no longer the beneficiaries of sustained, rapid growth. The second is the whole, different set of challenges arising from the emergence of quite different kinds of companies in the new industries comprising the economy's next drivers of growth. The survivors from the *old* economy (which, remember, was driven in large degree by automobiles, electrical appliances, aircraft and aviation, chemicals, synthetic fibers, pharmaceuticals, and radio and television) will be those who find new ways of managing to suit the characteristics of their maturity in a changing world. The winners in the *new* economy will be those which first develop appropriate forms of organization and accompanying management techniques that fit the characteristics of the new technologies, and the rapidly evolving environment they will have to deal with.

Richard Tanner Pascale has said that less than two percent of the American managers of the mid-Nineties have the skills to cope. Whether or not our global competitors are better off, surely this is the most important aspect of the challenge facing American management. If those competitors aren't in better managerial shape, we have a huge opportunity. If they are, our relative deficiency in managerial skill is the real competitive challenge we face. In either case the transformation of management, that is the way we manage our business enterprises, is clearly the most urgent task the leaders of our organizations must undertake. And on the quality of their response, more than anything else, will depend whether or not the year 2000 heralds a second, American century.

Pascale has also said, making a telling analogy to the development of medicine, that we are still in the Dark Ages when it comes to understanding how to keep organizations healthy over the long haul. Whether or not we experience the clearly identifiable form of a fifth wave in the coming years, we are certainly at one of those points when mammoth change and huge competition mean that maintaining or, in all too many cases, rebuilding the competitive health of our organizations is the primary management challenge. This book is the result of one person's journey through the early years of searching for the keys to maintaining the competitive health of our organizations. All of its insights are based on observation of what happened in practice, or in the recent history of organizations wrestling with the challenges of major, strategic change. The period covered has turned out to be close to the complete, second or "B" phase of the fourth, long wave of the American economy. It should therefore be in time to help some of you prepare for, and prosper from, the new economy that is taking its place. We continue our diagnosis with an exploration of what made one great company of both the third and fourth waves very sick indeed.

2   The Poisoned Inheritance: The Fall of the Giants

"We cannot learn without pain."   (Aristotle)

"To anticipate the behavior of an organization, assume it to be controlled by a secret cabal of its enemies determined to discredit it."

(Robert Conquest)

"There are six stages of decadence: political overcentralization; inordinate growth in taxation; the growth of a top heavy administration; promotion of the wrong people; the urge to overspend; and, the dominance of 'liberal opinion' – a feeble sentimentality moved by sentiment rather than by reason."   (C. Northcote Parkinson)

Whatever happened to the giants of the fourth wave? The likes of International Harvester, American Can, Continental Group, RCA, Sperry and LTV, all gone; GM, IBM, Westinghouse, Eastman Kodak all sick to the point of radical surgery, management overhauls, streams of job losses and much shareholder wealth destroyed.

Why did they fall? Was it inevitable? Or, is there a pattern of decline which we can learn to avoid next time round?

Professor Parkinson's six stages of political decadence have an uncanny parallel in several of the major factors that contribute to corporate decline, with very little adaptation of language: over-centralized decision-making; inordinate profit contribution expected from divisions; growth in overhead costs; promotion of the wrong people; the urge to overinvest; and the dominance of non-business factors in the way the company is managed – often cloaked as "compassion" to individual colleagues, employees and local communities. All of these have been part of the malaise that has overtaken much of corporate America in the last two decades.

In this chapter we will explore how they and other factors led to the decline of the giants of the fourth wave. We will begin by proposing a model of the processes of growth and decline of business empires, then use it to trace the history of one of the giants – Eastman Kodak. Other giants will appear frequently throughout the book – most notably IBM, perhaps the paradigmatic company of the fourth wave,

27

the car companies, and Johnson & Johnson – to illustrate various aspects of the challenge of maintaining competitive health over the long haul. Here we will confine our focus to one company so as to explore the processes of growth and decline in proper depth. Finally we will conclude by discussing the implications of this story for the new giants which will emerge as the new economy gathers pace.

THE RISE AND FALL OF THE GIANTS

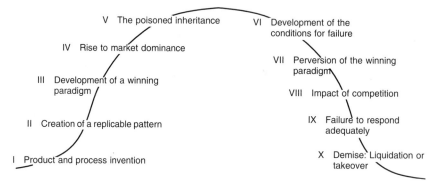

Fig. 2.1   *The rise and fall of the giants*

There are ten stages that mark the rise and fall of corporate giants, if carried right through from their start-up to their disappearance, through liquidation or, more often, takeover and relegation to the status of a much shrunken division of another company (see Fig. 2.1). Rather than dwell on just what these stages refer to here we will explain each of them, and illustrate what they entail, as we follow the story of Eastman Kodak.

THE RISE AND NEAR-FATAL DECLINE OF EASTMAN KODAK

This is a cautionary tale. It is not intended to be a complete history of all that happened, or a complete explanation of why it happened. Rather it highlights the impact of the major strategic and organizational forces with which this book is concerned, and spends less time on, for example, the legal and technological issues that also played a role. In a sense, therefore, it is selective – other forces were also at work and contributed to the outcome. However, it is not selective in the sense of misleading the reader as to the significance of what is portrayed. As the story should make clear, these forces were decisive. Irrespective of the contribution of other factors, what is described here by itself was enough to cause the near fatal decline of Eastman Kodak.

I suspect a very similar story could be told about IBM, or GM, or your favorite fallen giant. In addition to setting up the challenge which subsequent chapters will be tackling, the purpose of telling it is therefore also to warn the new giants emerging from the transformation of the global economy. For surely they will face the same twin challenges: first, how to avoid the hubris that their spectacular success will, unless consciously combated, inevitably induce; and second, how to begin to change what will still be working well in time to avoid a repeat of the competitive sickness, and resulting radical surgery, that has befallen our current generation of giant corporations. Hopefully they can learn from our pain and at least some of them will thereby avoid some repeating it in their turn.

The easiest way to understand what happened to Eastman Kodak is to use our model of the rise and fall of corporate giants to trace its evolution from the earliest days of the company through the years of world dominance and then through the process of decay that ended with a Chairman fired, and a Chairman hired from outside the company for the first time in the company's history.

I. Product and Process Invention

The initial invention of the core products that were to form the basis for the new industry – photography – came in the 1880s and 90s along with the other major innovations that were to drive the third wave of the American economy. In the late 1880s George Eastman, an enthusiastic amateur photographer, was experimenting with coatings that could be dried onto the glass plates then used to make photographic images, so that he could "avoid lugging around the dark tent and silver bath" the existing wet plate system required. As he put it: "At first I wanted to make photography simpler for my own convenience, but soon I thought of the possibilities of commercial production". And so was born a remarkable company which was to become a giant of both the third and fourth waves, before it stumbled into decline as the latter came toward its end.

Just before Thanksgiving 1880, Eastman was in the photography business. His first product was gelatin dry plates, and his first customers professional photographers and expert amateurs as he himself had been. But this was a business restricted by its dependence on glass. To fulfil Eastman's dream of a large, mass market for photography meant making the move to transparent film and a simpler process for taking pictures.

In 1884 the breakthroughs began: first to a "stripping film" – a transparent film on a paper base, which was stripped off the base after exposure, for development and printing. Next, on June 13, 1888, came a lightweight, portable camera, for which Eastman created the name Kodak, and in 1889, the transparent, nitro-cellulose, photographic film which had been his goal all along. Now he had "The Kodak System", a fundamentally new value proposition which forever changed the way people took pictures, how often they took them, and what they took them of. This was what he needed in order to tackle his dream of a mass photographic market. The breakthroughs provided the products he needed. Strategic success now depended, as it does with any genuine breakthrough, on the establishment of the internal capabilities and external positions to exploit their potential.

II. Creation of a Replicable Pattern

While his product genius, Henry M. Reichenbach, was working on the film, Eastman himself had been focusing on the process and equipment that would be needed to make it. In fact his vision had extended way beyond both the product and the associated manufacturing process to the whole of his business before he even started it. In the winter of 1879–80 he had established four business principles:

1. Production in large quantities by machinery
2. Low prices to increase the usefulness of the products
3. Foreign as well as domestic distribution
4. Extensive advertising as well as selling by demonstration.

In 1881 he added a fifth principle, in response to a material quality and supply problem that had put him in debt for the first time, and nearly bankrupted his company:

5. Control the alternative (way of doing everything)

Now he had the opportunity to apply these principles in earnest to the mass production and marketing of the world's first system of photography for the ordinary consumer.

Internally that meant that the critical, technical inventions had to be turned into simple products which did not require an expert to use, or a craftsman to make:

- One-off, technical performance had to be made robustly replicable by amateurs with inexpensive cameras and film
- A process that could make the products in large quantities and at reliable quality had to be developed
- And, rapid progress had to be made down the manufacturing and processing experience curves, both to bring costs to where a mass market could afford the product, and to establish a defensible lead over competition.

Externally it meant that the market, and a way to meet its needs, had to be found:

- The demand had to be stimulated
- Delivery and service systems had to be put in place
- And, a defensible market position had to be created.

The purpose of these moves, in product, process, sales and marketing, and delivery and service, were to create the *replicable pattern* of activity that is needed to turn a craft into a mass production industry. In the third wave Henry Ford was achieving the same strategic success by following the same path in the motor industry. The oil and chemicals companies were doing the same. In fact if you look back at the drivers of each of the four waves of the American economy you will find the same story repeated by all the companies which rose to become giants of their eras. It wasn't enough to be the inventor of either product or process. The inventions then had to be turned from art, through science, to technology that could form the foundation for mass production, sales, delivery and service. And technology by itself was also not enough. Just as much innovation was needed to learn to manage the new, large organizations it made possible. The winners were the companies that succeeded in putting it all together into a comprehensive system of management – a grand strategy that addressed all the elements of the business in a superior, more consistent, and more mutually reinforcing manner than their competitors.

III. Development of a Winning Paradigm

Eastman Kodak did these things with almost unmatched brilliance, establishing both the reality of, and the reputation for operational excellence in the way the company was run, and world-class salesmanship in all the major markets around the world. In so doing it also created a name, which is still the number-one brand in the world for quality and which, in a recent independent study, was calculated also to be the most valuable brand in the world. As someone once said to me, "Kodak film is the only product in the world which, if it doesn't work when I use it, I blame myself and not the product!" What a priceless asset.

These capabilities were guided in their implementation by an equally special set of values, which owe their roots to George Eastman and the small group of pioneers who helped him build the company.

On the sixth floor of Building Twenty, in the complex of buildings that is Eastman Kodak's headquarters in Rochester, New York, can be found its Management Development Center. In the foyer is an exhibit of six panels. Each is headed by one of the six great ideas that guided the development of a company which became one of the icons of business achievement. On each panel, next to each heading, is a picture of the man most closely associated with the implementation of that idea, and a few words of explanation. Here is what each of them says.

PEOPLE   *George Eastman*
Throughout his life, George Eastman was deeply committed to the perfection of photography. He discovered how to coat photo-graphic plates ahead of time, putting an end to the cumbersome wet plate process. More importantly, he also invented a machine to do it.

Eastman was also deeply committed to people. The legacy that has evolved from his feeling for fairness includes a bonus system, which first appeared at the turn of the century. Today, it is the largest profit-sharing plan in American industry.

To protect his employees at their workplace, Eastman organized a safety committee in 1911. The Square Deal and the Open Door policy further reflect Eastman's concern for the company's employees. Eastman's commitment to people was based on good business sense. He said, "We are running a very complicated and difficult business. I do not know any that depends more upon the good feeling and faithfulness of its employees".

QUALITY *William Stuber*

The manufacturing of emulsions – the light sensitive part of the film – involved a complex and sometimes temperamental technology. Eastman had good reason to know how temperamental: in 1882, a emulsion failure on dry plates forced him to initiate what may rank as the first mass "recall" in America's industrial history. "Making good on those plates took our last dollar", Eastman said, "but what we had left was more important: reputation". To guard that reputation, Eastman turned to a master emulsion maker: William Stuber.

William Stuber was so jealous of the quality of his emulsions that he arranged for there to be only one door to the emulsion building – through his own office. That door was kept locked, and not even George Eastman could open it without asking Stuber first. It was Stuber who discovered, through artful trial and error, the secrets of emulsion stability and quality. These he guarded as faithfully as the door.

Stuber's chemists worked with spectrophotometers, sedimentation balances, and ionometers. They bandied about such words as mono-methylparaminophenol, alpha-dimethylglyoxine, and kryptocyanine. Stuber knew that it was unceasing attention to minute details that gave Kodak products a reputation for dependable quality.

PRODUCTIVITY *Frank Lovejoy*

In 1896, eight years before mass manufacturing in the auto industry, Eastman's company was already measuring its output in miles – 400 miles of film and paper a month. The state of the manufacturing art using long glass tables did not satisfy George Eastman.

Frank Lovejoy, fresh out of MIT, was placed at the head of a taskforce to develop a radically new method for making film. Lovejoy figured out how to make film on a huge, slowly revolving wheel. Two nickel-plated wheels, each weighing seven tons, were ordered from Gleason Works.

Lovejoy's wheels constituted a massive retooling of an industry. But it was worth it. "It works like a charm", wrote Eastman. "This is greater accuracy than we ever obtained on tables". The new technique was also five times more productive and is still used today.

While he was general manager of Kodak Park, Frank Lovejoy extended productivity to all manufacturing activities at the Park, which soon became the largest photographic plant in the world. It still is today.

INTERNATIONAL   *George Dickman*

In keeping with his strategies, Eastman made his new company one of the very first American multinationals. On his appointment as general manager of Kodak's European headquarters in London, George Dickman received a message from Eastman, "So far as I am concerned I have confidence in you and will back you, mistakes or no mistakes, until you have had a fair chance to show what you can do".

In England, Kodak's Harrow Works began to make film and paper in the very same year as Kodak Park – 1891. Kodak's London office on Regent Street was where George Dickman received news from the United States of the financial panic of 1893 and that the company in Rochester was seriously strapped for funds. Cash was also scarce in London, but Dickman had one ace up his sleeve: unpaid subscriptions to the stock of the English company. He called them in and later cabled relief to Rochester. Eastman's multinational not only protected the domestic payroll but may have saved the business from going under.

George Dickman trained men in many languages so that he could market Kodak products throughout the world. Eastman wrote him in 1895, "We are getting things in shape in the camera works, so we can certainly beat the world on design, workmanship, and price, and there is no reason why we should not sell cameras anywhere in large quantities all over the world".

INNOVATION   *C. E. Kenneth Mees*

In looking about for someone to head a research laboratory, Eastman wrote, "I decided that Dr. Mees was peculiarly fitted for the position, both on account of his education and his practical experience, he being a chemist, a physicist, a practical manufacturer of color sensitive dry plates and of color screens for use in photography, and one of the best known authorities on color photography". It fell to Mees to take Eastman's invention of dry plates and develop the future of photography.

It was Mees, of all people, who first suggested a ceiling on spending for research. Eastman was surprised, but he agreed. Later, when he asked Mees to cut expenditures as part of a general economy measure, Eastman got his second surprise. Dr. Mees refused, pointing out they had already agreed to what the research lab would spend that year. "Why, so we did", came Eastman's reply. By putting a ceiling on spending, Mees had also placed a floor under it.

Kodak's success grew from a string of innovations – first, dry plates; then, flexible film and the Kodak number one camera. Mees said, "Industrial research is an adventure; it is even a gamble, though one in which the odds are on success, provided that the work is continued in spite of delays and discouragements". Despite delays and discouragements, innovations flowed from Mees' laboratories – Kodachrome film, Kodacolor film, Ektachrome film and speed film increases of millions of times.

CUSTOMER ORIENTATION   *Lewis B. Jones*

Unlike other inventors, George Eastman refused to regard an invention as successful until it had passed the ultimate test – at the cash register. "People who have an itching to manufacture goods," he once complained, "do not understand what they would have to encounter when they come to try to sell them."

So maybe it's no surprise that before he hired Stuber, Lovejoy, Dickman, or Mees, he first sought out Lewis B. Jones, his advertising and marketing genius. The most famous example of Eastman's marketing aptitude is, of course, the name "Kodak" itself. But the famous slogan, "You Press the Button, We Do the Rest," is attributed to Lewis B. Jones.

Once, after a trip to Europe, Eastman looked through ads Jones had created during his absence. Immediately he sent for Jones. "I've been reading these ads", announced the chief, "and it seems to me they're different somehow – better than usual. How do you explain that?" "Well", Jones answered, "maybe it's because I used to write the ads for you. These were written for the public". Eastman did not hesitate. "From now on", he said, "I don't want to see the ads until they are printed".

Here were the roots of the management paradigm that won the world market. Decades later they had become part of a dusty, almost mythical past. Yet many people saw those panels everyday. Almost everyone saw them occasionally. But no one talked about them, or referred to them in practice. They were like a church spire in the middle of communist Moscow – there, seen, but irrelevant to all but a hidden few. It wasn't the absence of values that caused the company's later problems; it was lack of fidelity to its values.

IV.   Rise to Market Dominance

Operational excellence, world-class salesmanship, the Kodak brand, and these six values were an irresistible force.

In 1891 the *Chicago Tribune* wrote, "The craze is spreading fearfully. . . . Chicago has had many fads whose careers have been brilliant and brief. But when amateur photography came, it came to stay". By 1896 the "craze" had resulted in the one hundred thousandth Kodak, and film and photographic paper whose manufacture, as we have seen, was being measured in hundreds of miles a month! Meanwhile, Edison, using Kodak film, was creating the motion-picture business and Roentgen was finding another use for photographic film – radiography.

Only fifteen years later Eastman Kodak had become so successful that, along with a whole group of companies which personified success in the third wave, it had become the target of a Justice Department suspicious of "big business", and determined to use the Sherman Anti-Trust Act to break them up. World War I intervened before this action could be settled and in January 1918 the Government formally suspended its suit versus United Shoe Manufacturing Company, the International Harvester Company, the United States Steel Corporation, the Eastman Kodak Company, the American Can Company, the Quaker Oats Company, and the Corn Products Refining Company. At the end of the war a new administration and a new mood favoring "big business" led to a peaceful settlement of the suits. This, and the post-war weakness of its erstwhile German and French rivals, cleared the way for Eastman Kodak to complete its rise to dominance of the world's photographic market.

In 1925 George Eastman, now in his seventies, moved up to the Chairmanship but management stayed in the hands of two of the men who had built the company with him, William Stuber as President and Frank W. Lovejoy as Vice-President and General Manager. Under their leadership the company's technical and market advance continued unabated.

A generation later, after the introduction of color, and another consolidation of its global position in the aftermath of another world war, Eastman Kodak enjoyed a dominance of the world market so total that it seemed impossible that it could ever be challenged. But it was this totality of success, creating a momentum that lasted beyond the institutional memory of how the original strategy had really worked, and what those values really meant, which became also the source of the corruption of that strategy and those values, when it was inherited by later generations of management.

V.   The Poisoned Inheritance

What is the greatest gift a management team can bequeath to its successors?

Without any question it is high market share, built on a solid foundation of the right internal and external capabilities to sustain it. To inherit high market share and a set of institutionalized, winning capabilities is to inherit the basis for extraordinary financial performance. This is what happened to the generations of Kodak management following the great product and market successes that led to the world dominant position of the 1950s.

The first two phases of the company's history had been invention, and the creating of a replicable pattern, i.e., a product that would work reliably time after time, a manufacturing technology that would produce the requisite quality in large volumes, and a distribution system that would get it to its customers. This was followed by the creation of the managerial capabilities to exploit that invention, the putting in place of a set of guiding values, and then the institutional embedding of this winning paradigm. The fourth phase was the exploitation of this paradigm to build the position of global leadership. All this had already taken place by the end of the third wave in the depression of the Thirties. But Kodak wasn't done. In one of the few cases of a company moving successfully from one wave to the next, it renewed its technology (in particular with the great step from black & white to color photography) and repeated its earlier explosive growth in the fourth wave.

From the Fifties onward, successive generations of management then inherited world market dominance and an *already built*, twice successful, engine of wealth creation, and *gradually lost sight of what was creating the wealth*. In reality it was the performance of *past* generations that was creating *today's* results. The activities of later leaders had very little, strategically, to do with those results. But they didn't recognize it. And in this sense the inheritance was poisoned. Without an understanding of the value of the position they inherited, later generations of management came to believe it was what they were doing, not what they had inherited, that was the primary cause of their outstanding financial performance. The consequent reinforcement was the key. It was not that they "forgot" the real basis for value creation, or did not understand the real cause-and-effect relationships. It was more like a simple case of classical Skinnerian, behavioral psychology. They did what they did, and earnings went up. Year after year. Then as errors crept in and went uncorrected, because for a long time they had no noticeable effect on performance, the winning paradigm gradually became perverted – a textbook example of the corruption induced by inherited success.

VI.   Development of the Conditions for Failure

It led to three outcomes that, by the Eighties, were destroying the company.

World market dominance meant the company was successful whatever it and, more important, any individual within it did. From this followed three things. First, as described above, it became unnecessary to look closely at mistakes. Gradually, uncompetitive practices either crept in, or developed out of past excellence unchanged in the light of industry changes. Second, extraordinary results became the norm. All stakeholders, but in particular stockholders, employees and the Rochester community, came to expect, as their due, the incredible largesse the company was able to dispense. And third, individual performance – good or bad – had little impact. So, because it made little difference to the bottom line, it became difficult and unnecessary to distinguish between good and bad performers. Other factors soon came to dominate the way people were managed and rewarded.

Uncompetitive practices, inordinate financial expectations, and a non-performance-based people management system created the conditions under which the viruses of competitive sickness could thrive. On the surface in its apparently enlightened behavior, its dominance of its traditional, western market-places and its financial results, the company appeared still to be in good health (as late as 1982 it was listed as one of the excellent companies in *In Search of Excellence*). But, internally, in the way it ran itself, a corruption of its management practices had inexorably set in. The perversion of the winning paradigm was under way.

VII. Perversion of the Winning Paradigm

By the Eighties the previously excellent functions into which the company was organized – Sales, R&D, Manufacturing, Finance, Personnel Relations, Communications – had become fiefdoms exercising all their negative power to stop happening what they saw not to be in their own, narrow interests. Operational excellence had degenerated into functional tyranny.

Success in the market-place had gone to the heads of the sales force, which was really an "order-taking" force, whose *esprit-de-corps* had by now deteriorated into ill-hid hubris, relative to its competitors, its customers and other areas of the company. World-class salesmanship had degenerated into sales arrogance. The result was inevitable – internally, an uncompetitive cost structure; externally, the end of value-creating growth.

And those six great values, corrupted by the power of total market dominance, had each also become a sad perversion of the original.

- *People*, with no ability or need to distinguish between individuals on performance, gradually became *Political Paternalism*. Loyalty was to the boss or the function, not the company. And it was rewarded by compensation, career progress and job security increasingly at odds with the underlying reality of individual performance.

- *Quality* became *No Expense Spared*, in a confusion that was to affect most of American industry.
- *Productivity* deteriorated into *Monolithic Mass*, function by function, through misinterpretations of scale economics and the power of the functional barons.
- *International* success, country by country, left the Country General Managers feeling they were running *Independent Kingdoms* or, as the French insisted, *Independent Republics*.
- *Innovation* became *Technological Arrogance* both relative to competition and the ability to move into totally new fields.
- And, *Customer Orientation* turned into *Benevolent Disdain* (as Jack Thomas, head of Imaging and initiator of its turnaround in the Nineties, put it, "In those days if someone called us with a problem our response was, 'send the product in, and we'll examine it and tell you what you did wrong!'").

And what about that glorious Brand? By 1991, in the most awful of parody of a licensing strategy, it had been authorized to a stream of uses by other companies that brought tears to the eyes of loyal Kodakers who, with much better instincts than their leaders, knew that this was strategic suicide. Christmas Tree Lights? Perfectly good ones by the standard of that product I'm sure, but we all have problems with Christmas Tree Lights – and this was the number one brand in the world, for *quality*!

These factors were compounded by a mentality of "monopoly-think" – the thinking patterns, attitudes and concerns induced in a company with a near monopoly of the market. The most potent threat in the Fifties and Sixties was not from competition but the Anti-Trust division of the US Department of Justice, which had real, managerial consequences. In particular it led to a whole set of non-competitive, management behaviors. Those few competitors that survived were deliberately ignored, lest Eastman Kodak's actions be perceived by the Justice Department as having monopolistic intent. It was not that Kodak management was wrong to worry about the Justice Department. It was clearly a very real threat. But to worry about it to the exclusion of nearly all else meant that more conventional, competitive threats were overlooked. Gradually that meant that competitive thinking almost disappeared from the corporation. "Nice guy" managers were promoted – even-tempered, non-aggressive folk – and lots of technologists. Naturally those managers promoted people like themselves. And through it all earnings continued to rise, providing layer on layer of reinforcement.

When real competition did arise it came from two quarters. In the traditional, silver halide side of the business, Polaroid in the Sixties, and Fuji in the Seventies were recognized as real competitors. But the company's head-on, technology-driven and ultimately disastrous response to Polaroid (which culminated in a payment of almost $1 billion after losing a patent infringement suit) absorbed so much management mindshare that insufficient attention was paid to Fuji. In the Seventies the threat of technology substitution from electronic imaging also emerged. Black & white, and then color video took away the news film market. The same thing happened to home movies. This elicited another, almost totally technology-driven response, which again contributed to insufficient attention being paid to Fuji in the more traditional part of the business.

By the mid-Eighties two huge waves of competition – from new technology in the broader imaging industry, and Fuji in the remaining silver halide dominated segments – were causing continuous loss of market share defined on either a wider, imaging industry, or narrower, traditional photography basis.

VIII. The Impact of Competition

The company was ripe to be taken. And the coming of new technology, and the rise of new competitors soon brought it about. A set of reinforcing cycles was created, driving deteriorating performance. Fig. 2.2 shows how the forces of competition and technology can impact a management unschooled in the arts of strategy.

On the left, New Technology meant new products, whose substitution for traditional photography in areas such as news film and home movies translated into lost volume. At the same time it led Kodak to invest in the new technologies, driving up its "R&D" expense broadly defined (e.g., including buying companies with different technologies) and, to compensate, driving down its investment in its silver halide technology. But in both old and new technology the investment was either unproductive, or below the level necessary for success. This caused lost share, both on a narrow definition of the market as its major competitor, Fuji, continued to

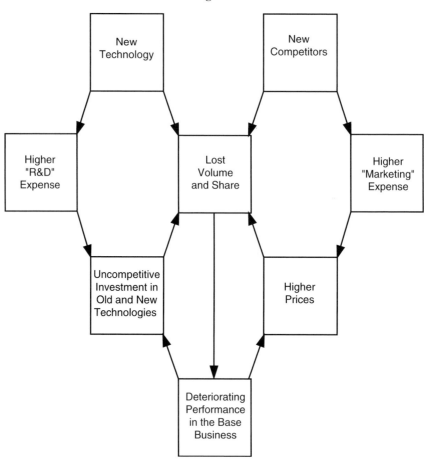

Fig. 2.2   *The impact of competition*

innovate and invest heavily in traditional photography, and on a wide definition as others were more successful in turning the new technologies into winning, new products.

On the right, New Competitors took share away and led Kodak to increase its "marketing" expense (meaning the expenditure of resources on just about anything that might boost demand except lower prices) to try to combat them. Even higher prices followed from the effort to recoup this marketing expense, so as to maintain the margins it had grown accustomed to – which meant a growing gap between its prices and its competitors', at just the time when the gap in relative product superiority, real and perceived, was shrinking. The result was more share loss.

In the center, lost volume and share, caused at first by the cycles depicted on the left and right, led directly to deteriorating performance in the base (photographic) business. Initially this was seen in a slowing of growth, first in revenue, then in profits. Then, even the *maintenance* of profit levels became impossible. Two of Kodak's reactions were to squeeze further on its investment in traditional technology to cut costs, and to raise prices even more to restore or even increase margins, and deliver profit growth that way. These actions had the effect of further lost volume and share, leading in due course to further deterioration in the financial performance of the base business, and so on, and so on.

The key to this accelerating spiral of deterioration was the box in the middle – Lost Volume and Share. For years this was masked by the growth in the world market. Kodak was achieving volume growth despite global share loss. The price escalation it was at the same time implementing meant financial performance went on improving by leaps and bounds. It became normal within the company to talk about "the Kodak markets" and "the Fuji markets", as if there was no crossover impact between them.

In fact, in the Seventies market share was not even discussed – monopoly-think had made it literally a taboo subject. The thermostat which could have warned of the impending meltdown had been turned off. Competition and competing were banned subjects. In their place was SPICE (Suppliers, Public, Investors, Customers, and Employees). All the right constituencies, if serving them was understood to be taking place in a competitive environment; but, without that understanding, a set of demands which were continually met at the price of further deterioration in the underlying competitive position.

In practice the company's basic strategy to continue to meet the inordinate expectations earlier success had created, was to "sell" its market share in its base, photographic business. By underinvesting in traditional technology relative to its principal competitor, and raising its prices without commensurately enhancing the value provided by its products, Kodak caused its market share gradually to erode year after year. But that lower investment and those higher prices translated, in the short-term, into wider profit margins and cashflow than a share-sustaining strategy would have resulted in. Those wider margins and that higher cashflow were the "price" the company realized from the market share it "sold".

But, unfortunately, a strategy of "selling market share" has built into it its own failure. Market share is a limited commodity – there is only 100% of it. Eventually there is no more to sell. In fact failure sets in much earlier because the underlying competitive and economic situation is changing to the worse with every sale. The share gainer's market position and underlying operating economics improve with every gain; and the share loser's deteriorate with every loss. Eventually this constant shift in relative position has its impact on profit margins. The leader can no longer dictate prices in the market-place, and the follower's now competitive, maybe even superior technological and cost base changes the rules of the game. Wider margins turn suddenly and shockingly into shrinking margins; and a now hungry and aggressive competitor has all the motivation to continue its share gaining strategy at the expense of the leader. Hence, the curve along which market share drops is ever-steepening, and what started as a strategy to improve profit and profitability eventually has the opposite effect. The size of the business simply cannot be shrunk fast enough to keep pace with the drop in market share. Graphically, the result looks as in Fig. 2.3. Many a successful career has been built on such mortgaging of the future, provided the next move comes before the profit decline begins!

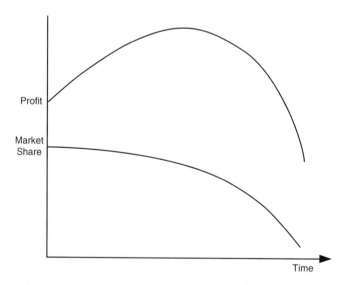

Fig. 2.3 *Profit realization and market share loss*

Reversing the process means making the profit situation even worse in the short term. The "seller" now must become a "buyer" of market share, and must convince those who were buyers first to stop buying, and then to become sellers. That requires changing the buyers' perception of the value of their share-gaining strategy that up till then has been improving both their volume and profitability. That can only be done by making it more unprofitable for them to go on than to stop.

Only a sustained and uncompromising competitive posture can achieve the necessary change in the competition's perception. This will translate into even lower profits until the desired competitive balance is regained. Not surprisingly this was a strategy that did not find much favor with a Kodak management still hoping to return to previous levels of profitability, without facing the fundamental changes that had taken place in the industry and their competitive position.

IX. Failure to Respond Adequately

Even after the decline in competitive position had become severe enough to translate into weaker financial performance, for a long time Kodak's response, rather than to undertake real change, came in the form of two kinds of overly ambitious, "more of the same" plans to get back to the previous level of performance, and satisfy the inordinate expectations that had become the norm. Overly ambitious because the underlying market, technological and competitive situation made such plans no longer feasible, and such performance no longer possible; "more of the same" because they basically relied on trying harder, and doing better, technologically and in the market-place, without any radical change in the way the company was run.

The first kind of plan typically involved the introduction of a major new product family, which it was forecast would unleash the next wave of volume growth and thereby avoid any need for restructuring or downsizing. This "home run" mentality was entirely consistent with the company's history of growth, which had indeed been fueled by periodic product breakthroughs such as Kodachrome, Kodacolor, the 126, and the 110 where it had led, and then the 35mm family of cameras and films, where it had followed but still had the market position immediately to become the leader. The "Disc" camera was a natural continuation of this line of strategy and the company's first major failure when the quality it provided did not meet customer expectations. The huge investment in electronic imaging technology in the Eighties was simply intended to be the biggest home run of them all. And, even as late as 1992, Photo CD was introduced as "the most significant product introduction since color film".

Here was a management which had "learned" that success came from unilateral introduction of significant technological change. It hadn't seen the need to listen seriously to its market-place for generations. In its own eyes it had always been the technological leader. And it was quite unaccustomed to thinking competitively. But in the real world of photography in the last quarter of the Twentieth century, what it had "learned" no longer worked. It could no longer dictate to the market-place. It was no longer the unchallenged technological leader, even in its base business. And it now faced a new set of large, sophisticated competitors in the electronic imaging arena. The plans, one after the other, simply failed.

The second kind of plan came out of the standard budget cycle, and involved promising significant improvement in financial performance relative to the previous year. Typically expenditure increases were budgeted to stimulate volume growth. These operating plans then met the reality of the uncompetitive practices that had been rigidifying the operational infrastructure, and the non-performance based people management culture that effortless success had created. The result much of the time was that the costs were incurred but the growth was not realized, and corrective cost-cutting action either was not taken, or initiated too late in the year, so that there was a continued deterioration in performance.

After a time people became aware of the lack of realism in this operational planning, but it was regarded as "poor teamwork" not to promise to achieve what everyone so desperately desired. Then, when the plans' goals were not met, because fairness was an important element of the company's value set, and because in their hearts most people knew the plans had been impossible in the first place, no one was held accountable. So the response, instead of candid evaluation of the real situation and corrective action, was to prepare another overly ambitious plan. A duplicitous cycle of unrealistic planning and lack of accountability for results had set in.

Eventually, in the mid-Eighties, two responses, typical of the times, were tried – organizational change, to create Business Units focused on specific product lines; and the squeezing of costs, through a series of headcount reductions. For a time these worked, the first providing better business focus, and the second temporarily improved results.

But the changes were only partial and did not get to the root of the problem. The functional and geographical fiefdoms were not broken up so that, instead of simplifying things, the Business Units added to the organizational complexity and structural excess. And the gains from the headcount reductions were lost as numbers crept back up through the lack of any centralized control.

Business focus rapidly deteriorated into divisional suboptimization, and improved results proved only temporary. The latter half of the Eighties going into the Nineties was a period of constantly recurring performance problems. At the same time there was a terrible fragmentation of some of the most important strategic resources (most notably product development and equipment manufacturing), and dreadful confusion in a market-place now dealing with multiple, often overlapping salesforces, as the Business Divisions tried to become autonomous, mini-Kodaks. Not surprisingly this was accompanied at all levels of the company by a pervasive loss of confidence in its ability to be master of its own destiny.

X.   Demise: Liquidation or Takeover

Eastman Kodak never fell completely to the point of formal demise, although takeover rumors were common at the end of the Eighties and the beginning of the Nineties. However the restructuring that took place in 1993 and 1994 meant it had to sell off everything except its core, imaging businesses to restore the health of its balance sheet. Several small, peripheral businesses were disposed of in 1992 and 1993. Then Eastman Chemicals was spun off as a separate company in 1993, Sterling's Ethical Drug business was sold to Sanofi in Spring 1994, and its over-the-counter business to SmithKline Beecham a few months later. That company promptly sold its North American Divisions to Bayer. Lehn & Fink, the last piece of the 1988 Sterling acquisition, was then auctioned off in pieces. Finally, the Clinical Diagnostics Division followed shortly after, going to Johnson & Johnson. By the end of 1993 management changes had taken the toll of its CEO and all but two of its top management team from only three years earlier. By September 1994 this restructuring proved enough to bring about an eighty percent increase in Kodak's stock price from its low in 1992. But, whether the actions it has taken will prove also to be enough to stem the tide of Fuji's advance, and enable it to compete in the new electronic imaging technologies will have to be the subject of another, hopefully happier story down the road.

THE FALL OF THE GIANTS

What is the moral of the story? Is this ten stage rise and fall the inevitable fate of the giants making up the industrial drivers of any, individual wave of economic growth? Or were there other possible, and more successful paths that could have been identified and taken without the benefit of 20/20 hindsight?

Let us deal with these questions in reverse order, going from the particular instance of Eastman Kodak, to the wider case of the giants of the last industrial era and then to the general insights we can distill about maintaining competitive health.

There are two aspects to the question whether Eastman Kodak could have taken a different path. First, was it possible, *for anyone*, to see what was happening and determine a better strategy? Second, is it reasonable to expect the company to have been able to implement an appropriate response?

The answer to the first question is very clearly yes. There were many people within and outside the company who had a clear enough understanding of what was going wrong, accompanied by, maybe not perfect, but certainly sufficient ideas about what to do about it, to have brought about a different story if they had been heard. This was not just a case of there being so many, essentially random diagnoses and prescriptions that one of them had to be right. It was not a long series of small, obscure slips in little understood areas of management that brought the company down. It was large, glaring errors in technology development, marketing strategy, cost control, and people management.

Moreover, many of the mistakes were not made because of a lack of serious argument in the other direction. Whether it was the instant camera, the disc system, ink jet printers, floppy discs, or electronic project after project, price increases, marketing programs, overhead costs, organization structure, early retirement programs, acquisitions, people decisions – and the list goes on – these were large, repeated errors of judgment by the company's leaders, certainly usually at the recommendation of someone or ones in senior management, but also usually in the knowledge that there was significant disagreement from other respected people within the organization. What these failures had in common was that the decisions which resulted in them were consistent with the perverted version of the management paradigm that initial success had embedded, and then sustained success had corrupted. The forces of change, of taking a different view, of trying a new approach, of suggestions that the past was no longer a reliable predictor of success, lost time after time. The same can no doubt be said for GM, IBM, and many others. The problem was much less that *no one* had the necessary insight or understanding, and much more that the *leadership* thrown up by the perverted management paradigm combined an inability to see the significance of a changed situation, with an unwillingness to act in the required way even when it did understand.

Which leads us to the second question and to the wider case of the fallen giants: was this kind of decline unavoidable? Or, is it reasonable to suggest that the giants could have given themselves leaders who could have taken different decisions?

This is a much more difficult question. And it goes right to the heart of the problem of maintaining the competitive health of the modern corporation. For it is a very human problem, one which we create for ourselves in the very processes that we use to build organizations and sustain their success. How do we retain the possibility of challenging what has been, and usually still is the bringer of success when it becomes necessary to change it? How can we tell the difference between the premature challenge which could damage a still vital management paradigm, and the desperately needed initiation of strategic change to cope with an emerging new world? How do we find and promote the kind of people who can lead the way to a new world, not just faithfully continue the pattern that led to past success?

With what was known about strategy, and organization and change at the time that Kodak's problems were setting in, it is tempting to conclude that there could not have been a very different outcome. On this argument, the paradigm simply took over, and when it became perverted no one could do anything about it. Internal cultural forces were so strong they created a self-perpetuating, decision-making process incapable of dealing with the reality that evolved. The leaders were merely puppets in the hands of these forces, mischosen, misdeveloped and misled by the past into creating a self-fulfilling future of failure.

But surely this is to fall into the same trap as treating criminals as victims, and blaming a disembodied "society" for their actions. The element of truth in the charge has been allowed to excuse the culpability of the individual. Whether we're talking of crime or organizational failure, there *are* individuals and organizations from similar backgrounds, in similar situations, subject to similar forces who have stayed out of trouble, or competitively healthy as the case may be.

Nor is the fact that it is clearly a very difficult challenge – to see what is coming, and take the necessary steps to deal with it – a sufficient excuse. It is to do just this that we elevate leaders to their lofty stations, give them the extraordinary power that goes with that and pay them significantly more than anyone else in their organizations. That's what they're for. Finally, where were their Boards? Isn't one of the main reasons for having a Board to detect and stop this kind of decline? In Eastman Kodak's case the Board presided over more than a decade when the return on investment in Kodak stock didn't even keep up with inflation, let alone the stock market's performance, before it did anything.

It finally acted in July 1993 removing its Chairman, Kay Whitmore, and replacing him with George Fisher from Motorola in November of the same year. IBM, General Motors and Westinghouse also removed their chairmen, and went outside their management ranks to replace them. As did many others. And it was appropriate that they should have done so, for what we have seen is a massive failure of leadership right across the highest, hubris-ridden reaches of American, corporate management. In too many places the generation that took charge during the recessionary phase of the fourth wave was not just not up to the job, but suffered from an arrogance, bred by America's post-war success, that did not even allow it to be told the truth. Moreover if the leaders of the new giants, that will emerge with the coming of new industries, do not learn from what happened to their predecessors we can be sure that we will be seeing some of the same kind of tragedies played out in companies we hardly know today, about four decades from now. The answer to the longest-term challenge facing the leaders of those companies is to build into their grand strategies the ability to change, right from the start.

Finally, what can the ordinary manager, far from the lofty peaks of the executive suites of the giant corporations, learn from all this?

First, for those who work for industry leaders, there is the old saying, "being warned, is being forearmed". Be on your guard against over-confidence, leading to complacency and finally to hubris. In every sphere of competition the most common cause for the favorite to lose is over-confidence. So, value your dissenters, those brave few who give you the contrarian's viewpoint, who puncture the smugness and sound the alarm. Watch out for signs that what was the vital insight that led to success has turned into an obsolete, but sacred cow that no one can question. Second, for everyone else, look for the same signs – in your competition. They mean opportunity.

Third, for industry leaders and followers alike, pay close attention to what follows! There *are* some rules that govern the interaction of competitors, the operation of complex organizations and the behavior of people faced with change. Learn them and you have the tools both to identify the threats to the competitive health of your organization, and to develop the appropriate responses.

3 Strategic Management: The Evolution of Executive Concerns

"The problem before us is not to invent more tools but to use the ones we have."   (Rosabeth Moss Kanter)

"Those who cannot remember the past are condemned to repeat it."
(George Santayana)

Kodak tried just about every management technique that came along during the twenty years of its decline. Rather than face the complicated, painful task of transforming the way it managed itself, it tried to graft technique after technique onto the body corporate in an endless chain of hope triumphing over experience until, like an overloaded Christmas Tree, the whole edifice was ready to be toppled by one little push from any direction. It was not alone in this search for the holy grail of a quick fix. Right across corporate America, for a whole generation, academics and consultants had a field day of offering the latest balm for the latest hot spot. I arrived in America right in the middle of it all, thinking I had come to the font of management wisdom.

I emigrated to the United States on January 1, 1979. Later that month I came across an article, in an eminent business publication, by William Ouchi entitled "Made in America (under Japanese Management)". That hurt, and maybe it hurt me, the immigrant, most of all. After all, what had I done? I had emigrated to a country that had lost faith in the one thing at which it was supposed to be the best in the world – management. And the reason for my coming was "management development"!

Unnerved by the dazzling success of Japanese manufacturing, too many of us took to trying to do it their way, with consensus, quality circles, kanban and on and on. The passion to imitate Japanese management techniques became a symptom of what happened to United States business in the Eighties: we experienced a crisis of confidence in American management.

For a long time we weren't able to find anything substantial enough to take its place. The result was a succession of diagnoses and solutions which came and went with bewildering speed. First, it was the techniques of strategic planning which, after rising as if from nowhere to extraordinary eminence and envy in the Seventies, were almost buried by the same managers, academics, and business press who had been lauding them just a few years previously. Then came the phenomenal rise and fall of *In Search of Excellence*, at that point the best-selling business book of all time. Regarded as a bible within months of being published in 1982, it had become a target of derision in many quarters by the end of 1984. Next it was the turn of all the ideas for improving innovation. This time disillusionment set in in most places before they were even tried. Most managers had had enough of the "consultant of the month" phenomenon even to take notice. As Terry Faulkner, the best strategic planner I ever met, told me, "I once kept a sign in my office that said, 'The only good consultant is a dead consultant,' with apologies to General Philip Sheridan". Yet the pace only accelerated – Corporate Culture, Total Quality Management, Time-based Competition, Restructuring, Reengineering, Benchmarking and on and on.

What did it all mean? Were, are all the techniques only so much snake oil? Is the art advancing so fast that future additions to the techniques of management can expect only a short life before they are displaced? Are some good, some bad? In which case, which? Or can we discern an underlying pattern that leads to a new understanding?

As Alvin Toffler pointed out many years ago, we are caught up in change that has become so extensive and so rapid that the result is confusion. Unable to separate multiple causes and multiple effects, we lost faith in all the tools and techniques that were being showered upon us. Toffler wrote *Future Shock* in 1970 just as the growth phase of the fourth wave was coming to its end, and since then, the rate of change has only continued to accelerate.

Twenty-five years later we have reached the point at which new techniques seem, in many places, to be adding less in greater efficiency or effectiveness than they cost in disruption and relearning. Yet there was a reason for all those techniques. They weren't invented for nothing. They were developed, and there were so many of them, because many people saw a need and tried to fill it. It is time to examine the ideas and trends that have occurred in business since the Second World War in an attempt to view them not as trends and fashions to be discarded, but as natural responses to the stages in an evolution of the tasks of management. We can then integrate what we have learned from the recent past into a synthesis that will give us a solid foundation for dealing with the debilitating change and complexity which are our latest challenges.

To explore the evolution of management concerns and tasks over the fifty years since the Second World War, we will look at the characteristics of the period in five separate phases, each time asking ourselves three questions:

1. What was the primary focus of the executive suite during this phase?
2. With that focus, what was the implied, major management concern? and
3. What was the managerial response offered by the academic and consulting communities of the times?

We begin, of course, with the good old days!

THE GOOD OLD DAYS

In 1945 we came out of a major war with demand exceeding supply for virtually every conceivable product and in particular for those coming out of the innovations in automobile, electrical appliances, aircraft, chemicals, synthetic fibers, pharmaceuticals, radio and television, that had occurred at the end of the previous, third wave. The growth phase of the fourth wave which, in Mandel's chronology, began in 1939, had been held up by the Second World War (as its length – 35 years – was to show). Pent-up demand, ready processes and ample manufacturing capacity, which had been built to produce material for the war and which had provided the testbed for many of the new technologies, created the conditions for long sustained prosperity. In many industries we hardly even needed salespeople. In Britain this was so much the case that the leading machine tool manufacturer of the immediate post-war period, Alfred Herbert, made a practice of granting sales positions as "rewards" to its technical and production people for many years of service!

There was easy access to cheap raw materials, the cost of money was low and stable, and the major markets of the world were cut off from each other by poor communications and expensive distribution. A reasonably well-made product was always able to find a ready market, so that the producer could easily charge more than its costs and make a profit. And constant growth covered up most of our mistakes. It was indeed rather difficult to fail.

As a result, chief executives had a single, rather simple purpose – to produce and deliver as much as they could at reasonable cost to meet the seemingly insatiable demand. The secret of success was efficiency. With operations that were always running at capacity, efficiency was the key to making the most profit. The natural, managerial response to this executive concern, as Fig. 3.1 shows, was to develop methods of budgeting and procedures aimed at running smooth operations, and controlling the use of the short-term resources (money and people) that were used in those operations.

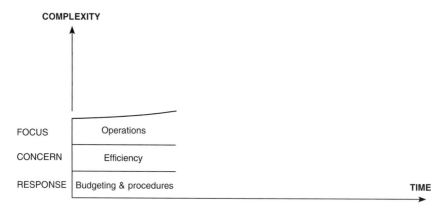

Fig. 3.1   *The evolution of executive concerns – I*

It might sound strange to us today to hear that as recently as the Fifties budgets and operational procedures were actually considered to be state-of-the-art tools. Discounted cashflow as a way of evaluating projects, which I doubt the modern manager can conceive as ever not being part of the management kit bag, did not make it until the early Sixties. From our current perspective, these things seem so elementary as to be relegated to an introductory course, if taught at all. Yet at the Harvard Business School, then even more than now the thought leader, many of the cases studied by the students of the 1950s centered on standard costs, marginal costing, variance analysis, and other aspects of the pursuit of efficiency. There was even an article in a business publication of that time entitled "Annual Budgets: State of the Art Tool to Help the Chief Executive Officer Run His Organization". Budgeting and procedures were a mainstay of booming accounting and industrial engineering firms. Operational research, developed to tackle the logistical challenges of the Second World War and offering sophisticated mathematical techniques to achieve efficiency, was the ultimate in management "science", which is the way we thought of the task.

All of this may seem incredible. But only because it's not at the forefront of our thinking anymore. More than thirty years of increasing change have impelled us to advance far beyond this stage of development. But if you consider the situation facing the CEO of the early Fifties, that response was both logical and correct. What's more, it's not too far off the mark today for the high-tech company facing explosive demand for its newly developed, breakthrough product. Story after story of the inefficient disorder of rapid growth start-ups reinforces the message. That point in their evolution is very like where much of corporate America, in particular in those new industries which were the drivers of the fourth wave, was at the end of the Forties. In fact this focus was right on target, and it worked very well for almost everyone until the orgy of consumer buying began to slow down after the Korean War. At that point it became less and less simple just to plan to produce more every year and expect to sell it all, with high profitability following inevitably from efficient operation.

A LITTLE CLOUD

In the late Fifties the economy began to become more complex and its old certainties started to break down. As the initial, relatively simple needs for basic goods were satisfied, demand both slackened and became more selective. As the growth phase of the fourth wave passed its point of greatest strength and began to slow down, economic cycles began to have a more significant impact. Spurts of growth alternated with slower periods, which resulted in temporarily lower profits and unused capacity. An increase in government regulations created uncertainty about whether current products and operating practices would be acceptable in the future. Finally, as machines began to displace labor, many industries tended to become more capital intensive. And automation, a direct result of the previous era's concern with efficiency, brought with it uncertainties surrounding what equipment to choose, how much capacity to install and when to bring it on line.

At the same time, because of the changes in the market-place, it began to be less clear that the "right" demand would indeed be present to meet supply. Chief executive officers became more concerned about the element of risk in making decisions about where to invest their resources. Moreover, since increasing capital intensity meant that considerable resources had to be allocated in advance of any return on those resources, there was a time factor involved, which became known as "lead time". From a planning perspective this simply means the period of time when a company is at highest financial risk, since its resources have been committed and the returns have not yet arrived.

Budgeting, the planning and control response to the previous primary concern of efficiency of operations, deals with the short-term, typically through the one-year cycle of the budget or operational plan. The need now emerged to plan in greater depth for a more extended period of time, to reduce the amount of longer-term risk inherent in the new situation. The response of the academics and other management thinkers was to invent another "planning and control" tool – long-range planning (see Fig. 3.2). In 1955 the Stanford Research Institute introduced the first of the services that have since developed into the huge industry that we now call variously "strategy, strategic planning or strategic management consulting". They called it "long-range planning", and that term began to appear in the management literature of the time. The second stage of the evolution had been reached.

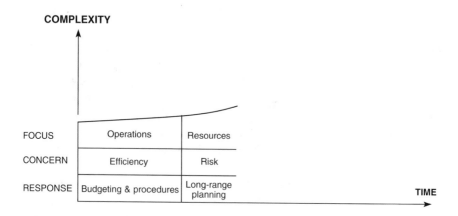

Fig. 3.2   *The evolution of executive concerns – II*

The primary focus of long-range planning is on determining what resources will be needed and when they should be committed, to deal with the problem of lead times in complex environments. The automobile industry provided and still provides a good illustration of the need for such long-range planning, since it takes several years to design and build new bodies and engines. This is true irrespective of whether there is significant competition or not. The notorious Edsel debacle, for example, was fundamentally a simple failure in long-range planning, independent of any competitive considerations. The designers had misread the future direction of demand, which was not for more complicated designs but for simpler ones. By the time the car was ready the market had disappeared. (Interestingly, after the Edsel debacle – the best researched yet biggest, new car introduction failure in the history of the industry – the researchers returned to their data to see what they'd missed. What they found was that, although at the time when the product was conceived the trend was still toward more complicated designs, the second differential had changed. That is, the trend was slowing. By the time the car was launched it had not just slowed, but stopped and reversed itself. That same data then gave birth to the Mustang – the most successful new car introduction in the history of the industry!)

The rosy business picture of the years immediately following the war was clouded by new complexities and uncertainties that arose in the mid-Fifties. The techniques of long-range planning were added to those of budgeting and procedures as the natural response to these challenges. Discounted Cash Flow made its entry as one of those techniques, specifically to recognize the "time-value" of money – that is its ability to earn a return over time, which was foregone during the period of highest risk, before a major investment began to be productive. "Operational Management" – the managing of today's business, and the allocation of resources for tomorrow's – had come to full maturity. It was now conventional wisdom to describe *the* management task as one of "planning and control". As we can now see this was only true, in the simplicity with which it was then regarded, for the immediately preceding generation, because that indeed had been the right managerial response to the prevailing conditions.

By the end of the Sixties, however, much darker clouds began to appear on the horizon, as a very new concern began to become apparent.

THE GATHERING STORM

As the Sixties turned into the Seventies, and the long expansionary phase turned into a recessionary one, we moved toward the environment of competitive intensity, unprecedented in our post-war experience, that is still with us today. Of course, competition had always been a factor in American business, but before this time, in the period since the Second World War, it had not been the matter of greatest concern. The long-range planners had focused more on trends in the market and in technology, and the budgeters more on efficiency in production and distribution than on competition. Now competition became the top priority and, growing more intensive over the next two decades as the fourth wave approaches its end, it remains one of the principal areas that most concern the executives at the top of our companies today.

All of a sudden we found ourselves living in a world in which economic success was relative instead of absolute. No longer was it enough to provide a product to meet an identified need. Absolute, economic results now required relative, competitive success. Business had become a race, and the race, after all, had always gone not to the swift but to the swifter. This was a competition to win a gold medal, not break a world record. But it was more than just an increase in *direct* competition. We have learned from the hard lessons of the past twenty years that the level of competitive intensity in an industry is a function of much more than the rivalry among existing firms that are producing the same product or service. From today's perspective, looking only at that rivalry, which is what most strategic thinking had been doing, was a crude assumption. As Harvard professor Michael Porter pointed out in a model that revolutionized strategic thinking the truth is that in considering competitive intensity there are four other forces that must be taken into account.

As Fig. 3.3 shows, it is also necessary to look at the threat of new entrants into the market and substitutes for the product under consideration, the bargaining power of suppliers, and the bargaining power of buyers. All these forces impinge directly on, not just the environment in which competition takes place, but on the actions competitors may take, and so on the level of competitive intensity in an industry.

My own experience at Continental Can is a case in point. In the 1970s the major US can makers – Continental Can, American Can, National Can and Crown Cork and Seal – were all faced with

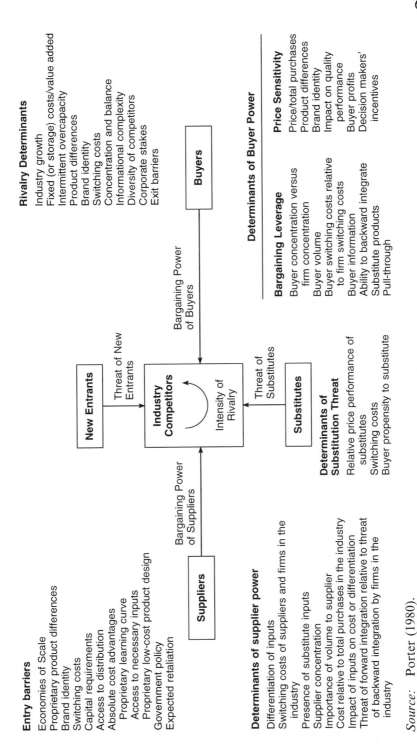

Fig. 3.3 *Elements of industry structure*

Source: Porter (1980).

overcapacity: too many plants making too few cans. Since steel workers were numerous and members of a strong union, it was very expensive to lay them off. It was difficult to get out of the business cheaply, so, in the emerging language of strategy, exit barriers were high. This encouraged can makers to lower their prices rather than reduce their capacity. The situation was further complicated by the entry of Metal Box, a British company, into the market, and then by the decision of brewers to make many of their own cans. With mature, purchasable technology and relatively low capital costs for a competitive unit of production, entry barriers were low. Finally, to add to the production capacity problem, first Monsanto, and then other companies (including a division of Continental!), began the manufacturing of plastic bottles as substitutes for cans. On top of all this, Continental Can was buying its raw material from giant companies like Alcoa and United States Steel, and selling its cans to the likes of Anheuser Busch and Coca-Cola. So, in a glutted market-place, with a major new entrant, self-manufacture on the rise, and aggressive introduction of substitute packages, we were caught between large suppliers, who were in a position to drive up our material costs, and large buyers, who could exert tough downward pressure on prices.

The result was a competitive inferno. And there was no happy ending, least of all for the people involved. With horrendous pressures on its profit margins, Continental took major write-offs and spent a whole decade continuously laying off people. By 1986 both Continental group (Continental Can's parent company) and National Can had been taken over and American Can had announced that it was selling its packaging business.

This was just one particularly dramatic example. What was happening in general? Though several forces were at play, they combined to define two basic realities: scarce, more expensive resources, and a leveling of the competitive playing field. The late Sixties saw the dawn of a real global economy. Its impact on raw materials availability and cost was brought home with particular harshness by the Six-Day War in 1973. And the cost of money, which had always averaged below three percent in real terms, had risen to the teens by the late Seventies. For the first time in the history of the United States resources became scarce and expensive. At the same time as this was reducing the margin of error in the way resources were utilized, a whole host of factors were making it more and more difficult to gain and maintain a competitive edge, and hence reducing the ability to achieve a higher price. Deregulation caused a leveling of the playing field in industries ranging from airlines to financial services. Barriers between industries were coming down and competitive advantage was becoming more and more difficult to achieve.

The playing field was further leveled by the "information explosion". Now everyone could gain ready access to technical and managerial expertise. Business schools and consulting firms queued up to ensure anyone could apply the latest technique the moment it was introduced. Reduced economic growth also made the going tougher. With high growth, many companies could still satisfy their corporate objectives even if they grew a bit more slowly than the market. But with slower growth we approached a "zero sum game", a situation in which there have to be winners and losers.

Finally, and apparently most difficult of all for corporate America to accept, it became clear that there really is no fundamental difference between the quality of the people in any two companies. Over nearly three decades I have lived in three continents, spent extensive amounts of time working in six countries, and studied a dozen or more industries, but I have yet to find a company that can *truly* claim that its strategic success, or failure, stems from a sustained difference in the quality of its people. Yet everybody keeps saying there is! I attend many management gatherings, and the ritual is almost invariably the same. The leaders give the last speech and, moving to their climax, they come to their clinching argument for their belief in the future success of their unit. "The *real* difference between us and our competitors", they say, "is the quality of our people". Fine, rousing stuff. Great to get the troops to charge up San Juan hill the next morning. But it has very little to do with strategy. The "raw material", the basic quality of the total population of the organization, simply doesn't vary very much. In fact, it would be surprising if it did since we tend to hire our people from the same schools, get the same consultants to teach them the same techniques and give them the same books to read. The prudent manager's assumption is that there is no difference in the quality of his or her people compared to his or her major competitors'. But this is not to say that there are not differences in the quality of the *performance* that different companies derive from their people. In fact, at bottom, what the highest form of strategy, grand strategy, and this book are all about is not better planning, or finer technology or cleverer marketing, but getting superior performance out of essentially the same bunch of people. And that more than anything else is a challenge of leadership. The *real* difference between competitors lies in the quality of their leadership – not just the leadership provided by top management, although that is often decisive because of its impact on everyone else, but leadership as it is exercised throughout the organization. And this applies to the individual contributor facing a decision over whether to undertake a possibly risky initiative or not, just as much as to anyone who has the responsibility of managing other people. The quality of a few brave people does make a difference, in fact the decisive difference. But it's not through genius or individual feats of performance. It's through leadership, by helping an otherwise ordinary bunch of people become an extraordinary team.

But recognition of the critical importance of the human factor did not come until much later. In the Seventies, occupants of executive suites attempted to deal with their new focus on competition by seeking, through the deliberate planning of what they would do with principally their financial resources, to determine how to create superior, competitive positions for themselves which would enable them to win in the market-place. The trigger was the competitive storm loosed by the shift from the "A" to the "B" phase of the fourth wave, compounded by the beginnings of a global market-place and the new scarcity and cost of resources. It was the first step away from operational management, toward strategic management. Academics and planners responded by developing a whole host of techniques to monitor the environment, to compare companies, to determine the characteristics of superior positions and to suggest strategies to achieve them. The first building block of grand strategy began to be put in place. As Fig. 3.4 shows, we made our first deliberate effort to add business strategy to the evolving management discipline.

The key to strategy as a management technique, as we will explore in considerable depth in a later chapter, is that it recognizes the addition of the element of competition to planning. What before only had to deal with where technology and demand were going, now had to factor in the unpleasant reality that there was someone out there who wanted to stop you achieving your aim. As an ex-naval officer once said to me, "If you're given the task of taking the fleet from Newport News to Scapa Flow in time of peace you certainly need an operational plan. If you're given the same task in time of war you need a strategic plan".

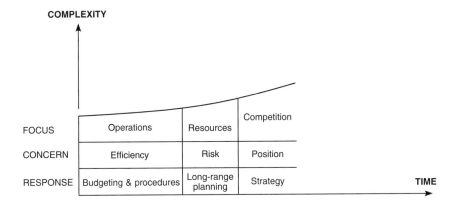

Fig. 3.4 *The evolution of executive concerns – III*

Strategy then involves a particular kind of planning – one that takes account of competition as well as every other kind of uncertainty – so as to achieve some kind of objective. In the Seventies we began to apply this new kind of planning to the objectives of business.

The ultimate objective of business is economic – a return on investment that justifies the risk the investor takes in contributing his or her capital. But business competes in the market-place for capital, as well as for the goods it provides. And that market-place is no different in the way its "buyers", i.e. investors, choose between competitive offerings. So, the true, financial aim of business is a *superior* return compared to other, similar investments available to the investor. Either a higher return with equality of risk, or the same return with less risk will achieve this aim. So the aim of strategy is to achieve such a combination and, at best, both higher and more secure returns at the same time.

But is this possible? Can one achieve returns that are both higher and more secure at the same time? One's immediate intuition says no. Think about the securities markets, where we expect higher returns on an investment usually to be accompanied by higher risk (typically stocks), and more secure investments to yield lower returns (typically bonds). The aim of strategy, we're saying, is to beat this expectation, to achieve both higher returns and more secure returns at one and the same time.

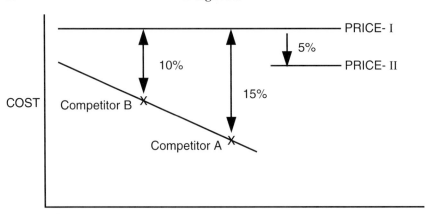

Fig. 3.5   *The importance of relative cost*

In the early Seventies, we had a simple, graphic way to show that this was indeed possible (see Fig. 3.5). Imagine two competitors making the same product and, because it's the same, selling it for the same price (*Price I* in Fig. 3.5). If one competitor has lower costs than the other it is immediately obvious that it will enjoy higher returns, the first goal of strategy (let's say 15% on sales compared to 10%, as the exhibit shows). Now think of what happens in a recession, or temporary downturn in the demand for the particular product. For a time supply exceeds demand enabling buyers to shop around more than before and forcing down the price, by say 5% (to *Price II*). The result is a 50% reduction in the margin for the competitor with the higher cost, but only 33% for the one with the lower cost. Competitor A's return can now be seen to be not only higher, but also more secure than Competitor B's, in the sense that it is less affected by the drop in price caused by a downturn in demand.

From this example we would draw the conclusion that strategy, therefore, must focus on relative cost: that the aim of strategy could and would be reached by achieving and sustaining a relative cost position that is superior to that of the competition.

The vast bulk of the strategy development work in the Seventies stemmed from that idea. As George Bennett, ex-Boston Consulting Group, ex-Bain, and ex-Braxton said, "Sixty percent of the work we did [in the Seventies] was cost analysis". Achieving and exploiting a sustainable cost advantage became the core idea on which most business strategy was developed. The previous era had concentrated on efficiency of operations as the primary source of profitability, and allocation of resources as the way to reduce the risk caused by the lead-time between when an investment is made and a return on it is realized. In retrospect we can see that the first wave of strategic management that followed was fully continuous with that focus, since it was concerned mostly with cost, and its aim was superior relative cost, or *efficiency*, as the way to deal with the new source of risk, competition. Efficiency is the first dimension of strategy, and was almost the total focus of that early era of strategy as a management discipline.

The dominant idea was the 'experience curve', introduced to business by The Boston Consulting Group at the end of the sixties, as the fourth wave approached its recessionary phase. Here is part of BCG's Perspective No. 16, published in 1968:

THE EXPERIENCE CURVE

There is a hypothesis that costs follow a definite pattern which is a function of accumulated production experience. If further research validates this theory then the implication for business management is far reaching . . .

Price and cost data show that *costs decline by some characteristic amount each time accumulated experience is doubled.* Given this, it is clear that not only can one's own costs be projected, but costs relative to competitors can also be estimated, given some rather straightforward information about the market.

The characteristic decline is consistently 20–30% each time accumulated production is doubled. This decline goes on in time without limit (in constant dollars) regardless of the growth of experience. The rate of decline is surprisingly consistent, even from industry to industry . . .

When accumulated units of a product are increasing annually at a constant percentage rate, then each year of product experience produces approximately the same percentage effect on cost. If competitors maintain the same relative market shares and have roughly equivalent histories of experience, then their costs will tend to move in parallel. If competitors' market position changes, so do their relative costs.

Again as with previous steps forward in the art of management, for a time it worked, at least for the early practitioners. But as individual companies, industries and whole economies matured and moved down to the flat part of the experience curve, where cost declines occurred more slowly because less and less was being added proportionately to accumulated volume, the absolute differences in efficiency that were sustainable became much smaller. So efficiency became less viable as a source of advantage that could by itself sustain strategic success. I can remember, as early as 1974, a disappointed client saying to one of BCG's Vice-Presidents, "It's a pity so many of your recommendations were based on the experience curve".

If lower cost than competition could no longer be relied upon, the only other way to achieve the desired higher and more secure returns was higher price. And to realize and maintain a higher price meant *differentiation* – supplying a more highly valued combination of products and services than the competition. Gradually, during the Seventies, attention shifted from efficiency toward differentiation, as the former lost its strategic power in more and more industries.

This does not mean that efficiency was then, or is now no longer a matter of concern. Nor does it mean that the Experience Curve somehow no longer holds, and that its users were "quacks" rather than purveyors of genuine medicine. Quite the contrary. It means that efficiency is still vital, and the importance of the experience curve to the building of a competitive cost base, particularly for a new product or service, is still central. But instead of being sufficient for success, efficiency has become for many just the condition for starting the race. By itself it is no longer enough: differentiation, the second dimension of strategy, has also become a condition for winning.

By the end of the Seventies, nearly all large companies, and many smaller ones, had adopted the discipline of strategic planning to address the needs for superior efficiency and differentiation if they were to compete effectively. Unfortunately, in most of them the promised performance did not result.

BACK TO BASICS

By the early Eighties strategic planning had fallen into disrepute. As Russell Ackoff described one CEO's conclusion: "Strategic planning is like a Chinese meal. After I eat it I feel full, but three hours later it's as if I hadn't eaten at all". The promised performance just didn't follow the enormous time and cost put into the planning. Whether the planning was good or bad we'll never know, because most of the plans were never acted on. One researcher, who studied the situation in Europe, suggested that over 95 percent of the strategic plans that were written in the Seventies were never fully implemented. From my experience that may have been a conservative estimate. At Continental we eventually concluded that the best thing to do with our strategic plans was to give them to American Can, since they at least might be fooled into thinking that was what we were going to do!

So, like jilted lovers the managers, who had only recently been such enthusiastic fans of strategic planning, took their revenge. And summarizing their reaction in its December 1982 issue, *Fortune* ran a cover story with the title "The Real World Strikes Back, Corporate Strategists under Fire" (see Fig. 3.6).

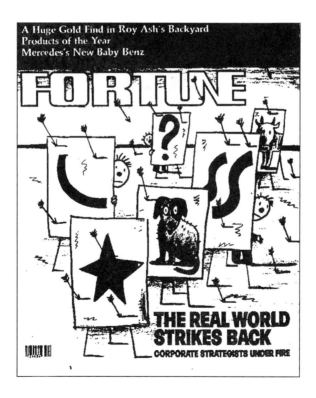

Fig. 3.6 *Fortune*'s **cover story, December 27, 1982**

There they were, all those strategists under fire, hiding behind the symbols that the arch-priests of strategy, The Boston Consulting Group, had made so famous during the Seventies – The Experience Curve, The Product/Life Cycle, and the four inhabitants of the Growth/Share Matrix: The Star, The Dog, The Cash Cow and The Question Mark.

The reality was in fact simple: if the strategy is not implemented and the position is not achieved then performance, unsurprisingly, does not follow. That was the overwhelming experience of companies in the Seventies, a decade of strategic planning but not of strategic management. But the managers weren't ready for that conclusion. It couldn't be *our* fault, it must have been the idea of planning, and the ideas of the planners. So, concluding that strategy did not work, managers moved back to what they had been doing before, the direct pursuit of financial performance. In good American fashion, and under our favorite slogan when we think things have become too complicated, "back to basics", the pendulum swung from strategy in pursuit of superior competitive positions to its philosophical opposite, the search for success, through execution, through better operational management. But it was the "basics" that had got us in trouble in the first place. Once upon a time they were the secret of our success, since what were the "basics" but the codification of the replicable pattern that had become conventional wisdom? But things had changed, so by themselves, they didn't work anymore. So when we tried to go back to them, this time things didn't improve. And that's where we lost our confidence. We began to look for new ways of doing things, not out of an innovative spirit but from defeatism.

The Vietnamese War, Watergate, a bankrupt New York, a falling dollar, the Iranian hostages, the debacles in consumer electronics, steel and cars – all these seemed to suggest in the early Eighties that we weren't the super-managers of the superpower that the whole world had been saying we were just a short time before. We reached the era of "Made in America (under Japanese management)". We began to copy other people, in particular the Japanese.

The new buzz words were "quality circles", "consensus", "lifetime employment", "Theory Z", whatever that meant, and of course "corporate culture". Just learn about these, the gurus said, and all your problems will be over. Just follow my nostrum and the performance you desire will be yours. Almost all of these ideas were borrowed. And even when they weren't they didn't seem natural to the real world of business. We were looking outside ourselves for solutions and none of them seemed to fit. Then in 1982 came salvation, in the form of a book – *In Search of Excellence*, with its subtitle, *Lessons from America's Best Run Companies*. Its emphasis on action rather than planning, and a message that was interpreted as a call for a return to the basics of management was irresistible. In some quarters so much so that the insights of the previous stage were all but forgotten, and the new message was used as an excuse to drop strategy as a serious discipline altogether. But elsewhere, in more thoughtful circles, it was understood that the lessons of excellence, as a contribution to the evolving management discipline, were complementary to those of strategy and the second element of grand strategy began to be put in place, as Fig. 3.7 shows.

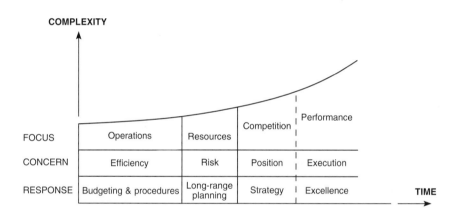

Fig. 3.7 *The evolution of executive concerns – IV*

For a book that was to be so successful, it had a curious start. The *New York Times* panned it. There was one story that Peter Drucker described it as "a puerile response to a recession" – delicious, but perhaps unworthy of the master. But business loved it, and I think for three reasons. First, it broke the spell. It reminded us that there *were* some American companies which had managed to perform in a truly outstanding fashion throughout this depressing period. It was thus the first step in finding a new, *American* way. Second, it provided a simple list of ideas that anyone could follow, feel they were doing what the best did and look confidently for the results to follow. How many of us remember that once famous list today?

1. A bias for action
2. Close to the customer
3. Autonomy and entrepreneurship
4. Productivity through people
5. Hands-on, value-driven
6. Stick to the knitting
7. Simple form, lean staff
8. Simultaneous loose–tight properties.

How many of us truly understood it? Or really tried to implement it? Third, and in my view most important of all, it legitimized the "soft" stuff. It allowed us to begin talking about beliefs, values, and how to deal with people. A famous saying of the time was "real men don't eat quiche". Whether that was true or not, what certainly was true was that real businessmen (there still weren't many women) didn't talk about values. These simple, basic ideas that all of us in business knew were important, but somehow weren't legitimate subjects in the previous era of hard-nosed, cost-focused, by the numbers management, suddenly could be discussed. The book struck a chord deep in the hearts of American management. They knew something was wrong, and that the world wasn't as simply reducible to numbers as was the dominant practice of the time.

In the Eighties two examples of companies with an ethic which encompassed the soft stuff, and wasn't simply "profit", reigned supreme: IBM at its best, in the Seventies and early Eighties; and Johnson & Johnson, in particular in its handling of the Tylenol disaster, in the early Eighties.

THE MOST ADMIRED AND MOST VALUABLE COMPANY IN AMERICA

By the mid-Eighties IBM had reached the peak of its perceived success. It was the most admired company in America. It was also the most valuable, and by a very long way. As we later learned, the seeds for its downfall had already been sown. So what we were really seeing was a company running on the momentum created by an earlier set of leaders, most notably a famous father and son – Thomas Watson, Sr, and Thomas Watson, Jr. Through a whole generation the latter, taking over from his father, had guided IBM to world dominance in computers, and pre-eminence as a management institution in the eyes of all the rest of us who used it as a model. It is an extraordinary testament to the power of what he and his father believed in, and what they instilled in IBM, that it took so long for the subsequent hubris and errors to bring the company down. As the quote at the very beginning of this book shows, central to what he believed about the roots of corporate success were "beliefs". His book about IBM is entitled *A Business and its Beliefs*, and in it he describes the three beliefs that were the rock on which he and his father built their success:

> [We put first] our respect for the individual. [Second,] we want to give the best customer service of any company in the world. [And third,] we believe that an organization should pursue all tasks with the idea that they can be accomplished in a superior fashion.

These values may not have worked for every organization; and the way IBM put them into practice may not have universal appeal. But it is very clear that, for a long time, IBM stayed true to Watson's thesis, and that its people believed this was indeed the foundation for the firm's success. Buck Rodgers, retired Senior Vice President of Marketing, in the mid-Eighties attested to how broadly these values were shared within IBM when he exclaimed, "If you don't share them, you leave quickly!" He also gave us an insight as to what it means to manage a major organization this way: "The top management of IBM does not manage the company. It manages the values. The next level down runs the company".

So, what went wrong?

Clearly there were errors in strategy, in insight on where the market was going and in devising the appropriate responses. But, from watching and talking to many of IBM's people from close at hand right through the Eighties, I'd say that more than anything else it was the failure to adapt those three beliefs to a new age, and then stay true to them as an operating credo, that was at the root of the company's decline. In fact it was worse. As at Kodak, enormous, sustained success led in practice to the perversion of IBM's beliefs into forms of behaviour which bore no relationship to the original intent.

It began to be reported in the market-place that IBM was no longer the service leader. And, when that happened, its higher prices, less than state-of-the-art product line and inattention to the new segments that were emerging began to erode its market share. The paternalism and heavy emphasis on job security that had been the company's way of giving life to "respect for the individual" in the uncertain days of the Depression, by the Eighties had turned into the right to a job for life under virtually any circumstances. And "superiority in everything we do", originally a call for excellence and attention to detail had become an attitude of "going first class", "no expense spared" and "only the best is good enough".

As I said earlier about Kodak, and as John Gardner has said of America, it was not a lack of beliefs that was the problem, but a lack of fidelity to its beliefs.

THE STORY OF JOHNSON & JOHNSON'S CREDO

The first version of the Credo (see Fig. 3.8) was written in 1946 by a young Brigadier-General, Robert W. Johnson, head of the family and the firm. In his preamble to it he wrote:

> Institutions, both public and private, exist because the people want them, believe in them, or at least are willing to tolerate them. The day has passed when business was a private matter – if it ever really was. In a business society, every act of business has social consequences and may arouse public interest. Every time business hires, builds, sells or buys, it is acting for the people as well as for itself, and it *must* accept full responsibility for its acts.

Little did he know how important his words would be in the handling of a crisis nearly forty years later.

Brigadier Johnson regarded the Credo and its use as the "public service" orientation of a business. Reading the Credo shows, as a later generation of management was to discover, that it was much more than that – it was a statement about a way of behaving, of setting priorities and of choosing between alternative courses of action when the chips were down. In short, it was and is a statement of values.

In 1975 Jim Burke, CEO of Johnson & Johnson, and some of his top managers became concerned "whether, in fact, we were practising what we preached". In a talk he gave to the Advertising Council in 1985, he described what they did about their concern:

> So we tried an experiment. We invited twenty-four of our managers from the United States and overseas here – to the Waldorf [Astoria, in New York City], as a matter of fact – for a meeting to challenge the Credo. I opened the meeting with the observation

OUR CREDO

"We believe our first responsibility is to the doctors, nurses and patients,
to mothers and all others who use our products and services.
In meeting their needs everything we do must be of high quality.
We must constantly strive to reduce our costs
in order to maintain reasonable prices.
Customers' orders must be serviced promptly and accurately.
Our suppliers and distributors must have an opportunity
to make a fair profit.

We are responsible to our employees,
the men and women who work with us throughout the world.
Everyone must be considered as an individual.
We must respect their dignity and recognize their merit.
They must have a sense of security in their jobs.
Compensation must be fair and adequate,
and working conditions clean, orderly and safe.
Employees must feel free to make suggestions and complaints.
There must be equal opportunity for employment, development
and advancement for those qualified.
We must provide competent management,
and their actions must be just and ethical.

We are responsible to the communities in which we live and work
and to the world community as well.
We must be good citizens – support good works and charities
and bear our fair share of taxes.
We must encourage civic improvements and better health and education.
We must maintain in good order
the property we are privileged to use,
protecting the environment and natural resources.

Our final responsibility is to our stockholders.
Business must make a sound profit.
We must experiment with new ideas.
Research must be carried on, innovative programs developed
and mistakes paid for.
New equipment must be purchased, new facilities provided
and new products launched.
Reserves must be created to provide for adverse times.
When we operate according to these principles,
the stockholders should realize a fair return."

Fig. 3.8 *The Johnson & Johnson Credo*

that the document was hanging in most of our offices around the world. If we were not committed to it, it was an act of pretension and ought to be ripped off the walls. I challenged the group to recommend whether we should get rid of it, re-write it, or commit to it as is.

The meeting was a turn-on, a genuine happening, as these managers struggled with the issues that the Credo defined. What we discovered was that we had a set of guiding principles far more powerful than we had imagined.

In the next three years Jim Burke and his COO, David Clare, held what were called "Credo Challenge meetings" for key Johnson & Johnson managers from all over the world. In small groups they met with the CEO, or COO, and explored the substance and significance of the Credo, testing the seriousness of intent of their leaders in making it the supreme guide for how the company should be run. The result was the document in Fig. 3.8 at the beginning of this section. Since then there has been one change – "mothers", on the second line, has been changed to "parents" – to reflect a changing world.

At the end of this process, in June of 1979, Burke brought the managers of J&J's 150 companies from all over the world to New York, where, as he put it: "The centrepiece of that meeting was the revitalized Credo – a statement of purpose that everyone now not only understood, but had had the chance to contribute to".

Three years later, on September 29, 1982, they learned that a madman in Chicago had decided to use Tylenol as a murder weapon. Seven people died. Potential panic. The seeds of chaos. The first decision Johnson & Johnson had to make was what to do about the product. Was this an isolated incident in Chicago? Could it affect all of Illinois? The Mid-West? The whole country? What should they do? No one knew how many other "killer capsules" might be out there in stores, in handbags, in consumers' homes. The conversation must have gone something like the following:

Well, what does the Credo say?

The first sentence of the Credo says, "We believe our first responsibility is to the doctors, nurses and patients, to mothers and all others who use our products and services". And three years ago that's how we said we were going to run this company. We don't have any choice. We have to take it, the product, Tylenol, perhaps our highest profit maker, off the shelf right across the country."

They did, at some huge cost, certainly hundreds of millions in 1995 dollars. And every expert in the country forecast they'd never get their market back. Ten months later they had over 90% of their original share. Today, after another disaster which forced a major product change to ensure it could never happen again, they have a higher share than before it all happened.

Jim Burke has said that he didn't believe they could have got through the crisis without the Credo to guide them at the top, and for all the other people in the company called upon to take some form of action, or make some kind of statement. But this wasn't enough for Burke, or Johnson & Johnson. They had spent a huge amount of money in being true to the first paragraph of their Credo. But, what about the last paragraph, "Our final responsibility is to our stockholders. . .". Was it a good investment? Did it pay off? Jim Burke was sure that it did. As he said, "I have long harboured the belief that the most successful corporations in this country – the ones that have delivered outstanding results over a long period of time – were driven by a simple moral imperative – serving the public in the broadest, possible sense better than their competition". But was there any concrete, financial evidence that doing the right thing would translate into superior financial performance, and be rewarded in that most cold-blooded of forums, the stock market? They decided to see if they could find out.

With the help of the Ethics Resource Center in Washington and The Business Roundtable's Task Force on Corporate Responsibility, they set out to find other companies like Johnson & Johnson. Not companies with identical credos, nor even "perfect" companies in the sense that they had never slipped. Nor even companies in businesses with which no one could find any fault. But companies about whom there was strong, external evidence that they had indeed tried to run themselves with a sense of their broader mission to serve the public, as it accorded with the world and the times in which they were doing business.

"We decided to look at companies who had been in existence at least thirty years and, at the same time, fulfilled two very rigid criteria", said Burke. "First, they had to have a written, codified set of principles stating the philosophy that serving the public was central to their being. And second, there had to be solid evidence that these ideas had been promulgated and practised for at least a generation by their organizations".

They eventually identified twenty-six companies on which there was sufficient data to conclude that this was the case. They had to drop eleven who weren't public, had been private or didn't exist thirty years earlier (so that they could not examine their stock market record) – for example, Prudential, Hewlett Packard, Levi Strauss, Johnson's Wax and McDonalds. The final group of fifteen companies was as listed in Table 3.1.

Table 3.1   Values-driven companies, 1983

AT&T	IBM	Procter & Gamble
Coca-Cola	J. C. Penney	R. J. Reynolds
Eastman Kodak	John Deere	Sun Co.
General Foods	Johnson & Johnson	3M
Gerber Products	Pitney Bowes	Xerox

Each of us may find reasons to quarrel with this list, particularly after another decade has passed. Many of them have since slipped – one, Eastman Kodak, we have explored at length. Another – IBM – we have just referred to, and will again. R.J. Reynolds was in a business, cigarettes, which ten years later would be regarded as almost definitional of lack of regard for the public. But during this period (1952–1982), with the world the way it was then, and the evidence the researchers were able to gather, they felt justified in concluding that these companies met Jim Burke's criteria. Then they examined the financial performance of the group.

In November 1983 when they did their analysis, the Dow Jones Index was standing at just over 1200. The question for you, the reader, is: what do you think it would have been standing at, if it had been comprised of those fifteen, superior public service or values-driven companies? In years of asking this question the highest bid I have ever received was 4,500. The actual answer is 9,399! Those fifteen companies outperformed the Dow Jones Index by a factor of almost eight, by apparently making their first priority not profit, but serving the public better than their competition. In fact, Jim Burke used to say that the most common question he was asked about the Credo was, "Why do you put the stockholder last?" His answer has always been the same: "If we do the other three jobs properly, the stockholder will always be well served". $30,000 invested evenly in each of the fifteen companies in 1953 would have been worth over a million dollars thirty years later when the analysis was done – their stockholders were indeed well served. As Burke put it in a speech when receiving the Public Service Award on behalf of his company, "The results are, at the very least, provocative".

And I thought I'd found the crowning piece of evidence to support the idea that the best course of action, even when measured in the most directly financial way imaginable, is indeed to do the right thing.

But, unfortunately, I am a mathematician and one day it dawned on me that there was a huge flaw in the reasoning – the sample had been chosen looking backward. Maybe, following rigorous, scientific procedure, if the sample had been chosen in 1953, looking forward, there would have been another fifteen, or fifty or five hundred companies, with equally strong values, all of which had gone under in the interim, so that they couldn't be found by Jim Burke's researchers in 1983. Include them and the return on an investment in them *all* would not have looked anywhere near as good thirty years later.

Disheartened, I was looking at the list of fifteen when it struck me that there was another characteristic that these companies shared, in addition to being guided in their behaviour by a clear set of values. They were all run for much, if not all, of the thirty-year period by superb, focused businessmen. (I use the last word literally. The good news is that it is already apparent that the term is obsolete in this context. Dynasties of the future will be led by women as well as men. This is not just because the opportunity is at last emerging, but because, as we shall see, "managing change", the new management paradigm, requires much more of the feminine than the old one, "command and control", which was almost entirely masculine.) These were not charitable institutions. A clear, broadly inclusive philosophy they may have had, but they were in business for some very clear, hard-nosed purposes – to satisfy demanding sets of customers, to win in the market-place, to grow and above all to make a handsome return on the significant sums many of their leaders personally had invested in them.

Maybe, therefore, there was another factor operating here in addition to values – the determined pursuit of a set of clear, business purposes, in particular recognizing that the primary purpose of all is to make a superior return on investment. Maybe Jim Burke was gilding the lily just a bit when he said that the only thing you had to concern yourself with was taking care of the groups represented by

J&J's first three responsibilities. And maybe if we looked at both values and purposes at the same time we could gain a deeper understanding of the nature of companies, and the kind of performance to be expected from them.

DAVIDSON'S SEMI-SERIOUS TYPOLOGY OF COMPANIES

So was born Davidson's Semi-Serious Typology of Companies (see Fig. 3.9). *Semi-* because the world is clearly a more complicated place than this simple little idea might suggest; but -*serious* because there are some real truths here, which seem to hold up very well when applied to situations one knows about.

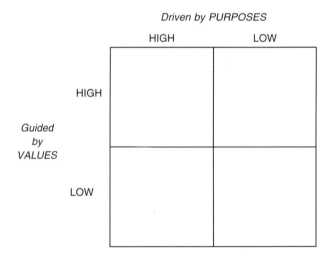

Fig. 3.9 *Purposes/Values matrix*

Naturally, being the brainchild of a consultant, the typology requires a matrix – with Purposes on one axis, and Values on the other. We have explored the nature of values in some depth above, and we will do the same for purposes in a later chapter. Here what matters is that possessing a set of clear purposes implies the tough-mindedness to insist on not compromising the very reasons to be in business in the first place, most notably the making of a superior return on the stockholder's investment. Now, what can we say about the performance of the four kinds of companies so defined?

High on Values, High on Purposes

The fifteen companies in Johnson & Johnson's sample fall in the top left-hand corner. As we have seen their thirty-year performance put them in a class of their own, so let's call them Dynasties.

High on Values, Low on Purposes

On their right are the companies which didn't make it into the J&J sample, despite their high values orientation, because their low purposes orientation had caused them to fail sometime before the research was done at the end of the period. This kind of company has the cultural foundation for long-term success, but its lower, or less rigorous attention to its business purposes continually gets it into short-term trouble. If they don't go out of existence in one of their down periods, the performance of these companies will oscillate between good and bad. Let's call them Roller Coasters.

High on Purposes, Low on Values

In the other corner we have the opposite kind of company, with a high emphasis on its purposes, in particular its financial ones, but no foundation of values to sustain it over the long haul, or build the foundation of trust with its public that J&J's Credo does. Here we find the financial conglomerates and asset strippers of the late Sixties and early Seventies, like ITT and Litton, who rose rapidly on the back of short-term profit measures, and then petered out when their strategies proved to have no staying power – Roman Candles.

Low on Purposes, Low on Values

Turkeys! Waiting to be taken over, and carved up because their pieces are worth more in other hands than the whole is under its existing management. These are the sleepy, asset-rich companies that did very well in the good economic times of the expansionary phase of the fourth wave, but lost their way under poor leadership thereafter.

Summarizing these descriptions, we can now lay out the corporate typology (see Fig. 3.10):

Driven by PURPOSES

		HIGH	LOW
	HIGH	**"Dynasty"** *Sustained high performance*	**"Roller Coaster"** *Mediocre short-term performance* *Better long-term performance (if it survives)*
Guided by VALUES	**LOW**	**"Roman Candle"** *Good short-term performance* *Mediocre long-term performance (if it survives)*	**"Turkey"** *Waiting to be taken over and taken to pieces*

Fig. 3.10   *The Davidson typology*

Now, let's use this typology to think about investing our own money, and let's look back over the last three decades to see where the action was, and where we were being advised to put our money.

In the Sixties, great economic times, a rising stock market and opportunity galore, the investment community touted the conglomerates. They seemed to be able to do no wrong as they used their high-priced stock to buy up less glamorous companies and apparently grow forever. The Roman Candles were where the action was, rapidly rising stocks which everyone tried to take advantage of, creating a self-fulfilling prophesy until the whole thing collapsed under its own weight.

The Seventies were much less exciting economic times as the fourth wave began to slow down and recessions began to hurt. The Roller Coasters lived up to their name. The Investment Community loved them. Why? Because of the inflection points, i.e., the changes in direction of their performance and hence their stock price. These inflection points were opportunities to recommend "Buy", or "Sell" – and stockbrokers make their money out of transactions, i.e., when you and I follow those recommendations!

Finally, in the Eighties, as the fourth wave approached its end, the old-line companies began to have serious economic problems. Many of them were managed by leaders who had fallen prey to The

Poisoned Inheritance. Their values had long since lost their vibrancy if they hadn't actually been perverted, and their leaders were incapable of taking the actions needed to restore profitability. The game was takeovers, and leveraged buyouts. The focus was on the Turkeys, opportunities to make a killing when a company was "put in play" and its stock price was bid up in the subsequent takeover battle.

In the Sixties it was the Roman Candles, in the Seventies the Roller Coasters, and in the Eighties the Turkeys. Where would you like to have had your money? In the Dynasties, of course; unless you wanted to spend the time, and take the risk, of playing the market. But most of the time the Dynasties weren't as exciting as the others. They didn't swing much, they didn't have rapid stock price run-ups and they weren't takeover targets. They just performed, over the long haul, better than anyone else.

We are now in yet another kind of economic time – where the fourth wave is ending and a new economic era is beginning. Who are going to be the Dynasties of the next wave? We know some of the Industries to look in – telecommunications, biotechnology, material sciences, microcomputers and software, and robotics. But which companies? And how to tell?

The answer is to look at their leaders. Find this generation's Thomas Watsons, Robert Johnsons, and Robert Woodruffs in the industries that will drive the emerging economy, and you will find the new economy's IBMs, J&Js and Coca-Colas. The Venture Capitalists have known this all along. They bet not on the product or on the market but on the people. Napoleon said, "The Psychological is to the Physical as three to one in war". And so it is in the competition that will determine the business winners and losers as we enter a new era.

So, values matter *and* purposes matter, and *In Search of Excellence* was the trigger that unleashed a renewed interest in the "soft stuff" of management that put the two together again. It was a return to more basic insights and the idea that if you do the right thing, the world will do right by you. In short, it was wonderful. "Excellence" became *the* subject. Tom Peters became an instant celebrity. Next he gave us *A Passion for Excellence*. Others jumped in with *Creating Excellence*, and *Managing for Excellence*. A whole new industry seemed to have been born.

Then, two-and-a-half years later in its November 5, 1984 issue, *BusinessWeek* punctured the balloon (see Fig. 3.11).

Fig. 3.11 *BusinessWeek*'s cover story, November 5, 1984

FASTER AND FASTER AND FASTER

The life cycle of management ideas seems to grow shorter and shorter. What happened to discredit Peters and Waterman's book in the brief span of two years? Many people read *In Search of Excellence* eagerly looking for the golden rule, the thing that would make their companies successful forever. And in so doing they forgot that it is a history book. The authors looked at the decade of 1965–1975. They examined the performance of America's largest companies and then looked more closely at what the outstanding companies were doing to achieve "excellence". That was fine and good, and a great service to business, in particular American business. However, it led many of their readers to make the faulty generalization that if their companies just behaved in future, as those people had behaved in those organizations during that ten-year period, their companies would succeed as well. But conditions change. What worked before may not work again. The focus on the executive suite moved on to change.

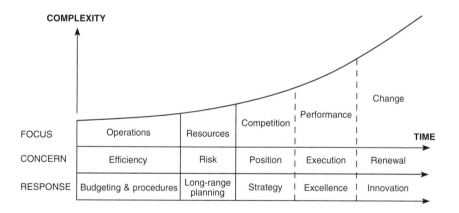

Fig. 3.12 *The evolution of executive concerns – V*

As John Gardner has written, "One of the ominous facts about growth and decay is that the present success of an organization does not necessarily constitute grounds for optimism". And even more pessimistically before him Arnold Toynbee wrote, "In evolution 'nothing fails like success' is probably always right".

Peters and Waterman were criticized for giving insufficient attention to change. I believe this was a correct charge, and it was a serious omission for a book that purported to provide management ideas in an era when, as the fourth wave petered out, and the industries that will drive future growth were being created, change was beginning to be described as the only constant.

Peters tried to answer the charge by pointing out, albeit correctly, the emphasis they had put on innovation within their eight characteristics. He missed the point. And his generally disparaging remarks about strategy confirmed his blind spot at the time. The determining changes occurred not just within the areas he had focused on but *outside* the eight characteristics altogether. Those characteristics are heavily oriented toward execution and operations. While critical changes were occurring in these areas, there were other equally important ones taking place in the domain of strategy, i.e., the dynamics of global, competitive relationships. When those shifted, no amount of excellence at operations, that had correlated with outstanding financial performance in a previous era, could surmount the new reality.

BusinessWeek missed the point, too. Those companies were still just as "excellent" – *at what they had been doing before*. It was just shown to be not enough, or maybe not even the right thing to do anymore. The failure of the fallen excellent companies was in their inability to cope with change. They could not adapt fast enough to the changing environment. Waterman got the point – his next book was called *The Renewal Factor*.

A good example of the problem faced by the excellent companies, and all others for that matter, comes from the energy industry. In Fig. 3.13 the thick line shows what happened to the price of oil between 1970 and 1984. Each of the thin lines shows what the best experts, in the largest energy companies, said would happen to the price of oil (i.e., at each point "O" they forecast it would go to an "X"). Other than maybe for a short time in the early Seventies, and then again in the late Seventies, if you ran your company in the way we were all taught, based on the best predictions of the future money could buy, you'd be in trouble, big trouble.

Even more revealing, let's look at the two times they nearly got it right. Who was setting the price of oil in the early Seventies? They were called the Seven Sisters – the major oil companies. The same people who were forecasting the price of oil! Not very difficult to forecast the price of oil when you're setting it. Now what about the late Seventies? Who was setting the price of oil then? OPEC, another cartel, and what did they tell us about their intentions – that they

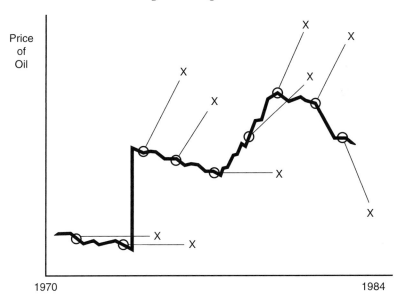

Fig. 3.13 *Oil price forecasts, 1970–1984*

were going to raise the price of oil in real terms forever. The point is that the only times this giant, sophisticated industry could get right the one and only assumption which really mattered – the price of oil – was when there was a monopoly. The message to us as strategic managers is clear. What we used to call "hard" – the numbers – have gone soft. So we had better make what we used to call "soft" – mission, goals, values, beliefs – hard, because they are the only things that can survive this kind of wrenching, unpredictable change.

By 1981 demand began to lessen. Other sources of oil were developed. There were major advances in alternative energy sources such as nuclear power and more efficient uses of coal. Most important, cars, oil-burning heaters and other heavy oil-using equipment were re-designed so that they saved on energy costs. As a result, the price of oil began to drop. In the summer of 1985 the *Wall Street Journal* said that the assumption in 1981 that the price of oil would continue to rise forever was probably the single most expensive mistake in the history of business. Failed energy companies, tax shelters, and banks, and finally a deeply troubled economy in states and counties dependent on their oil revenues, have attested to the accuracy of that assessment.

We began to experience dislocating change in the mid-Eighties for many reasons, among them the explosion of information, the speed of communications, and the massive amount of technological discovery. Remember the quote in Chapter 1: Bruce Merrifield, Undersecretary of State for Technology and Innovation in the Reagan administration, said, "Mankind has discovered more in the last ten years than in its whole history before that time. And we're going to do the same thing in the next ten years!" That's an exponential curve run riot! The decade since has lived up to his expectations. Competition itself is a force for change. In a new era characterized by unprecedented competitive intensity it drove companies to strive faster and faster for innovation, and for the differentiation that would give them an increasingly elusive competitive edge.

By the late Eighties executives of all kinds of organizations were focusing on this latest challenge. Their concern was the renewal of their organizations as the demands on them began to change with frightening speed. Innovation was the day's hottest topic. Entrepreneurs and entrepreneurship became what everyone wanted in their people. The word "intrapreneur", coined by an American, Gifford Pinchot, to mean entrepreneurial activity inside a corporation, was the next buzzword. The ForeSight Group, formed in Sweden in 1979 and renowned for new product development, established a School for Intrapreneurs for the sole purpose of teaching corporate managers how to nurture innovation.

All of this ferment about innovation represented a legitimate concern with the problem of finding ways to cope with a whirlwind of change. Yet somehow, the proffered solutions were strangely unsatisfying. They didn't even achieve the earlier, Chinese-meal status of strategy. And by themselves, that is as a single, self-sufficient solution, they didn't last any longer than excellence. At last a reluctance to buy the latest tonic was evidenced. Why? Because we were beginning to realize that we were dealing with a far more complex situation than we had imagined. One that could not be broken into discrete parts to be examined and acted upon separately. One where the solutions were going to have to be as complex as the problems. We were finally being forced to recognize that the management challenge has many dimensions, and those dimensions are all interrelated. Simplistic, one-dimensional solutions were just not going to work, in fact they almost certainly made things worse.

So, at last, we were ready for a synthesis of all that was good that had been discovered about management during the fourth wave. The time was ripe not for yet another new theory or methodology, but rather for a grand synthesis, and a discipline following from it that, utilizing and combining all that we had learned into a new and superior way of running the business, would therefore be the greatest competitive advantage of all.

4 Grand Strategy: An Agenda for Leadership

"The ultimate goal of the corporation is survival."   (Peter Drucker)

"The highest type of strategy – sometimes called grand strategy – is that which so integrates the policies and armaments of the nation that the resort to war is either rendered unnecessary or is undertaken with the maximum chance of victory."   (Edward Mead Earle)

"The crux of grand strategy is in policy – the capacity of a nation's leaders to bring together all of the elements, both military and nonmilitary, for the preservation and enhancement of the nation's long-term interests."   (H. A. Sargeunt and Geoffrey West)

Let us stop and take stock of what we have learned. By the end of the Eighties we had been through five stages of the evolution of the business leadership task in the period from the end of the Second World War, which coincided with almost the whole of the fourth wave of the American economy. In that time executive concerns moved from efficiency of operations in the late Forties and early Fifties, through risk in allocating resources in the late Fifties and Sixties, to position versus competition in the Seventies, execution to get performance in the early Eighties, and finally renewal to cope with change just a few years later. Our responses to each of the five stages, once they had matured and the false starts had been weeded out, were flawed only because they could not stand alone. Each contained great insight, but was only a partial solution. Each was necessary; none alone, nor any subset, was sufficient as the task grew more complex.

The critical issue was were they, together, sufficient? The most common question I was asked when I started presenting these ideas during the late Eighties was, "What comes next? You've explained the past very nicely. But how is that going to help me deal with the next challenge? What's the next concern and, more importantly, the next response? Tell me the tool I'm going to need for what's going to happen to me tomorrow".

There were two answers to this question. The first was that were indeed new challenges coming, some of which we might already be

91

able to see, but most of which we couldn't even guess at. But asking to be told the next technique was a bit like demanding a more certain prediction of the price of oil to cope with the energy management challenges of 1978–84. It would be wonderful if it were possible; but what we really needed was to recognize that we had to learn to manage without depending on predictions and forecasts at all. As Rosabeth Moss Kanter said, what was needed was the flexibility to cope with whatever happened. Shell Oil had already understood this. Its planning concentrated on the development of a range of scenarios. Implementation then meant putting in place the contingent ability to respond to whichever scenario occurred. That obviously works when one of the scenarios captures what then does happen. However it also gave Shell an advantage even if what happened was not one of the predicted scenarios. The practice its managers had in strategic thinking, and the flexibility built into the organization from the acceptance of uncertainty, enabled it to respond better to whatever occurred. Eventually change was to become so rapid, and so unpredictable that Kanter's response – the flexibility to cope with *whatever* came along – was the only solution.

The second, and more telling answer was that this five-stage evolution was in fact a circle. That the next stage, after innovation, was budgeting and procedures. Invent a new product and the first challenge is how to manage operations so as to produce and sell it at a profit. From this would rapidly follow the need to plan for capacity, new product generations, and all the other elements of long-range planning. Soon we'd be back to competition as others entered, then performance problems as the business matured and back again to innovation all over again. The set of five tasks that had been, each in turn, our primary concern over a forty-year period were in fact a description of a cycle that frames the whole management challenge.

But if the first two, as I described earlier, comprised the task of operational management, what were the last three – strategy, excellence, and innovation? And what was, if indeed it was anything different at all, *strategic* management?

Strategy, excellence and innovation, our responses to the last three sets of executive concerns, are the elements that make up grand strategy. It includes them but it is also above them, and goes beyond them. It is the highest form of strategy since its field is the totality of what happens in the organization, and its focus is the totality of its competition with rival organizations.

Its aim is to achieve a competitive advantage in all three areas: i.e., stronger strategic positions, higher quality execution, and more effective renewal. But grand strategy is not just a broader definition of strategy, or a new approach to planning. Its focus is on what our very purposes and values should be and how we actually run our organizations to achieve them in the face of competition. It is an agenda for leadership, not a recipe for strategic planning. Thus its real goal is a *pre-eminent management technique*, a better way of running the business, in the belief that in the long-term the better managed organization will win. Indeed that, faced by unpredictable and accelerating change, superiority in management technique is the ultimate and only reliable, long-term competitive advantage. Grand strategy is the discipline needed to achieve it.

The term "grand strategy" originated in its modern usage after the French Revolution. In the era before then, wars were about armies fighting armies, with the risk of the destruction of the nation not at issue. After the French revolution, in which the entire population of France became the source of a citizen's army, war grew to mean whole nations fighting whole nations. Total war does not mean war without rules. It means absolute, or all-encompassing warfare. It means calling forth the resources of the entire nation – its labour, its money, its food, its loyalties. Survival is at stake, so nothing can be withheld from the struggle. Grand strategy at the national level is the art of conducting *every* aspect of a nation's competition with other nations including, if need be, total war to assure its survival and long-term prosperity.

When applied to management, grand strategy has the same ultimate goal – the survival and long-term success of the organization – and is characterized by the same broadness of its concerns, which are *everything* about the organization. It therefore differs in scope from what Michael Porter has called "competitive strategy", which merely looks outward and seeks positions of advantage. Grand strategy looks outward at the competition too, but it looks inward as well, seeking, in addition to the goals of strategy, superior execution and the ability to cope with change. It thus deals with every management concern, and puts all of those concerns in a competitive context.

Consider two armies marching across a plain. On the other side of the plain is a hill, and the armies are expecting to do battle. Strategy dictates that we try to get on that hill first, since the hilltop is the stronger strategic position. Even if we succeed, it is still possible that we could lose the ensuing battle, if the opposing army outfights us. Therefore, grand strategy needs to be concerned with the quality of execution as well as with gaining the superior strategic position. The problem we have in business today, that those two hypothetical armies do not face is that the hills can move! As Kanter has pointed out, change moves faster then the decision-making process, let alone how long it takes to execute our response. For us, the hill may have moved by the time we get there. So we have to be able to renew our strategies more effectively than our competition, and do that in addition to executing them better, and gaining a superior position for ourselves through them. And finally, we have to ask ourselves why we are going to fight at all? What result is it aimed at achieving, what is the purpose it is intended to serve? Why, ultimately, do we indeed exist as an organization?

That is what grand strategy looks like. It addresses the ultimate goals of the organization. It encompasses the whole range of concerns, and it seeks superiority throughout. It starts by addressing the fundamental goals of the organization. It then comprises strategy, for position against competition; excellence of execution, in order to achieve performance; and innovation, for renewing anything and everything about the organization to cope with change. And the purpose of doing all these things, if they are to have any practical impact, is to determine how to manage today's operations and how to allocate resources to tomorrow's; because operational management is still the way we run our organizations. Grand strategy aims to give us a superior way of doing that, so we can cope with the most intense competition and highest rate of change that we have ever faced. Strategic management is simply operational management driven by grand strategy.

A study by the American Business Conference examined the financial performance of 525 mid-size companies (up to $200 million in revenues) over a period of five years and compared their performance with the possession of the six key traits set out in Table 4.1. It found that Return on Investment for these companies was related to the possession of these traits as set out in Table 4.2. Not proof maybe, but a good indication that we are on the right track! It turns out that many, maybe even most, of those techniques that had evolved during the fourth wave had value. But none of them by itself was sufficient. And most of them were being used in most places with a superficiality and lack of top management conviction that was doing more harm than good in company after company.

Table 4.1 Financial performance and key traits

Trait	Grand Strategy Element
Niche competition	Strategy for Position
First or second in market share	Strategy for Position
Selling on value, not price	Strategy for Position
"Overspending" on critical functions	Excellence of Execution
Frequent innovation	Innovation for Renewal
Product pioneer/early market entry	Innovation for Renewal

Table 4.2 ROI and possession of traits

	Possession of this number of traits *(not necessarily in the above order)*					
	0	1	2	3	4	5/6
ROI (%)	9	12	18	18	23	35

The recent evolution of the management task has simply reinvented in a modern business context what has always been true. In the Introduction we saw how human groups have always faced the same three issues – how to deal with the outside world in which they are placed, how to deal with the inside world of member interactions, and how to cope with the changes which make obsolete their responses to the first two issues. As we look at modern organizations, and not just business ones, these challenges imply the need for three capabilities, corresponding to the three fundamental challenges all of them have to meet in order to succeed over the long haul.

1. The ability to survive in the external environment . . . implying the challenge of Competition
2. The ability to align the internal environment, so that the organization can implement its external strategy . . . implying the challenge of Performance
3. The ability to gain competitively from environmental shifts, whether internal or external, so that the organization remains one of the fittest that survive . . . implying the challenge of Change.

And then there is the fourth, easily forgotten challenge that all organizations share and that I touched on above – to define the purposes that justify their existence. We tend to underestimate this challenge as it seems to be so self-evidently answered, often by the very name of the organization – "family group", "hunting parties". But the seductive simplicity of things we take for granted in old and simple institutions masks the complexity of the concept when it is applied to large, modern, multi-constituency organizations. And, even when satisfactorily answered for such organizations, as was clearly the case for the several decades of success of the giants of each economic wave, major change – such as is occurring as the fourth wave gives way to a new era – puts such answers in question. The "certainties" of the waning era – which were in fact the very successful answers that grand strategy gave to these fundamental questions for that era – give way under the pressure of the driving forces of the next era. Organizations, new and old, then have to deal with the issue of the very legitimacy of their purposes and values – they face the challenge of Mission.

Moreover the four challenges of grand strategy are not discrete problems. They all interact with each other. So, in practice, it is necessary to find a solution to the larger challenge of how to run the whole organization in such a way that all four problems are adequately addressed all the time, in a consistent, mutually reinforcing fashion. Finding this superior way of running the organization, implementing it and when appropriate changing it is *the* distinctive task of organizational leadership. The leader's job is not so much to manage the organization, as to manage the way the organization is managed. This is true even in the smallest of units, where the leader may also have other, individual responsibilities. In large organizations it is the all-absorbing task for its top management. This is what Buck Rodgers was referring to when he said, "The top management of IBM does not manage the company. It manages the values". And when it stopped doing so, IBM began to get into trouble.

As described earlier, this search for the ultimate competitive advantage – a pre-eminent way of running the organization – is the challenge that grand strategy addresses. It provides the reasons for an organization's existence. It then encompasses strategy to deal with competition, but it goes beyond strategy. It addresses excellence to ensure performance, but it goes beyond that, too. It seeks the innovation that can maintain the organization's superiority over its competition, and hence its competitive health whatever happens in the environment around or within it. It harnesses the total resources of the enterprise behind the task of survival. At its best it integrates internal policies with external strategies ensuring one, cohesive whole, focused on the purposes of the organization and changing what needs to be changed to ensure its continued health from one era to the next.

As indicated above, grand strategy becomes of particular importance in times of major change, since all the assumptions on which the organization's current activities rest then come into question. In calmer times it may be possible for CEOs to regard themselves, as Bob Hatfield, Chairman of Continental Group in the Seventies, used to say, as "stewards", or guardians of a company's human, financial and technological assets, with all the conservative and conservatory implications of that role. But when major technological and socio-economic changes are going on, it calls for a different kind of leadership, to wrench the organization from its comfortable patterns of past success, and fit it for a whole new set of challenges. Bob Hatfield's successor in the Eighties proved not to be up to the task, and Continental Group was taken over and taken to pieces – the fate of the turkey it had become.

In the second half of the Eighties, Strategy was evolving rapidly as new methods of competing and new techniques of planning were developed and tested. It soon comprised much more than the focus on efficiency and differentiation which had been its primary concerns in the Seventies. Time-based competition added a third dimension to our model of strategy. Benchmarking became *the* tool of the early Nineties, and Economic Value Added had its day. Strategy moved from upstart fad of the early Seventies to mature, universally used technique in the Nineties.

We discovered that "Excellence" was in fact only part of the solution to the larger challenge of integrating everyone and everything in the organization into the cohesive whole needed to address the challenge of Performance. And we soon learned that "Innovation" too only dealt with some of the aspects of change. So we began to talk about the components of grand strategy as a discipline being Mission, Strategy, Integration and Change since the latter two seemed a better description of the overall challenge in those areas than the terms and techniques of Excellence and Innovation, that we had derived simply from the responses we observed in our examination of the recent history of management techniques in Chapter 3.

As we have seen, today's organizations only started really to come to terms with the newly intensified problem of strategy in the Seventies, and that of integration in the Eighties. Then, all of a sudden, before either problem had been adequately understood let alone solved, massive, discontinuous change threatened their very existence. In the historical sense this was not a genuinely "new" challenge, any more than the need to deal with competition, and ensure the desired performance of the organization had been before it. The same phenomenon occurs toward the end of each wave of economic growth. At the end of the first wave, in the middle of the Nineteenth century, the clipper ship builders faced the same threat and succumbed to it, as did the steam locomotive builders, two waves later, in the Thirties. The long wave cycle repeats itself, and new generations of management condemned, unlike Bismarck, by their inability to learn from the experience of others, re-learn the same old lessons one more time. In each case the failure to adapt means a new set of companies takes the place of the old ones as one wave gives way to the next.

Competitive health means the superior fitness and adaptability to be one of those organizations which survive over long periods. At its best it means being able to cope with times of major change as well as those of relatively greater stability. Moving from one long wave to the next is the definitional time of major change for business. And, as the repeated story of the rise and fall of corporate giants shows, at that time very few companies make the grade. We are in such a period right now. Grand strategy is the overarching, integrative, management discipline that we need to identify a new way of managing to match the new economy.

It is of vital importance both to the old companies seeking to transform themselves in order to be able to compete in the new economy, and to the new companies which are the potential dynasties of this new era. In the fourth wave the personal characteristics of the individuals at the top of a small number of companies built the values-driven, profit-oriented organizations which define dynasties. In the new era there will be others like them, with the natural abilities that fit the new world. This is natural selection at work. But most of us won't have this rare match, any more than most of us don't have the natural talent of the great athletes. What do we do? Give up? Let evolution do its work and pray we end up in one of the winning organizations? The promise of grand strategy is that this fate is avoidable, that it is possible to beat evolution and that we can take control of our own destinies. What grand strategy offers is a way of thinking and a set of tools to help those of us with the desire and the willingness to work at it, beat evolution and thereby deliberately create the dynasties of the emerging global economy.

Let us now turn to these tools of grand strategy to answer the four great questions we must address if we are to create our piece of a new, or renewed dynasty.

Part II
Prescription

Introduction

In Part I we diagnosed the nature of the challenge facing organizations as each economic wave, and each phase of those waves gives way to the next. We explored the nature of the earlier waves and how their characteristics had given rise to the forms and methodologies of management that have developed over the past two hundred years. Next we saw, by looking closely at what happened to Eastman Kodak, how a lack of understanding of the driving forces of corporate success led to the dreadful competitive malaise that has assailed the giants of the fourth wave. We then looked more closely at the development of management thought in the economic era formed by that fourth wave, which began in the late Thirties and is now coming to an end. This showed us how the primary concerns of the leaders of companies evolved as the challenges posed by their economic environment changed. We learned that the flurry of management fads and fashions of the last two decades, far from being in some sense peculiar, or a sign of weakness was, in fact, the healthy search by an innovative managerial community for the new ways of managing that the recessionary phase of the fourth wave demanded. Finally we used all these insights to develop a definition of the task, called grand strategy, that encompasses the totality of achieving and maintaining the competitive health of our organizations.

With this understanding of the problem, and the nature of the managerial challenge it poses, we turn now to the development of a prescription for dealing with it.

In Part II we will address the four great questions facing the leaders of all organizations, large and small, that grand strategy must answer if it is to meet its goal of maintaining the competitive health of the enterprise:

1. *Mission* – What are we trying to accomplish?
2. *Competition* – How do we gain a competitive edge?
3. *Performance* – How do we deliver the results?
4. *Change* – How do we cope with change?

These questions correspond directly with the four challenges that all organizations share, which we explored in the last chapter of Part I – what is their reason for existing, how do they deal with the outside world within which they are placed, how do they deal with the inside world of member interactions and how do they cope with the changes which make obsolete their answers to the first three challenges? Our purpose in exploring these questions is not to add to the flood of specific methodologies of strategy, integration and change that are already overflowing the management bookshelves of the world. Our subject is grand strategy, whose aim is a preeminent management technique. Thus it is how the aims of strategy, integration and change impinge on the way we manage in general that concerns us. Or, to reverse it, what we are seeking is the characteristics of a way of managing that causes the needs of strategy, integration and change all to be met continuously and consistently over time and throughout the organization. While there will be recommendations for specific elements of technique in what follows, our greater goal is a way of thinking about, that is a *philosophy* of the management task, that can guide the day-to-day behavior of every manager, so that every aspect of the enterprise's activities is truly managed in a strategic manner.

We start, as must any organization and those who lead it or any unit thereof, with Mission.

5 Mission: Shared Purposes, Shared Values

"The secret of success is constancy to purpose."   (Benjamin Disraeli)

"To accomplish great things we must not only act but also dream, not only plan but also believe."   (Anatole France)

"The desire of this age is for a doctrine which may serve to condense our knowledge, guide our researches and shape our lives so that conduct may really be the consequence of belief."   (George Henry Lewes)

"Even bad doctrine is better than none at all. You can test it, differ from it, your mind has something to bite on. You need the rock to plant the lighthouse."   (Joyce Cary)

A few years ago, I gave a series of seminars for Business Week Executive Programs called "How to Become a Strategic Manager". In preparation for one of them a participant wrote me the following letter about an incident that happened in one of America's largest companies. As you read it, think about two questions: How could the disaster have been avoided? and, What is the moral of the story?

Dear Mike,

You asked for a "disaster" to share with the Seminar participants. Here is one that I sadly witnessed.

About four years ago a few sales managers, with the support of an influential and feared Corporate Vice-President who was their boss, put together a Business Plan for a new venture in one of the Divisions that would represent some vertical integration. It would also compete with some middle men who were currently our customers. The plan was "rammed through" and approved by the CEO. Another Vice-President, in fact the CEO's right-hand man, had misgivings about the venture and the plan to implement it. He hired a consulting firm to quickly review the business plan but this was not able to be completed before the CEO's approval.

The consultants' report on the plan proved to be highly critical. They stated clearly that there were some very unrealistic assumptions about the available returns in the marketplace, coupled with a gross over-estimation of the internal capabilities to execute the critical tasks on which success would depend. In fact it became evident that the numbers in the plan had been "backed into" after its authors had chosen some financial "results" which would sell the project.

The Vice-President who had initiated the study now indicated that the venture could not be stopped at this point; that would embarrass the Division head since he had already received the CEO's approval. In addition the powerful Vice-President pushing it would likely run round the Division head to the CEO (who encouraged this kind of behavior) and cause still more embarrassment. He would probably also succeed in keeping the venture alive.

The consultants' report unsurprisingly received very limited circulation, and their presentation was attended only by the initiating Vice-President, the Controller of the Division and the assistant to the Division head. Although the report strongly recommended setting six-month goals that would be grounds for cancellation if their analysis proved correct, this was not done.

The venture did not come anywhere near any of its goals; in fact it never made it into the black. After about 18 months, when failure was beyond denial by even the most ardent supporters, it was finally shot down and the individual who had initiated it left the company. Total losses were $3–4 million, which was a substantial fraction of the Division's profits. The Vice-President who had been the original force behind it died six months before the venture was discontinued.

As we considered the letter in the seminars, we focused on some of the telling phrases that gave us a clue about how the disaster happened. Phrases like "feared Corporate Vice-President", "compete with some middle men who were currently our customers", "rammed through", "very unrealistic assumptions about the available returns in the marketplace", "gross over-estimation of the internal capabilities", "numbers in the plan had been backed into", "run round the Division head" and "CEO (who encouraged this kind of behavior)" would always be identified as symptomatic of what was going on. I would then ask the participants to make a list of their thoughts about the nature of this organization and the decision-making process in it. This would elicit comments like "politically run", "insufficient market analysis", "power oriented", "dominated by line management", "poor integration of information", "weak headquarters staff", and "lack of understanding of strategy". All the comments that participants would raise fell into two broad areas, which suggested to us two basic conclusions:

1. Decision-making in this organization was a political process
2. Poor judgment on the specific, business-related variables was not adequately challenged.

I believe we should not find these conclusions surprising. Nor should we imagine that our own organizations are any different, because the main moral I take from the story is: this is the rule not the exception. In the modern American corporation most major decisions are taken by a political process, and the judgment of the initiators of business plans or investment proposals on business-related variables is not deeply questioned. Moreover this is the way it must be! The problem is not to try to change this reality but to find a way of managing that ensures it doesn't get out of hand, and create disasters like the one that befell this organization.

First, why must it be so?

The modern corporation is in reality controlled by its management not its owners (unless they happen also to be its managers), or their representatives, the Board of Directors. The last named behaves rather like the Central Committee of the Communist Party in Russia used to do. It acts independently only when things have got so far out of line that it has to do something, and it does so typically only on one matter; the replacement of the CEO. The initial elevation and later removal of Khrushchev as General Secretary of the Communist Party by the Central Committee is a rather apt parallel to what happened to Kay Whitmore at Eastman Kodak, John Akers at IBM, and Robert Stempel at General Motors. If things don't get truly bad, the top management group and those loyal to it (the Party) are left to run the company (the Country) as they see fit. Naturally, in such circumstances, the company behaves like the political institution that it is. It sets its direction and chooses its strategies according to the weighted desires of those who have an influence on the process, within the constraints of the relationships it must maintain with the various constituencies (or "stakeholder" groups) who can affect its performance, and ultimately its survival.

Things get out of hand when those with power wish to follow radically different agendas, either because they allow parochial concerns to take precedence over those of the whole, or because they hold different views about where the overall organization should be going. These are the circumstances that leadership must, and can, act to avoid, rather than trying to deny the reality of the political nature of the institution. The principal tool they use to do so is Mission – the putting in place of an overarching agenda that dominates local preferences and commands allegiance throughout the organization.

There has been much said and written about mission, vision, values, commitments, goals, credos, statements of philosophy, guiding principles, principles of governance, and numerous other terms for elements of the same basic idea in the last ten years. Views of their importance that I have personally heard vary from Jim Burke's comment after the Tylenol crisis that "the guidance of the Credo played *the* most important role in our decision-making"; through the down-to-earth Chairman of a New York Law Firm, "I understand the importance of being clear about what we stand for, but I can't stand the buzzwords"; to "semi-religious claptrap" from the cynical, old, managing director of the English subsidiary of an American Multinational.

Reading many mission statements leaves one with a lot of sympathy for the skeptics. At one extreme there is narrow short-sightedness – a pharmaceutical company: "to grow sales 15% next year". At the other there's bland generality – a computer company: "to meet the needs of all our stakeholders". In both instances, why bother? In the first case the annual budget already meets the need. In the second, we learn nothing at all. Then there's the self-serving – Seagram's: ". . .to be the best managed beverage company in the world". Who cares? To what end? And, how do the massive investments in DuPont's and Time Warner's stock, and purchase a controlling interest in MCA fit? And the ones that suggest the company's leaders have missed the point altogether – "The mission of The Coca-Cola Company is to increase shareholder value over time". Boy, that'll excite our customers. And get our people charged up for a hard day's work tomorrow morning!

So, how do we use a tool that seems to be fraught with some danger to the user?

We have had two strong clues. First there was the typology of companies using the dimensions of Values, and Purposes in the last chapter. Together, I suggested, these seem to provide a recipe for sustained, superior performance. And second there were the quotes at the beginning of this chapter, in particular the one from Joyce Cary:

Even bad doctrine is better than none at all. You can test it, differ from it, your mind has something to bite on. *You need the rock to plant the lighthouse.*

Values are the rock on which organizations that survive and succeed over the long haul are built. Without them there is no foundation, and, like the house built on sand, organizations without values will be swept away when the winds and the storms of hard times come. But values alone are not enough. We also need purposes, the lighthouse to guide our way. Together values and purposes solve the problem of the company that went ahead with the disastrous venture by providing two vital, overarching and organization-wide disciplines:

Shared Purposes provide FOCUS by driving strategy, and
Shared Values provide CONTROL by guiding implementation.

Without shared purposes each part of the organization will go its own way, maybe even adopting strategies that hurt the company, as the division described in the letter did by competing with some of the corporation's customers. An internal strategy of decentralization will be positively dangerous, but without it every decision will have to come to the top. And when that happens, the reality of institutional politics make it virtually impossible for a senior, and powerful line manager to be turned down.

Without shared values the behavior adopted by people to get their own way in the company described in the letter must be expected. In fact it was mild compared, for example, to what happens in a partnership where collegiality has disappeared, and money is the only thing keeping it together. The law of the jungle then prevails, with attempts to steal credit, steal clients and sometimes even steal money common in the stories of the survivors. In the declining days of ancient Rome, when the values of the Republic had been perverted into those of the late and corrupt Empire, murder was an accepted tool for political advancement! It still is, in the minds of not a few modern leaders who do not extend the sharing of their values to citizens of other countries and, sometimes even of their own.

We saw, in the Tylenol story, how shared values can work to guide people's behavior. There was a time in IBM when its leaders could rely on any of their several hundred thousand employees, faced with two options, always choosing the one which resulted in better service to the customer. Why? Because "the best possible service" was one of the three fundamental beliefs on which Thomas Watson Senior, and then his son, built IBM.

Causing people to behave in a certain way, determining which option they will adopt faced with a choice in the marketplace – this is a control system at work. But it is a control system that doesn't depend on voluminous books of procedures, the enforcement of rules, and fear of the consequences of not following them. Rather it works because people share a common set of beliefs about what is important, what is appropriate behavior and therefore what their priorities should be in any given situation.

So let us now explore what is involved in creating a Mission – comprised of statements of Shared Purposes, and Shared Values – that can provide the overarching agenda an organization needs to keep its politics in check.

SHARED PURPOSES

Although economic theory (and Coca-Cola's Mission Statement) may say that companies exist solely to maximize the return they can achieve on their equity, the money invested in them by their shareholders, in the real world they owe obligations to a much wider group of "stakeholders". Such stakeholders include in particular customers, employees, suppliers, and the communities in which the company conducts its business. Any or all of these groups not only have a large "stake" in the performance of the company, but also can have a major impact on that performance. There therefore exists the basis for a set of *mutually beneficial relationships* between the company and each of its sets of stakeholders.

Further, there exists the possibility of making the quality of these relationships in some sense superior to those achieved by a competitor with the same groups. Here we see the beginnings of the concept of grand strategy at work – bringing strategic thinking to bear on the totality of an organization's relationships, encompassing all those who have a stake in, or impact on its performance.

From this we can derive the two questions that need to be answered to develop the statement of an organization's purposes.

1.   Who are our key stakeholders?
2.   What need of theirs are we trying to satisfy better than anyone else?

Let us return to IBM, in its heyday of the Sixties and Seventies, and see what its answers might have looked like.

Information Equipment Users

In the Seventies IBM's market was just about everyone, and in that sense we were all part of its customer, stakeholder group. But we clearly need to be more specific than that for it to be useful. In fact one of the lessons we can learn from others' experience using the tool of Mission is that the more specific we can be, the better. Since the whole point of the tool is to provide focus, it is better to err on the side of specificity than generality. One of the most important things I learned from Bruce Henderson, founder of The Boston Consulting Group and father of the Experience Curve, was: take care of the core of a market segment, and the edges will take care of themselves. So we will call IBM's core, most critical set of customers "Information Equipment Users".

Now, what need of theirs was IBM trying to satisfy better than anyone else? It certainly wasn't low price – the cheapest information equipment. Or speed, or power – the fastest, or most powerful computers. Or even being state-of-the-art on the latest feature, or add-on. What they were clearly trying to do was provide better service than anyone else supplying their range of products. They were so successful that the name of the company IBM became virtually synonymous with Service, not just to Information Equipment Users but, more importantly, to their line bosses. Remember the slogan: "nobody ever got fired for specifying IBM".

This emphasis on service had its roots in the second of IBM's three fundamental beliefs, and it had been heavily reinforced by the company's policy, right up to the Seventies, of leasing not selling its computers. (When you continue to own them, and your revenues depend on their operation, you take good care of them!) Finally in that era of the introduction of computers, when no one really understood how they worked or what they could do, and when breakdowns could and did occur, service was more important to the vast majority of customers than any product feature, or even price. Here was an example of strategy, values, and purposes coinciding perfectly in both their current application, and their consistency with the company's history. Here was the root of IBM's success.

Creative, Intelligent, Career Seekers

Again, trying to be specific, the group is not just employees but that set of them that IBM wanted to attract. IBM followed a policy of promotion from within. And for its whole history from when Thomas Watson, Sr, joined the company until very recently its boast was that it had never laid anyone off because of industry conditions. Its policy regarding its people, founded in the difficult times of the pre-war years, was to give them security. The word "membership" has been used to describe the relationship but really the more powerful term "tenure" is even more apt.

To show this definition of purpose isn't just the proverbial "motherhood", i.e., something so obvious and so widely shared that no one could quarrel with it, contrast it with another highly successful company, Club Med. In its heyday, Club Med had a policy of moving its GOs (gentil organisateurs) – the mostly young and rather low-paid people who run its vacation villages – from one village to another every six months. Not only did they move them, they split them up, so that each member of a team went to a different place. As a result they maintained a freshness and spirit of innovative renewal at each village which was highly attractive to vacationers. But, as another result, they lost most of their GOs after only two or three years. The psychological impact of breaking often very close friendships every six months (without high pay to compensate) was more than those young people could take. (As a further result, Club Med needed to reserve very much less for pensions than a more conventional company!) Here was a very different relationship with a very different set of employees, but in its own way equally consistent with the company's strategy, and for a long time spectacularly successful.

Suppliers of Relevant Components

Again it is a specific set of suppliers that has to be focused on. And to them IBM offered a secure market. Notice how different that and its relationship with its employees was to the equivalent element of the American motor industry's grand strategy for most of its history. The motor industry was where the term Variable Cost was first used to include, principally, materials and labor. Can you think of a better insult to give your people than to describe them as variable cost? And when I was with Ford, in the late Sixties, we gave our suppliers six-month contracts. How much maintenance or investment for the future gets done under six-month contracts?

Under the pressure of Japanese competition the American car companies, in the Eighties, were finally forced to move toward more security of employment for their employees, and longer-term contracts for their suppliers. Why? Because without the first they couldn't get the co-operation they needed to increase productivity; and without the second they couldn't achieve the quality improvements they desperately needed. Productivity increases and quality improvements are the stuff of strategy. The relationships with employees and suppliers is grand strategy – changing them means changing major aspects of the way a company is run. Before the motor industry could take on the Japanese at the level of strategy, it had first to change at the level of grand strategy. This is indeed not motherhood!

Software Writers

In the early days of the mainframe computer IBM jealously guarded its software and regarded independent software writers as an enemy who might steal its secrets, and reduce the dependence of its customers on it. By the time the mini, the micro and the personal computer came along, IBM had at least partially recognized that future computer wars were going to be won on the software, not the hardware battlefield, and developed a "partnership" relationship with independent software writers. Its extraordinary, come-from-behind success with the introduction of the IBM PC was in part due to this huge change of policy, at least in that division. Rosabeth Moss Kanter, author of *The Changemasters*, said a few years ago that it was the best example of flexibility – which she cited as *the* distinguishing feature of successful companies in the future – in a giant company, she had ever seen. Ironically IBM's accompanying failure to see the true, ultimate impact of its own insight about the importance of software within a decade led to its own terrible decline, and the ascension to industry leadership of Microsoft (writer of the operating software for the IBM PC, but not under exclusive contract).

Investors Seeking Capital Appreciation

In the Seventies the yield on IBM's stock (the return the dividend gave on the stock price) was around 1%. This was not a company to invest in if an immediate steady income from a high dividend payout ratio was what you were looking for. But its stock price grew and grew and grew. Capital appreciation was what it offered, and capital appreciation is what it delivered until the middle of the Eighties. And when that appreciation stopped, the whole reason that most of its shareholders had for owning its stock disappeared. Despite raising its dividend, and buying back its own stock, the change in shareholder motivation for owning the stock drove its price down by two thirds, from its high to its low, in just a couple of years. It had to. As a stock in the market for capital, IBM, no longer a growth company, was now competing with high yield alternatives. Its competitive weakness meant it couldn't raise its earnings to provide a higher dividend, so its stock price had to fall, to bring the return to the shareholder in line with his or her alternatives.

To summarize, in the Sixties and Seventies IBM's purposes, although all of them were probably never stated this way, were in practice those set out in Table 5.1.

Table 5.1   IBM's purposes in the Seventies

Stakeholders	*Needs*
Information Equipment Users	Service
Creative, Intelligent Career Seekers	Membership
Suppliers of Relevant Components	Secure market
Software Writers	Partnership
Investors Seeking Capital Appreciation	Superior returns

And remember, its fundamental beliefs were

1. The individual must be respected
2. The customer must be given the best possible service
3. Excellence and superior performance must be pursued.

IBM's truly remarkable, and long-sustained success is perhaps less extraordinary in the light of the simple power and self-sustaining integrity of these two lists.

Defining the distinctive purposes of an organization in this explicit and specific fashion is the critical, *sine qua non* step to providing the focus needed to drive the development of strategy. Most organizations find a second step – the creation of a comprehensive statement summarizing its purposes (which in fact is usually called a "Mission", not "Purposes" Statement) – is needed to release the communicative power without which the tool is not very useful. Here style becomes important as well as rigor, because the purpose of the statement is certainly to inspire as well as to inform. These purposes must be seen as superordinate goals dominating parochial concerns, as goals worthy of single-minded pursuit as well as goals clear enough for developing strategies to achieve them.

In the mid-Eighties I was lucky enough to get the opportunity to contribute to this second step in a rather public forum, though without knowing it at the time! Let me explain.

I was invited to make a presentation on strategic planning at a conference of the Internal Revenue Service's senior executives. In preparation they sent me a copy of their recently completed, first, formal strategic plan. (Yes, the IRS does compete – with other countries in the efficiency with which it raises taxes, with other employers for university graduates, with the temptation not to comply with the voluntary US system, . . .) Policy Statement P-1-1, at the plan's very beginning, was a statement of the IRS's Mission:

> The mission of the Service is to encourage and achieve the highest possible degree of voluntary compliance with the tax laws and regulations and to conduct itself so as to warrant the highest degree of public confidence in its integrity and efficiency. The Service should advise the public of their rights and responsibilities, determine the extent of compliance and the causes of noncompliance, and do all things needed for proper administration and enforcement of the tax laws.

There were several things I didn't like about this statement – it's really a statement of means, not ends; it's uninspiring to read and to look at; and it leaves out two, I thought, important points: fairness (without which, *and* the perception of which, a voluntary system will fail), and a sense of striving to do better (which all of us desperately want to see in our rather complacent seeming, public institutions). So I decided to re-write it as a presentation device to show them how one of the tools of grand strategy could be applied directly to their situation.

The speech seemed to be well received, and a few months later I was invited back to give the same speech to a group of middle managers on a training course. To my surprise, before it was my turn to speak, I was called up onto the stage and presented with a plaque bearing the following, etched in brass:

Mike Davidson –

On November 4, 1983, you gave a presentation on Strategic Planning in Washington, D.C., to a nationwide conference of all Internal Revenue Service executives.

During your excellent presentation, you contrasted our mission statement with corporate mission statements and then put the Service's mission in your own words.

On December 28, 1983, we issued a newly worded mission statement which follows. The words you will quickly recognize – they are yours. We thank you.

Roscoe L. Egger, Jr.
Commissioner of Internal Revenue
August 15, 1984

THE MISSION OF THE INTERNAL REVENUE SERVICE

The purpose of the IRS is to collect the proper amount of tax revenues at the least cost to the public, and in a manner that warrants the highest degree of public confidence in our integrity, efficiency and fairness. To achieve that purpose, we will:

- Encourage and achieve the highest possible degree of voluntary compliance in accordance with the tax laws and regulations;

- Advise the public of their rights and responsibilities;

- Determine the extent of compliance and the causes of noncompliance;

- Do all things needed for the proper administration and enforcement of the tax laws; and

- Continually search for and implement new, more efficient and effective ways of accomplishing our Mission.

Fig. 5.1 *Revised IRS Mission Statement, 1983*

They had dropped their mission statement, withdrawn literally thousands of copies of an internal newspaper that was about to publicize it, changed maybe five words from what I had written, and now it was in every IRS office in the country! Not often does a consultant, and in this case I wasn't even that, see a recommendation taken and acted upon so fully and rapidly, and without his even knowing it.

Having said what's "wrong" with the first version, here's what I think is "right" with the second:

- It has a clearly stated end: "The purpose of the IRS is to collect the proper amount of tax revenues at the least cost to the public . . .".
- This purpose is carefully phrased. It's not the maximum, or optimal but *proper* amount of tax. And it must be collected at the *least cost*, leaving no doubt about the *fairness* of the Service. All these words add direction to those with the responsibility for developing its strategy.
- The means have been subordinated to the end, and clearly recognized for what they are, by being included in bullet form.
- Each of these means starts with a verb. It is difficult to overstate the importance of verbs in high level strategy documents, which are intended to be used as communication devices to guide the behavior of large organizations. Nouns describe destinations so are well suited for "visioning" exercises, which aim to create a vivid picture of a state that will inspire people to change. But verbs are vital to tell people what you want them to do to achieve those visions. Each of the five bullet statements provides clear guidance for action and priority-setting, for anyone, at any level of the Service.
- The first four bullets respond to grand strategy's concern for execution to get performance. Here are the major things the Service will *do* to fulfill its purpose.
- The fifth bullet statement is an addition, to nail the idea of continuous improvement to the mast, and add the fourth element of grand strategy – change – to the mission.
- And, finally, the layout of the statement is now more attractive and easier to read.

SHARED VALUES

In Chapter 3 we saw Johnson & Johnson's Credo (Credo, for those of you without a classical education, means "I believe"), how it had been renewed as a document to guide behavior, and how it had worked to help the company through a terrible crisis. Even earlier we saw the six great ideas that guided Eastman Kodak's founders as they built that company. Thirdly I have referred more than once to IBM's three fundamental beliefs, and their role in guiding the creation of that once great dynasty. All these examples vividly illustrate the concept of Shared Values as a control system, and as an integrating device to do for what goes on inside an organization the same as Shared Purposes does for its strategy to deal with the outside.

We'll look at one more example. But first, a question:

Of all the major, multinational organizations in the world that you've ever heard of, which has the least number of layers of management?

Very rarely do people get it right. The answer is in fact the largest organization of them all – the Roman Catholic Church: Pope, Archbishop, Bishop, Priest. Just three levels below the Pope (Cardinals are just super-Bishops, not an additional layer of hierarchy). How does it do it? The Church calls it doctrine, which means the teaching of its shared beliefs or, in our more secular terminology, values. Now what about the organization with the most layers?

The most common answer people give is the Government or, in America, the Pentagon, and they may be right. But, until a few years ago, there was one worse – the Communist Party in Russia! Why? Because they didn't trust each other! Remember, originally when it was an underground organization, it was organized into cells of three so that no individual could betray more than two people. That same attitude of suspicion, mistrust and paranoia over betrayal carried over into the multiple layers that formed the most hierarchical, stifling management structure in the world for seventy years.

Shared Values: flat organizations, minimal supervision, people trusted to do the right thing of their own accord. No Shared Values: layer on layer of hierarchy, management of every detail, people ordered to do what they're told without question, or reason.

In 1985 a very tough manager, trying to create what he described as "the most competitive company in the world", gave us another, very practical example.

Here is Jack Welch, CEO of (American) GE in the final paragraph of the company's 1986 Annual Report to its shareholders:

The removal of an entire layer of upper management structure in late 1985 gives significantly more responsibility to the leaders of GE's various businesses, freeing them to compete more effectively in world markets. We were able to make this major organizational change because of the growing recognition by GE people that, while we profit from the cultural diversity of our many businesses, we are governed by common policies and united by shared values. Our shared values include a recognition that:

- Excellence can be measured only in terms of customer satisfaction.
- Change must be accepted as the rule rather than the exception.
- Open, candid, interactive, continuous communication up, down and across the Company is the key to gaining trust and commitment.
- Effective leadership involves the acceptance and management of paradox. For example, we must function collectively as one Company and individually as many businesses at the same time. Similarly, we must meet our short-term commitments while investing for long-term success.
- Our resource allocation process must be dynamic. Sometimes a business benefits as a net importer of dollars, ideas and talent while at other times the same business will be called upon to be a net exporter for the benefit of the Company as a whole.

As we look to the next five years, our combination of different business cultures and shared values gives GE the ability – and flexibility – to win in world markets. It provides the bond that stimulates our people, the most important asset of any organization, to pursue a common goal – achieving excellence in everything we do.

Not words anyone at the time expected to hear from Jack Welch. For he was not, and still is not known for his soft-heartedness. In fact in the early years of his tenure as Chairman (shortly before this Annual Report was written), when he enforced a massive effort to reduce the number of people in the company and shed businesses he didn't feel could be "number one or two in their industry", he was given the nickname of Neutron Jack – because GE's buildings were all still there but there was no one in them anymore! Yet here he was espousing a way of managing that in most organizations was still regarded as "soft stuff", "motherhood", and not what real managers spent their time on. He had recognized that the combination of low costs, flexibility in the face of change, and collaboration across the company to meet the customers' needs, which was needed if GE was truly to become the most competitive company in the world, could only be achieved by a "control system" that removed the bureaucracy of micro-management, rules and turf.

As the Eighties turned into the Nineties Welch's rhetoric moved more and more toward this emphasis on the kind of culture GE was going to need in order to maintain its competitive health. Here was one of the few business leaders who not only saw that there was a new world of unprecedented competitive intensity and accelerating change coming, but tried to anticipate it in the way his company was run. Here are three examples (taken from *Take Control of Your Own Destiny or Someone Else Will* by Noel Tichy and Stratford Sherman):

ON WORK-OUT
(GE's process to increase productivity by empowering its people to remove unneeded activity and waste from the organization)

Ultimately, we're talking about redefining the relationship between boss and subordinate. I want to get to a point where people challenge their bosses everyday: "Why do you require me to do these wasteful things? Why don't you let me do the things you shouldn't be doing so you can move on and create? That's the job of leader – to create, not to control. Trust me to do my job, and don't make me waste all my time trying to deal with you on the control issue".

ON BOUNDARYLESSNESS
(Welch's term for the culture of openness and collaboration he is seeking to create)

Trust is enormously powerful in a corporation. People won't do their best unless they believe they'll be treated fairly – that there's no cronyism and everybody has a real shot.

The only way I know to create that kind of trust is by laying out your values and then walking the talk. You've got to do what you say you'll do, consistently, over time.

It doesn't mean everybody has to agree. I have a great relationship with Bill Bywater, president of the International Union of Electronic Workers. I would trust him with my wallet, but he knows I'll fight him to the death in certain areas, and vice versa.

He wants to have a neutrality agreement in GE's non-union plants. He wants to recruit more members for the union.

I'll say, "No way! We can give people everything you can, and more".

He knows where I stand. I know where he stands. We don't always agree – but we trust each other.

That's what boundarylessness is: An open, trusting, sharing of ideas. A willingness to listen, debate, and then take the best ideas and get on with it.

If this company is to achieve its goals, we've all got to become boundaryless. Boundaries are crazy. The union is just another boundary, and you have to reach across the same way you want to reach across the boundaries separating you from your customers and your suppliers and your colleagues overseas.

ON VALUES
(In response to the question: What's your response to those who dismiss your talk about values and empowerment as bunk?)

I think any company that's trying to play in the 1990s has got to find a way to engage the mind of every single employee. Whether we make our way successfully down this road is something only time will tell – but I'm sure this is the right road.

If you're not thinking all the time about making every person more valuable, you don't have a chance. What's the alternative? Wasted minds? Uninvolved people? A labor force that's angry or bored? That doesn't make sense!

If you've got a better way, show me. I'd love to know what it is.

Shared purposes and shared values then are the foundation for strategic success, and the first element of grand strategy. Every organization must have a clear mission comprising its shared purposes, the relationships it seeks to build with all who have a stake in its success; and its shared values, the guide to how it will behave as it pursues its purposes. A word-picture of the organization working this way is what we mean by strategic vision, the irresistible goal that the transforming leader is able to put in place to create common cause and bring about the winning effort. The question now is: how do we turn that vision into reality?

TURNING VISION INTO REALITY

In the company with which we began this chapter each division, and each department was heading off in a different direction according to its selfish reading of its parochial interests. So it must have looked something like Fig. 5.2.

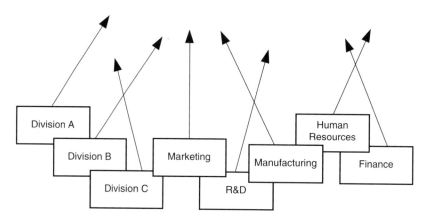

Fig. 5.2 *Organizational parochialism*

The purpose for developing a Mission, dominating these local concerns, is to provide a common focus (Shared Purposes) and a common code of conduct (Shared Values) so that, every element of the organization can be integrated into the effort to achieve the common vision. When this is achieved we will be able to draw a far healthier picture (see Fig. 5.3).

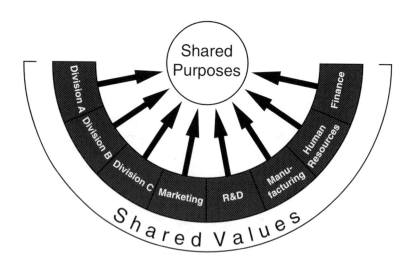

Fig. 5.3 *Organizational integration*

The question now is how do we actually make this happen? We've defined the common focus for strategy, and the control system for behavior. How does each division and department now know what to *do* to fulfill the organization's mission? We'll look at two industries to answer the question. As Fig. 5.4 shows, in 1960 the U.S. Motor Industry accounted for 52% of world car production, and the Japanese for 1.3%. By 1980 the U.S. share had fallen to 22%, and the Japanese had reached 24%. By all the rules of strategy this should be impossible, so how did it come about?

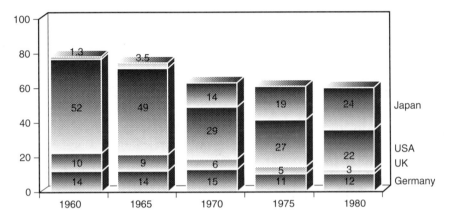

Fig. 5.4 *World car production, national market shares, 1960–1980*

Let's look at each of the decades in turn. What drove the first leap forward of the Japanese motor industry from 1.3% in 1960 to 14% in 1970? Remember those cars? They weren't very attractive, they were rather small compared to American cars, and they weren't marketed or distributed with anywhere near the sophistication of their American competition. What they were was cheap. And the Japanese found a lot of people – first in a Japan recovering from the Second World War, and then in the rest of the world including America – who wanted a cheap car. Initially exploiting its cheap labor, but quickly turning from that to the strategic driving force of *productivity*, the Japanese avoided head-on competition with their American competitors by concentrating their efforts on that part of the market that above all else wanted a low-cost car. The Americans let them have it perceiving it as a small, unprofitable part of the market-place.

What then drove the second decade's advance from 14% in 1970 to 24% in 1980? By this time the American car companies were having their profit margins fiercely squeezed as they tried to become more price competitive with the Japanese in a market that, in harsher economic times, was becoming more appreciative of low-cost transportation. The initial route they took to cost-cutting resulted in a severe loss in quality. In 1979 when I immigrated to the United States I rented an American car and my four year-old son found he could put his hand into the car between the body and the door without opening it, the tolerance was so wide! It was the conventional, manufacturing wisdom that you could have low cost, or high quality, but you couldn't have both. The Japanese thought otherwise. They retained their emphasis on productivity and now added to it a focus on quality, achieving a major point of differentiation to their American competition, even where the latter could match them on price. By the Eighties they were able to turn this differentiation into superior price realization, so that those Japanese imports, which less than two decades earlier were only able to sell because they were cheap, were now not only selling at a higher price but continuing to gain market share while doing so.

Productivity in the Sixties, exploiting the first dimension of strategy, efficiency, followed by Quality in the Seventies exploiting the second dimension, differentiation, in each case was a *capability* the American motor industry was unable to match and which produced a product a large part of the market wanted to buy.

What happened next? Let's look at Fig. 5.5.

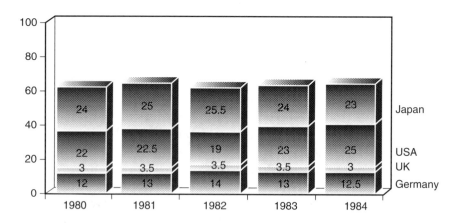

Fig. 5.5 *World car production, national market shares, 1980–1984*

The US industry hit its low point of market share, 19%, in the Reagan recession of 1982. By 1984 it had recovered to 25% and caused its Japanese rivals to stop their advance, and even decline a little in the final year to 23%. How did they do it?

Putting aside their help from a little matter called import restrictions (which after all only leveled the playing field somewhat since the Japanese had been using them for decades to protect their domestic manufacturing base), what the American motor industry basically did was fix the problems – of productivity and quality; maybe not completely, but at least getting back into the competitive ballpark.

Productivity and quality were essentially defensive strategy, aimed at neutralizing the Japanese advantage in these basic characteristics, so that other factors influencing the consumer's purchasing decision where the Americans might have an advantage (e.g., Buy American, familiarity, market coverage, marketing flair) could come into play. During the Eighties one American car company was the clear winner – Ford Motor Company. We know what its defensive strategy was (loudly proclaimed in the advertising slogan, "Quality is Job 1" which is still being used over a decade later), but what was its offensive strategy?

The answer is Design: Ford aimed to produce the best-designed cars in the world to enable it first to get its volume back, and then return to the superior price realization it had once enjoyed. The first car with the new design concept was the Tempo, whose styling the industry rather scornfully dubbed the "jellybean" look (we had a President with a jar of jellybeans on his desk). The second was the Thunderbird, which was allowed to have the "aeroflow" look, with a little, grudging respect. Then came the car that put Ford over the top – the Taurus – which by now was declared to have the "Ford" look. And the problem General Motors then had for several years was that every time it produced a halfway decent-looking car, it looked like a Ford!

Ford in its turn had achieved a distinctive capability – in this case Design – which enabled it to differentiate its cars from its competitors and provide something which a significant part of the market-place found special. Unfortunately its advantage didn't last long and, by the end of the Eighties the American motor industry was back at the low point where it had been at their beginning (see Fig. 5.6).

By this time the data we are using have become more difficult to draw conclusions from, since the Japanese had begun a significant

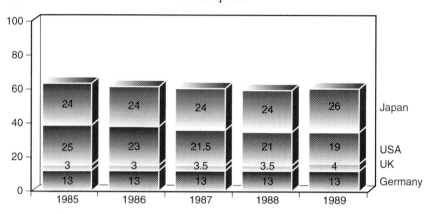

Fig. 5.6 *World car production, national market shares, 1985–1989*

amount of overseas manufacturing, and the Americans were at last integrating their companies around the world into common vehicle programs, so the numbers do not line up neatly by country and national industry.

With that caveat there are a couple of points we can still make from Fig. 5.6 about the competition between the American and Japanese motor industries:

1. The Japanese success in maintaining their global share manufactured in Japan, and the American loss of share manufactured in the US was driven by 1) the faster growth of production in new, national, automotive industries, e.g. Korea, increasing the global market faster than the Americans were growing; 2) the ability of the Japanese constantly to find new export markets; and 3) the failure of the Americans to do the same. That translates into the Japanese having developed yet another distinctive capability – in exporting.
2. The Japanese also found another, new, distinctive capability during this period: time-based competition. Not Just-in-Time manufacturing, which they introduced earlier and which was aimed at reducing inventory cost, but faster cycle times across the board, most importantly in the development of new cars. As a result it took the Japanese significantly less time to engineer a completely new car than the Americans. Thus they brought the third dimension of strategy – time – into play following their earlier exploitation of efficiency and differentiation, in order to

match the tastes of a rapidly changing market-place better than their competition.

What we have seen in this long-term example is how strategic success is maintained by developing *distinctive capabilities* that match the evolution of the market-place and the competitive forces within it. Over three decades the Japanese were able to add successive capabilities that gave them the ability to provide something of special value to a particular part of the market-place. For one short period Ford was able to match them sufficiently well on productivity and quality that a superior design concept gave it a differentiation edge. Now all three dimensions of strategy are in play and it will be superior combinations of the use of efficiency-, differentiation- and time-based competition which will determine success in the future.

Let's look at one more piece of competitive history to solidify our understanding of this idea that it is distinctive capabilities which turn vision into reality. Look at Fig. 5.7.

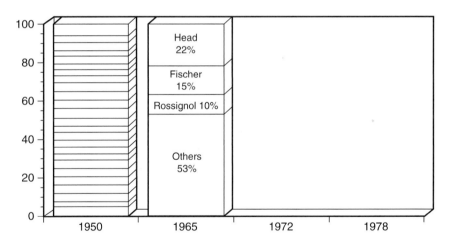

Fig. 5.7 *World ski producers, market share, 1950–1965*

In 1950, there were many, many small ski manufacturers, nearly all of them in Europe. In the next fifteen years, three companies, led by Head, moved into a position of clear industry leadership relegating all the rest to half the share they had enjoyed in 1950. What did Head do that revolutionized the competitive structure of the ski industry? Metal skis. Anton Head was a metal worker and avid skier. He put his trade together with his hobby and, after years of experimentation, came up with a superior ski which revolutionized both the sport and the industry. Then, just as dramatically as the company he had founded had won, it proceeded to lose (see Fig. 5.8).

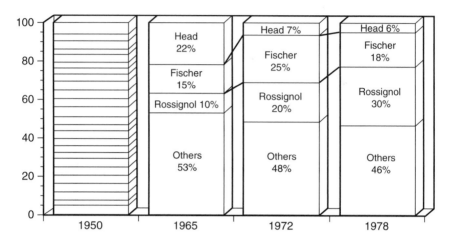

Fig. 5.8   *World ski producers, market share (1950–1978)*

Two things led to its demise. First it lost its focus, and began making all sorts of equipment for all sorts of sports. Second, Fischer introduced fiber glass skis, and then Rossignol took the lead with composite materials. This idea of a distinctive capability with special value to a particular part of the market-place turns out to be a little more complex than maybe it first appeared. It wasn't metal, or fiber glass or even composite materials that was the required capability, but material science applied to the making of skis. Moreover single-minded focus on the ski business was needed for leadership to be sustained.

The message is clear: when you have a focus on doing something that someone out there in the market-place puts a special value on, you win; when you don't, you lose.

For Anton Head the story has a happier ending. He sold his first company to a conglomerate at its peak and went on . . . to develop the first wide-bodied tennis racquet, the Prince! Guess what he did then. Right, he sold the company – to a conglomerate! Here was a man who understood. Twice he revolutionized a world sport and the industry that supplied it. Twice he built an industry-leading company. And twice he cashed out to an undiscerning buyer at the right moment. And he was "just" a metal-bender!

Although I doubt Head would ever have put it this way (but the Japanese might), we can now summarize what it is that turns vision into reality:

> Competitive success follows from focusing every element of an organization on a strategic vision. Achieving that requires the development of superior competence, or the ability to excel, in a set of distinctive capabilities which have special value to a particular part of the market-place.

Note that there are three focus words in that last sentence. It must be *distinctive* capabilities and they must have *special* value, and it must be to a *particular* part of the market-place. Gone are the days of *General* Motors, i.e., of being all things to all people. There are too many competitors in too large and too varied a market-place for that to be possible. A decade ago, Michael Porter, in his best-selling book on strategy – *Competitive Strategy* – said there were three generic strategies: Low Cost, Differentiation and Niche. Whether that was right or wrong, today it is clear there is only one – Low Cost, differentiated and focused, *and* fast and flexible enough to match the ever-increasing pace and unexpectedness of change.

Note also that excellence by itself is not enough. It must be excellence in areas of strategic significance, i.e., that determine the outcome of competition in the market-place. One reason the "excellence" practitioners went wrong in the mid-Eighties is that, in their enthusiasm for attention to detail and admiration for those who wanted things to be the very best they could be, they went overboard. Tom Peters, in his second book *A Passion for Excellence*, told the story of an author of gourmet cookbooks who flies in from the West Coast to New York one day to observe the taking of pictures for his next book. He arrives late in the photo session and, seeing a quiche on a table, tastes it and then, because he doesn't like the taste, makes them re-take all the pictures! This is not aiming at strategic excellence but at irrelevant perfection; and as a client of mine (with *very* high standards) once said to his people at a strategy session, "Always remember that perfection is the enemy of good enough".

John Gardner in his book *Excellence* tells a story that puts it just right:

That there are many varieties of excellence is a truth of which we must continually remind ourselves. The Duke of Wellington, in a famous incident, revealed an enviable understanding of it. The government was considering the dispatch of an expedition to Burma to take Rangoon. The Cabinet summoned Wellington and asked him who would be the ablest general to head such an undertaking. He said, "Send Lord Combermere". The government officials protested: "But we have always understood that Your Grace thought Lord Combermere a fool". The duke's response was vigorous and to the point. "So he is a fool, and a damned fool, but he can take Rangoon".

We live in a relative world where resources are scarce, not an absolute one where we can afford the best that is theoretically possible. Thomas Watson's third belief was *superiority* in everything we do. And *economy*, as we shall see, is the fourth Principle of Competition.

Let us now turn to the second element of grand strategy, competition, to see how the arts of strategy provide the tools for developing a distinctive, strategic vision and devising the actions to turn it into reality.

6 Competition: The Arts of Strategy

"What we need today, perhaps, is not a new theory, concept or framework but people who can think strategically."   (Kenichi Ohmae)

"Supreme excellence consists in breaking the enemy's resistance without fighting. Thus the highest form of generalship is to balk the enemy's plans; the next best is to prevent the junction of the enemy's forces; the next in order is to attack the enemy's army in the field; and the worst policy of all is to besiege walled cities."   (Sun Tzu)

"Force and fraud are, in war, the two cardinal virtues."
(Thomas Hobbes)

"In strategy the longest way round is often the shortest way home."
(Basil Liddell Hart)

Sustained, high performance – the manifestation of competitive health – stems from either luck (I found a diamond mine), inheritance (Kodak's dominance of the photographic market), or the rigorous application of strategy. Both of the first two eventually run out. For long-term health, the application of strategy is needed. It can happen in two ways. In the first, the leader is a superb strategist and dictates his or her strategy; everyone else implements it. In the second, the team, led by the leader, engages in rigorous situation assessment, strategy development and implementation follow-through. The first is high risk. What happens if he or she isn't as good as we thought? Or is, but gets run over by a bus? Only the second is a prudent way of managing for success over the long haul.

Most companies in fact pay lip service to something like this belief. They engage in extensive information gathering, implement elaborate strategic planning processes and hold long strategy review meetings. But somehow all this doesn't translate into improved performance. In most organizations the reality is that, despite all the activity, strategy isn't taken very seriously by the people who matter. Many of them don't even really know what it is. Most of the work is delegated to staff. Not much senior management time is spent on it; and only a few people (and they're all staff) ever look at the plans again after they have been submitted. Consequently strategy development is not done very well, strategic planning is not regarded as a serious activity, and implementation, as planned, is the exception not the rule. As I said earlier it has been estimated that 95% of the strategic plans in the Seventies were never fully implemented, and that was probably a conservative estimate.

The trigger for an organization to take strategy seriously has usually been poor financial results. These always stem from some kind of failure in the marketplace. I say "always" because, even if the only problem truly is just *internal* costs – that is, not product features, or reliability or service, or customer relations – it will eventually show up in the attempt to maintain margins, hence the raising of prices higher than the market will bear, or competition needs on its cost base. The result will be either lower prices than desired, hence shrinking margins and a deteriorating bottom line, or a loss of market share which, even if not initially regarded as in the category of bad "results" as at Kodak, will still ultimately translate into poor financial results.

So strategy must start with what's happening in the marketplace, and then explore for connections between that, and what's going on internally to seek the source of corrective actions. Today this is essentially a team learning process, because no one person or department possesses all the information needed for a winning synthesis. It is the *interactions* between functions, not just what goes on within each of them, that determine the success of the whole enterprise. And the better we get at performing each function the more this is the case because, (1) all our competitors are doing the same, so there is less room for competitive advantage on a function-by-function basis, and (2) functional optimization in a vacuum, as systems theory has taught us, always goes too far. The whole is never optimized by optimizing each of the parts separately.

Once upon a time neither of these reasons mattered as much as they do now. The first great advances in both efficiency and effectiveness were made function by function – the potential for these individual gains far outweighing any frictional losses through less than optimal interactions with other areas of the organization. Systems theory came along, when it did, precisely because it was needed. Interactions between areas of the organization had become more important than individual, departmental gains.

So it is now, with the elements of strategy. The early advances of the Seventies which focused heavily on the need for cost management, brought about by the slowing of growth that came with the onset of the recessionary phase of the fourth wave, did not need much subtlety. There was enough to be gained from a superior relative cost position. And the same was true with the next wave, differentiation, in the early Eighties. Again, early on, there was enough to be gained from superior price realization without worrying about the costs that differentiation added. (Notice the close parallel to what happened in the motor industry sixty years earlier. The recessionary phase of the fourth wave started in 1913 and the Model T Ford, exploiting the cost reduction potential of the assembly line, was the initial winner. Then General Motors, with Alfred P. Sloan's view of the market as five distinct segments to be pursued separately by Chevrolet, Pontiac, Buick, Oldsmobile and Cadillac, overtook Ford in the Twenties.) Next it was the turn of innovation, which developed into time-based competition, the in-technique of the late Eighties and early Nineties. But, eventually, the iron law of competitive economics – leads shrink, ultimately to negligibility – reasserted itself. Followers learned these techniques, too. Gradually strategy took on a much more complex hue, requiring an understanding of the interactions of all its elements, to come up with distinctive combinations that would provide an edge in particular parts of the market-place.

But to find these combinations meant learning, team learning. And to make them useful meant planning, team planning. The most successful organizations put them together, recognizing that there was no better way of learning together than planning together. As they did this they found that there was a second skill they had to develop: strategic thinking. Neither this nor strategic planning proved to be natural skills, at least not to the hands-on, analytic, action-oriented, "ready, shoot, aim" managers by whom most organizations in the Eighties were populated. In this chapter we will explore some of the things the winners have learned about strategic thinking and about strategic planning, as they sought to become better at both.

Before we explore these two areas, let's step back a moment and take a hard look at the key word – strategic – that distinguishes each skill from other types of thinking and planning. What does it mean? What in fact *is* strategy?

We can see from the above and from Chapter 3 that the elements of strategy as it has actually been used, have evolved out of responses to real competitive challenges, rather than as a body of concepts theoretically derived from first principles. Today, with the more perfect vision of hindsight applied to a generation of experience with strategy as a business concept, we can lay out a clearer synthesis of what strategy is, and how it can be applied.

I was first prompted to take the time to define strategy rigorously by an experience I had while I was preparing the material for the seminar series I mentioned in the previous chapter, which were to be called "How to become a Strategic Manager". I didn't think any special attention was needed to the key adjective until I was approached, just before the first seminar, by one of the major international consulting firms to be part of an effort to build a strategy consulting capability, which they did not have. They sent me a copy of a magazine they publish to showcase the ideas of some of their thought leaders. At the back were two pages of pictures and career sketches of the article writers, about twenty of them. Seventeen had managed to get either the word "strategy" or "strategic" into their descriptions of their current roles; and this was a firm that readily admitted it didn't have a strategy consulting capability! Clearly there was a need for greater rigor in the use of the term if it was to have any distinctive value in describing my seminars.

So I looked "strategy" up in the dictionary and, to my horror, I found the wrong meaning! "A long-range plan of intended actions", it said. My initial reaction was that America had ruined another good, English word. Then, looking at the inside front page to see who had published this monstrosity, I discovered I was looking at what is called a "Usage Dictionary", one that records the current, common usage of a word, not necessarily its original or primary meaning. Given my recent experience with the consulting firm's magazine, there was no question that the dictionary was doing its stated job accurately after all. I am pleased to record that when I turned to the same company's Collegiate Dictionary I also found equal integrity with regard to the English language:

Strategy: a plan, method or series of maneuvers or stratagems for obtaining a specific goal or result

. . . and the two words on which this meaning depends. . .

Maneuver: a planned and regulated movement or evolution of troops, war vessels, etc.; an adroit move or skillful proceeding, especially as characterized by craftiness

Stratagem: a plan, scheme or trick for surprising or deceiving an enemy; any artifice, ruse or trick to attain a goal or to gain an advantage over an adversary for obtaining a specific goal or result

These are words to re-read, to dwell on, and to let work on your imagination. The richer the images you let them conjure up, however far afield they seem at first from the business of running an organization, the richer the understanding of strategy you will develop. For me they contain five ideas which are of particular importance:

1. Strategy requires specificity about the intended "goal or result"
2. Strategy involves a carefully orchestrated combination of actions for its effect
3. Strategy consists of the deliberate commitment of precious, and powerful resources
4. Strategy, works through craftiness, artifices, ruses and tricks to surprise and deceive
5. Strategy is not about actual, direct competition, but the gaining of advantage.

I chose the above words carefully not just to capture the ideas but also to move us from the dictionary and war, to practice and business. In Chapter 3, I described how modern thinking on business strategy developed as the responses we adopted to deal with the newly intensified challenges of competition, that arose as the expansionary phase of the fourth wave turned into the recessionary phase at the beginning of the Seventies. Before then "long-range" and "corporate" planning were already a part of the executive's tool-kit, but it was only in the Seventies that titles and departments of "strategic" planning began to appear on the organization charts of major companies.

The key is that word "competition". It is the presence of competition, actual or potential, making every task a "relative" as well as an "absolute" one, that turns the need for operational planning into the need for strategy. "Best" and "better" become the operative adjectives, not "good" – superlatives and comparatives, always relating every aspect of performance to the rival organizations which have to stop you achieving what you want to achieve, if they are to achieve what they want to achieve. After all, the race, as I said earlier, never did go to the swift, but to the swifter – or, perhaps even more insightfully, to the less slow!

I remember listening to Bob Crandall, Chief Executive Officer of American Airlines, talking to 2,000 of the airline's employees in Chicago in the late Eighties. It was a time of huge price competition led by Continental which had unilaterally canceled a labor contract and dramatically reduced its labor costs while operating under protection of the bankruptcy laws. Crandall was asked by an employee if a voluntary giveback by employees of some of their benefits would help the airline. His response (my comments in parentheses): "I don't want anyone here to give up any of your benefits. What I do want you to do is write to Senator Kennedy (Secretary of the Labor Committee of the Senate, who was holding hearings on employee benefits at the time), and tell him that it is unconscionable that any major company in this day and age does not provide post-retirement medical benefits for its employees (as Continental didn't)". It wasn't *lower* costs he was after, but *competitive* costs. Is it any wonder that seven years later American Airlines was one of the very few major companies that supported the employer mandates (as a way to pay for universal coverage) in the Clinton Health Care Bill? American is under a terrible, competitive handicap as long as it has its expensive employee benefits and major competitors can avoid them.

Absolute economic performance in this age of unprecedented competitive intensity is dependent on relative, competitive success. We saw it in the example that I gave in Chapter 3 to illustrate how, in the Seventies, we showed the aim of strategy – higher and more secure returns (themselves both comparatives) – could be achieved through superior, relative costs. We saw it again in the way this first insight of business strategy as a modern management discipline was followed by superior price realization through differentiation; which in turn was followed by the faster response times and shorter new product development cycles of time-based competition. The motto of the Olympics says it all: "Faster–Higher–Stronger". As I've said, this is a competition for a gold medal, not an attempt to a break a world record. The best in business receive the highest rewards, not because they are good, but because they beat their rivals when it matters, just as it is in every other sphere of human competition.

So strategy is:

the commitment of combinations of significant resources in ways that deceive or surprise competitors, and thereby result in the achievement of positions of advantage, which lead to the attainment of specific aims, with or without ensuing, direct competition.

That is not just a mouthful but also about as dry and general a definition as we can get! So let's look at how these concepts apply more specifically to the different levels of strategy that an organization must address.

A HIERARCHY OF STRATEGY

At the top of the hierarchy we find the subject of this book, grand strategy. It was called "the highest type of strategy" in one of the quotes at the beginning of Chapter 4, because its aim, at the national level, is to so integrate "the policies and armaments of the nation" that its goals are achieved without resort to war at all, or with the maximum advantage from the very outset if war cannot be avoided. Its "crux" was described in a second quote as "the capacity of a nation's leaders to bring together all of the elements" of competition. It is thus "grand" both because it operates *above* strategy, at best to avoid the need for strategy at all, and because it goes *beyond* strategy to address every aspect of the nation's competition with other nations.

Using this understanding, for organizations we therefore can define it as follows:

Grand Strategy

The definition of policies and capabilities covering every aspect of an organization's activities that, when implemented, result in a set of such superior, mutually beneficial relationships with all key stakeholders that, at best, competitors find it impossible to challenge, and if they do maximizes the probability of success in the ensuing competition. Its aim (as Chapter 4 described) is a pre-eminent management technique which results in stronger strategic positions, higher quality execution and more effective renewal than competitive organizations, so as to fulfill its purposes – the set of superior, mutually beneficial relationships with its key stakeholders.

Beneath grand strategy, and guided by it, come the two forms of strategy that the vast bulk of the literature deals with, addressing the questions of first *where* to compete, and second *how* to compete.

Participation (or Corporate) Strategy

The choices of which businesses, and which segments of those businesses a company will compete in, the positions it will seek to achieve in them, and the distinctive set of capabilities on which it will base its participation.

Operating (or Operational) Strategy

The comprehensive program of resource commitments to achieve the goals of Participation Strategy. It has three principal components:

1. *Business Strategy*
    A program of resource commitments aimed at breaking the competitive equilibrium in a particular business and then resetting it to your advantage, so as to achieve higher and more secure returns than your competitors.

2. *Process Strategy*
    A program of resource commitments aimed at achieving the defined performance levels required from each of an organization's critical, business processes in order to implement its Strategies.

3. *Functional (or Departmental) Strategy*
    A program of resource commitments that enables a function to implement its pieces of the organization's strategies in conjunction with the units with which it interacts.

Armed with this understanding about what we mean by strategy in its various forms, let us now turn to the skills a management team needs to use it – strategic thinking, and strategic planning.

STRATEGIC THINKING

We have already learned that strategic thinking is . . .

*   Relative, not absolute, and is needed because of the existence of competition standing in the way of the achievement of one's aims;
*   Concerned with the deployment of combinations of significant resources to meet specific aims, which, in business, usually means it is also long-term in its effect; and

- Multi-dimensional in its need to consider both every aspect of an organization's activities, and their interactions along the three dimensions of strategy – efficiency, differentiation and time;

and that it must consider. . .

- Customer segments and the sets of needs they represent, which determine what they want to buy, and who they are likely to buy it from;
- Existing and potential competitors' capabilities, and their needs, which are likely to determine their behavior;
- The organization's existing and potential capabilities, and the needs of its various stakeholders, which it must meet in a superior way.

Here we will explore three tools that strategic thinking uses as it determines its aims, what resources it will utilize and how it will allocate them to meet its goals:

- The Dimensions of Value, which determine the return on investment the organization can and will make;
- A Philosophy of Competition, which can guide us in the creative task of devising the combinations of resource commitments which comprise a winning strategy;
- The Principles of Competition, which provide us first with the list of elements we must consider in the allocation of specific resources which moves strategy from intent to action, and then with the means to test our strategy's robustness when we are ready to put it into effect.

As I said earlier, it is not my intent to try to compete here with the already vast and continuously growing body of literature on strategy, so why these three tools?

My goal in this book is to give the reader a way of approaching every management task in a strategic frame of mind. The first element of this approach was described in the previous chapter – the explicit definition of the sets of shared purposes, shared values and distinctive capabilities which distinguish an organization's aims and its unique approach to achieving them. In addition to driving the development of strategy, this element of grand strategy, once set, guides the everyday decision-making and resource-allocating behavior that implements strategy. The purpose of the second element of grand strategy is to meet the need for a competitive edge in each of the same two aspects of management – the development of strategy, and the everyday behavior that implements it. What these three tools give us, beyond some valuable techniques (which are included in Appendix 1) is the essence of what it means to think strategically, so that, having mastered them, the way we approach every management decision automatically builds into our thought processes the need for whatever we choose to do to create, enhance or maintain competitive advantage. The Dimensions of Value, A Philosophy of Competition and the Principles of Competition form a mental model which enables those who master them to build strategy into everything they do.

THE DIMENSIONS OF VALUE

"Value" here means stockholder value. The purpose of this tool is to instill into our thinking the characteristics of a business that lead to the creation of value for the stockholder, so that all our everyday, as well as our longer term, decision-making constantly seeks to bring them about. Empirical results, for example from BCG and the PIMS project and then much enhanced by Margeaux Cvar, to whom I am indebted for many of the insights that follow, not just theory, have found three sets of characteristics that lead to the superior creation of stockholder value (see Fig. 6.1).

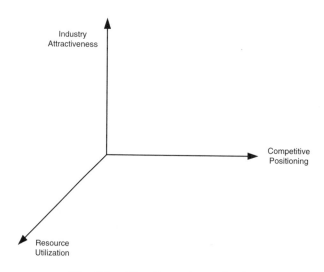

Fig. 6.1   *The dimensions of value*

Industry attractiveness provides the basis for predicting the average returns available in an industry and their risk. It looks at the forces which determine the general pressures on the profitability available to all players in an industry (or business, or market segment depending on the level of analysis) to assess how high that is likely to be, and how much it can be expected to vary over time.

Competitive positioning provides the basis for predicting how a given company will perform relative to its industry peers. It looks at the strategic (i.e., relative) characteristics of companies that have been shown to correlate with profitability to assess how high that is likely to be for each player.

Resource utilization then provides the basis for predicting how well a given company will translate the potential for profit defined by the first two dimensions into an actual return on investment. It looks at the way resources are actually utilized and assesses how this will turn into future cashflows.

There are ten variables that need to be considered in the exploration of what makes an industry attractive as a place to participate for those already in it. In Appendix 1 is a full explanation of each of these areas for the reader who wants to explore them in depth, plus exhibits to enable their application to his or her organization. Table 6.1 lists the variables that make up each dimension. There then follow some general comments on their significance.

Table 6.1   Industry attractiveness variables

---

1. Growth Rate
2. Number of Competitors
3. Number of Customers
4. Product Significance to buyer (*i.e., its criticality vs. how much it costs*)
5. Number of Suppliers
6. Regulation
7. R&D Intensity (*i.e. R&D as a percentage of Sales*)
8. Cyclicality (not *seasonality*)
9. Experience Curve effect (*ability to turn learning into lower costs*)
10. Marketing Intensity (*i.e., Marketing Costs as a percentage of Sales*)

These variables address major characteristics that have been found empirically to correlate with the general profitability in, and cashflow available from participation in an industry, or segment thereof.

Seven of them deal with forces from Michael Porter's competitive intensity model – Number of Competitors (Rivalry among existing firms); Product Significance and Number of Customers (Bargaining Power of Customers); Number of Suppliers (Bargaining Power of Suppliers); R&D Intensity, Experience Curve Effect and Marketing Intensity (Potential New Entrants, Potential Substitutes) – since the level of competitive intensity is a primary determinant of the return it is possible to make in a business.

The other three – Growth, Regulation, and Cyclicality – have also been shown to have a significant effect on profitability. The first, because growth requires funding, which means that when it is high there are fewer spare resources to spend on competitive strategy, and when it is low competitors seek to raise their own by taking share from their competitors, which depresses profitability. The second is a little more complicated – there is "good" regulation, and "bad" from a profit potential point-of-view. The American trucking companies, Savings and Loans (Building Societies), and Airlines used to enjoy the former, since price was effectively taken out of the marketing mix by regulation. What has happened to all three since de-regulation is evidence enough. "Bad" regulation, which from this viewpoint essentially just means price and/or profitability controls, is more obvious in its effect, and the return available from a Utility illustrates the point.

Moving now to Competitive Position, there are seven variables to be considered (see Table 6.2).

Table 6.2   Competitive positioning variables

1.   Market Share
2.   Market Rank
3.   Quality Image
4.   New Product Intensity
5.   Product Line Breadth
6.   Cost Position
7.   Selling & Distribution Integration

Here the variables help us understand how much better or worse the individual company has the potential to perform compared to its competitors, given its position relative to them. The first six variables all deal with the first two dimensions of strategy – efficiency and distribution – which we showed in Chapter 3 were the basis for competitive success, that is higher and more secure returns than the competition at a point in time. They speak to whether the subject company is likely to have a better relative cost position, and/or superior price realization than its competitors, hence higher returns. The seventh deals with how close it is to its market-place, since this has also been found to correlate positively with higher profitability – because of the greater sensitivity it gives to customer needs, and the absence of a middleman to siphon off profits.

The third dimension of value is Resource Utilization, and here there are eight variables (see Table 6.3).

Table 6.3   Resource utilization variables

1.	Value-Added per Employee
2.	Unionization (or labor rigidity)
3.	Capacity Utilization
4.	Value-Added per Overhead Dollar
5.	Vertical Integration
6.	Working Capital
7.	Fixed Investment
8.	Long-Term Liability

This dimension determines how well the potential of the first two are turned into realized returns. Each again has been included not just for theoretical reasons but because empirically they have been shown to correlate with actual profitability performance. However these are not simple relationships where the more of one of the variables the higher (or lower) is profitability. It turns out that it is possible to "go too far", and that wherever there is a "normal" rule there are also exceptions (for a discussion of which see Appendix 1). The importance of this finding to the would-be grand strategist is that subtlety in the management of these variables is conspicuous by its absence in most corporations today. There are optimal points for each of these variables for each competitor and, nearly always, finding them means a team effort, because of trade-offs between the traditional functions that make up a business. Here it is critical to recognize the "system" nature of modern business, requiring the management of functional, departmental and divisional interactions if the potential of industry attractiveness and the power of competitive positioning are to be turned fully into the reality of profitability.

To summarize, The Dimensions of Value tell us the characteristics that lead to superior profitability. The first dimension, Industry Attractiveness, sets the bounds of profitability that are possible, and describes the environment in which competition is to take place. The second, Competitive Positioning, defines the elements in which to seek the "stronger strategic positions", which it is the first aim of grand strategy to achieve. The third, Resource Utilization, lays out some of the key relationships between the way resources are used, and profitability.

Thus the Dimensions of Value help us address three critical "what" questions: what parts of the market-place to participate in, what positions to seek in those areas, and what patterns of resource utilization to try to establish. In conjunction they provide a very powerful tool for understanding the forces that drive a company's profitability, and hence a host of insights on actions that might improve it. Many of these actions depend on trade-offs between different aspects of the company's operations, vividly demonstrating the "systems" nature of the challenge. Using this tool is a team task which can be frustrating, but the payoff is very high. It leads not just to actions which improve profitability, but also to the enhanced sensitivity of functional specialists to the impact of their areas of responsibility on others, and through that the profitability of the whole enterprise.

Having addressed the characteristics it is seeking, i.e. the "what", the team then needs to address the three corresponding "how" questions, to develop strategies that will achieve the industry participation, competitive position and resource utilization profiles that result in superior value being created for the stockholder. So we turn now to the way of approaching this challenge which the history of competition has shown to be the key to the creative art of strategy.

A PHILOSOPHY OF COMPETITION

Our aim is to devise ways of deploying resources that enable the organization to achieve its desired results, in the face of competitors who must stop this from happening if they are to achieve their goals. Here is where "artifice" and "ruse" and "trick" have their place, and where "craftiness" is the skill that is needed to surprise and deceive competition. The need for these skills stems from two fundamental, competitive truths known in the military as the importance of mass, and the superiority of the defense. Let us see why.

A group of twelve redcoats meets nine minutemen in the open field. The range is such that one shot in three causes a casualty. After the first volley the redcoats are reduced to nine and the minutemen to five. The original 33% advantage in mass has increased to 80%. The minutemen hold their ground and a second volley is fired. Now the redcoats' advantage has grown to seven-to-two, or 250%. The groups have not even approached close enough for hand-to-hand combat but, if they do, the outcome is already determined. The greater initial mass of the redcoats has determined the victor.

Now suppose, instead of meeting the redcoats in the open field, the minutemen await them behind a wall, which reduces the effectiveness of the redcoats shooting by half so that only one shot in six causes a casualty. The effectiveness of the minutemen is unchanged, so stays at one shot in three causing a casualty.

After the first volley the redcoats, as before, are down to nine men, but the minutemen, in their defensive position, still have seven standing. After the second the redcoats are reduced to seven but only one more minuteman has fallen so they are at six. Parity has almost been reached, and the probability of the outcome of a continued battle is that the redcoats will lose. The same advantage of mass that was overwhelming in the open field is nowhere near sufficient to deal with the superiority of the defense.

Of course if the stronger side also has the advantage of the defense, as it normally does in business, the attackers are annihilated. Twelve to nine becomes eleven to five after one volley, and ten to two after two.

From this it is but a short step to conclude first with Basil Liddell Hart that "No General is justified in launching his troops to a direct attack upon an enemy firmly in position." And second, because of that, with Sun Tzu, "In all fighting the direct method may be used for joining battle but indirect methods will be needed to secure victory."

Finally, we can go to Bruce Henderson and the meaning of these truths for business, "Business success always requires repeated displacement of lower cost, entrenched competitors. Therefore all long continued success is based upon an indirect approach that depends on misperceptions by competitors."

THE STRATEGY OF THE INDIRECT APPROACH

The importance of mass, or scale as we refer to it in business, and the superiority of the defense imply that a direct challenge to competitors is both the most likely to fail, and even where successful is very costly in resources. The aim of strategy therefore is to seek a strategic position so advantageous that, if it does not of itself result in the objective being achieved, the competition that then follows is sure to achieve it, and at the least cost in resources. We want the advantage of both higher scale and the defense if we have to compete. Ideally, as we discussed earlier, we want our competitor to give up without even trying.

IBM used to announce its new computers well in advance. Jack Welch, in charge of GE's plastics businesses, used to give his competitors long notice of his intent to add new capacity. In both cases the aim was to freeze competition, to get them to conclude it wasn't worth the effort – in other words, to win without fighting. In both cases the target of the strategy was the mind of the opposing managers. The goal was the psychological dislocation of competitors in advance of any head-to-head competition that might result. One of Napoleon's maxims, that I've mentioned before, was "the psychological is to the physical as three-to-one in war". And the Duke of Wellington used to say that Napoleon's presence on the battlefield was worth fifty thousand men (and the Iron Duke only had 67,600 on the decisive day at Waterloo!).

In business, a "winning" strategic position is comprised of the set of distinctive capabilities which have special value to a particular part of the market-place that, we learned in the last chapter, is the way mission is implemented, and vision turned into reality. If we have them and competition doesn't, in that part of the market-place we enjoy the advantages of both scale and the defense. Whether we are aiming to hold or gain share, competition has to try to stop us without the advantage of the key set of capabilities.

Let us look at some examples.

The Demise of the British Motorcycle Industry

In the late Fifties the British had 95% of world trade in motorcycles. Thirty years later they had none. What happened? The British dominated the world market with the grand old marques such as

Triumph, Norton and Villiers. They made most of their money from what are now called the superbikes – the heavy 500cc and 1000cc machines that, like heavy-weight boxers, were the most glamorous part of the business. When the Japanese began to invade world markets with the small, light, 50cc and 125cc bikes the British, believing there was no money to be made there, and that the secret to profit was share in the larger bike segment, let them have the market. Unfortunately, while it was true that the secret to superior price realization might have been share of the superbike segment, as we have learned there is a more fundamental condition for strategic success – low cost, which in this business comes most of all from manufacturing scale. The production line did not distinguish between the number of cc in the engine of the bike it was making. Scale was the number of engines and bikes, designed and made. The basic technological capabilities were shared.

So the Japanese took the small bike segment, then the medium (250cc) segment and finally the superbikes. The British motorcycle industry followed what is now perceived as a classical pattern of segmentation retreat – away from the low-price/high-volume market toward the higher-price, more brand-sensitive segments, eventually losing the scale to be profitable and to develop a technologically competitive product, even at those higher prices.

Was this deliberate, superior Japanese strategy right from the start? Not at all. Tell the story in California and you'll learn that the Japanese, copying the British, tried initially to compete in the larger bike segments, with no success. Then a dealer who had imported a couple of the tiny bikes for his family suddenly found a demand for them. The rest, as they say, is history. The Japanese genius was to learn from their market-place experience, cut their losses in the larger bike segment and refocus on the small bikes, where the British weren't competing. This indirect approach eventually gave them the superbike market which had been their initial goal, and which they had failed even to dent by a direct assault.

L'Eggs Pantyhose

Once upon a time women's stockings, and then pantyhose were sold exclusively in department stores, with the huge variety and personal service that channel provided. By focusing only on a small number of high volume ("commodity"?!) items, utilizing a unique, new package (the egg) and moving distribution to channels (Supermarkets and Drugstores) that these characteristics fit well, L'Eggs broke the competitive equilibrium and reset it in its own favor.

Procter & Gamble's New Product Screen

I once heard a management lecturer describe P&G management's three rules for new products during its major growth period up to the mid-Eighties. First they would only enter large, which usually also meant mature markets, which broke the first rule I had been accustomed to using: namely enter markets when they are small and immature, and pre-empt the growth. Second they wanted stable markets, which they measured by the presence of major competitors already in them, which broke the second rule I had been taught: to enter markets where competition is fragmented, and gain share from the weakest competitors.

But P&G knew what it was doing. First, it is a huge company and, unlike most, had recognized it didn't know how to compete in niche markets. Its culture and embedded management paradigm meant it had to focus only on large markets. Second, its core competence is brand management in consumer advertising and merchandising. Launching a new, branded product into the crowded world of consumer goods requires a massive upfront investment in advertising, which it takes years to recoup. P&G can't afford, therefore, to be in fashion-sensitive, unstable businesses. It has to be able to rely on the market being there for a long time so that the later years' profitability can make up for the initial investment in marketing.

So the first two rules made eminent practical sense. The necessary indirection came in the third rule, which was that it would only enter a new market with a truly superior product. P&G's strategy was to use its merchandising capability to get shelf-space and its advertising capability to get customers to try the new product, and then rely on its true product superiority to get repeat buying and eventually the displacement of existing offerings.

The introduction of Duncan Hines cake mixes was a textbook example. An industry researcher had discovered the ingredient that makes baked goods go stale, and that its removal did not have any negative side effects, for example on taste. Only P&G initially realized the significance of this discovery for cake mixes. As the story was told to me, a cake was taken into a senior management meeting by a new product champion who then announced it was one week old and proceeded to cut it with a feather! Itself a wonderful example of indirection.

P&G then bought permission from a famous chef – Duncan Hines – to use his name and hence (another indirection) add an extra element of credibility to its product claim. It duly introduced its new line of cake mixes, rapidly gained share on the previously dominant Betty Crocker line, and in a very short time displaced it for leadership of the segment.

Minnetonka

In the early Eighties a small company called Minnetonka came up with an indirect way of competing with the giants, such as Procter & Gamble, and Unilever, who had a lock on the soap business. Minnetonka launched a consumer-oriented liquid soap and, finding a market that no one knew was there, experienced explosive growth, becoming one of the "in" presents for one memorable holiday season. Unfortunately the story does not have a happy ending, at least for Minnetonka. Indirection is a wonderful strategy for bypassing the strengths of existing leaders, and establishing a bridgehead in a market. But it comes with a question that it is *mandatory* be answered if a short-term breakthrough is to be turned into long-term success: What are you going to do about the inevitable counter-attack?

When P&G responded, the next year, with an equally good product its huge marketing clout removed Minnetonka from the business as dramatically as it had entered it, thereby putting the company under.

Empires don't take kindly to pieces of their territory being annexed by upstarts. The gains of the smaller competitor will only be held if the quality of the defensive position it creates matches the creativity of the offensive strategy it adopts.

Humana's Artificial Heart Transplants

Humana was one of the first companies to build a chain of hospitals and seek to create a "brand name" in health care. After the first successful heart transplants, as the story was told to me, Humana asked the leading surgeon if he would like to move to one of their hospitals and, if he did so, how many operations he would like to perform if they funded him for the next couple of years. As the story goes he answered, "How about four?" To which the Humana representative replied, "How about 120!" The surgeon had been thinking of an intensely expensive operation, the Humana manager was thinking of free publicity. After the surgeon moved, in that early period for these astounding operations, each time he performed one, Humana would be mentioned on the news every evening, on all three US networks. Within six months the company went from zero to 15% unaided awareness among the American public.

IBM's Pillow Ad

My favorite IBM advertisement was a full page of the *Wall Street Journal* with just a pillow in the middle of it, and at the bottom of the page the caption: "What you want from your computer is a quiet night's rest".

The Soft Drink Wars

The first round of the soft drink wars lasted from the establishment of The Coca-Cola Company until after the Second World War. During that long period Coca-Cola built an apparently impregnable position based on the unique image of the shape of the bottle, its identification with the establishment and tradition and what became known internally as "ubiquity" – availability just about everywhere in America in particular, and most importantly in huge numbers of Soda Fountains and Vending Machines. These represented not only mass, but an extraordinarily strong defensive position – there were hard, Coke assets in these channels with contracts attached to them, which Pepsi had to replace if it was to penetrate at all. Pepsi Cola survived, at times barely, as a much smaller competitor under the Coca-Cola price umbrella, for a long time after the Second World War using the slogan "Twice as much for a nickel too" (a 12-oz, in the early days refilled, beer bottle, at the same price as a 6.5-oz bottle of Coke for the same 5¢).

Then, in round two, Pepsi began a whole series of indirect approaches to whittle away at Coca-Cola's dominance of the soft drink industry. It went to countries like Saudi Arabia where Coke was banned because it was selling in Israel. It went to Russia. A young sales manager called Howard Kendall arranged for the famous TV shot of Vice-President Nixon and General Secretary Krushchev sharing a Pepsi . . . and ended his career three decades later as Chairman of the Company! But these were small victories. The breakthrough came through the combination of a new package, cans, and a new channel, supermarkets. Cans are a much superior package to bottles for the take-away market because they don't break when dropped, and are lighter to carry. Pepsi's strategy was to exploit these features – which was initially, culturally difficult for Coke to follow because its whole identity was so tied up with the famous 6.5–oz, contoured bottle – along with the rapid growth of supermarkets, using an aggressive pricing strategy which both appealed particularly well in that channel, and drew a stark and immediate contrast to the price of a Coke only a few feet down the same aisle. The package was one indirection, the channel another. The importance of the latter was that there were no contracts, and no fixed Coke or Pepsi assets in place in a Supermarket. It was all working capital which turns over very fast – and with a low-price based push on volume, it was very much in the interests of the supermarket manager to help an aggressive Pepsi gain share. Inside a generation Pepsi had overtaken Coke in the supermarket channel and has been running at least even ever since.

Then Pepsi began a line extension which Coke again found it difficult to follow because of its historical identification with the one, flagship product. Next Pepsi changed the focus of its advertising to young people, "The Pepsi Generation", using popular music stars and offbeat humor to bypass Coke's identification with traditional America.

To each of these attacks, Coca-Cola's response was "direct" in every way – same packages, same line extension, same focus for its advertising and, eventually, same price. It was enough to stop the losses but, unlike P&G's response to Minnetonka, it was not enough to turn the tide the other way, first because Pepsi was both relatively larger so had the resources to defend itself, and second because Pepsi had put in place a very special defense for its newly won position – The Pepsi Challenge.

In shopping malls all over the country people were asked take a blind taste-test, first sipping two Colas and then saying which one they preferred – and 55% of the people preferred Pepsi! It must have sent the executives in Coca-Cola's marble, Atlanta palace crazy.

Every night on the television were all these people, whom Coke thought they owned, discovering that they preferred the taste of Pepsi. If they had no advantage on taste, being equal on all the characteristics, which they had just followed on, was not going to be enough to reverse their losses. What were they to do?

So began the project that was finally to remove the Edsel from the pinnacle of American marketing debacles.

On April 23, 1986 I was in the middle of a training workshop where I was teaching a group of consultants about strategy. The Soft Drink Wars was one of my case studies and I was going to ask my students the next morning how Coke should respond to The Pepsi Challenge. I went back to my room that evening and there on prime time news was the story that Coca-Cola had announced a new recipe for its flagship product. "It was the easiest decision I ever made", said its Chairman, Roberto Goizueta. Now, where in the world, would all three major networks lead off their most important news program of the day with the change in recipe of a soft drink? No wonder the Russians thought we were crazy!

In the next couple of months Pepsi had a field day poking fun at the new product, and taking advantage of the cry of dismay, and even outrage that emanated from the American consumer.

On July 11, I was teaching another group of consultants the same course in the same place, as I had been on April 23. Again I was to use The Soft Drink Wars as a case study the next morning, only this time there were going to be two questions: What *should* Coca-Cola have done? and, What should both Coca-Cola and Pepsi do *now*? Before I could get to them, Coca-Cola announced it was bringing back the old recipe, as Coca-Cola Classic!

That, of course, was the answer I was going to lead my students toward the next morning. But what should Pepsi have been planning to do, if Coca-Cola had not taken this step? A little over a year later I found out what it *was* planning to do – and it would have been brilliant. Here is Roger Enrico, then President of Pepsi Cola USA, in his book *The Other Guy Blinked*, published in November 1986:

> What would *you* do if you were running the second-largest company in your industry, and the largest company trashed its biggest-selling product?
> First, you'd be amazed.
> We were.

Then you'd have some fun at the giant's expense.

We did.

But what if your surveys showed that 80 percent of the people who tasted the giant's new product thought it was a lousy idea?

What if your surveys told you that 70 percent of the people who tasted the giant's new product just plain didn't like it?

And, knowing all that, what would you do after two or three weeks went by and it was clear that a lot of consumers really wanted the old product to be returned to the marketplace?

Right, you'd do what we did: You'd wait for the giant to change his mind.

But what if – knowing all that – the giant still refused to bring back the old product everybody was now demanding?

What would you do *then*?

No, you say, You wouldn't. Not *that*.

But you would. You're damn right you would. If the Coca-Cola Company won't make the real thing, you'd say, we'll have to do it for them.

That's why I ordered the Pepsi R&D lab to reinvent Merchandise 7X – because if Coke wouldn't make Coke, I decided, Pepsi would.

In about two minutes, we even had a name for it.

Savannah Cola. Savannah "Classic" Cola, to be exact.

It didn't take us long to crack the Merchandise 7X code. Or to come up against a problem.

To make Old Coke just like the Coke many people knew and loved and were now mourning, we'd need some coca leaf – with the cocaine extracted, of course. Unfortunately, there's just one company I'm aware of that specialized in this product. And guess who its biggest – and practically only – customer is?

If we ordered that coca leaf, Coke would know what we were up to in *seconds* – and even the most stubborn New Coke supporter at Coke headquarters would vote to bring back the old formula.

So R&D went back to work, trying this time to simulate the taste of cocaine-removed coca leaf.

We imagined that we'd have Savannah Classic Cola ready for the world by mid-September 1985.

With that timetable, we'd be able to announce it on Labor Day. Happy picnics, America! Have a Coke and a smile – compliments of your friends at Pepsi!

Just in time – with less than two months to spare – Coca-Cola had avoided this even greater disaster by bringing back the old recipe.

Thereafter the Soft Drink War deteriorated into a First World War style, head-on battle of attrition between the two giants where price was the principal weapon. The consumer benefited hugely – the price of a 2–liter bottle of Pepsi or Coke stayed effectively unchanged for the better part of a decade. Meanwhile both companies missed the really important, long-term trend toward "Gourmet", "Fashion", and "Health" Soft Drinks and allowed a major erosion of their share of the broader beverage market by not responding effectively to the stream of indirect competitors – New York Seltzer, SoHo, Clearly Canadian, Arizona Iced Tea, and Snapple just to name a few – who took advantage of their fixation with each other and the Cola product.

Coca-Cola, in 1993, showed its continued and extraordinary addiction to direct strategy in its domestic market-place by taking the "owner" of sports drinks, Gatorade, head on with Power-Ade without a significant product, or any other kind of advantage at all. Again the consumer benefited from the impact on price, but even if Coca-Cola succeeds and holds onto a reasonable share it will be at a very heavy cost to its stockholders. And this is the company that declared its sole mission to be "to increase shareholder value over time!" In 1994 Coca Cola at last began seriously to consider how to compete in the "new age" segments which it had allowed to grow unchallenged for a decade. Meanwhile, ironically, outside the US it was extraordinarily successful, by one of the great indirect strategies available to all American "icon" companies – don't sell your product, sell a piece of The American Dream.

Indirection then is the key to the area of strategy that is most an art – exploiting competitors' misperceptions of their strengths, where the market is going and what threat you pose, to find segments you can take, and ways of doing so that surprise your competition. It implies risk because, as Bruce Henderson said, it involves the displacement of powerful, entrenched competitors. Moreover, if they see the world the way you do soon enough, they usually have the resources to negate the indirection, and turn the competition into a direct form where they have the advantages both of scale and of the defense. So the strategy must be carefully crafted, and the plan to implement it prepared with great thoroughness. To enable us to do so there are a set of universal principles derived from the basic characteristics of competition, to be followed first in developing, and then in evaluating the quality of our plans.

THE PRINCIPLES OF COMPETITION

"War is nothing but a duel on an extensive scale", wrote Clausewitz. So let's start there, with that most basic form of conflict, to derive some principles for testing our strategic ideas.

A duelist, let us say a boxer, has to do four things – to think, to guard, to move, and to hit. Before fighting, each fighter must have a plan of how he is going to beat his adversary. What is his objective, i.e., how is he going to win? Knock his opponent out? Disable him? Win on points? Then, with the actual experience of putting it into practice, he must have the mental agility to alter his tactics, and maybe even his objective. For, as General Patton once said, "No plan ever survives contact with the enemy!" Next he must be able to guard against his opponent's offense. Third he must be able to move into a position where he can take the offensive, so that, finally, he can hit his opponent and knock him out. From these four basic elements of what goes on in a fight we can derive four corresponding principles – The principles of The Objective, of Security, of Mobility, and of The Offensive.

Staying with our boxer, as he develops the skills that come from experience, he will soon recognize three further keys to his success. He will seek to economize his strength so as not to exhaust himself prematurely; he will try to use his weight to apply superior strength, e.g., leaning on his opponent or hitting him harder than he himself is hit (which of course is why boxers fight in weight-determined classes); and he will attempt to surprise him, that is catch him off guard by doing something he is not expecting. So we arrive at three more principles – of Economy, of Mass and of Surprise.

Now, when we take this rather basic form of competition up a level of complexity, so that it now involves two groups of fighters, we find that, to achieve the aims of the first seven principles, we have to add two more. We need to ensure that all the members of our force understand the objective, and that all their actions are co-ordinated toward it. And, finally we will find that the more people involved, the more propensity there will be for confusion, misunderstanding and misinterpretation of orders. We will need to keep things as simple as possible. So we come to the last two principles – Unity of Command, and Simplicity.

These nine precepts are known as the Principles of War. Making them useful in the context of business strategy requires only a couple of small adjustments. First business is not, in general, about discrete "campaigns" and "battles" but a general situation of competition. So instead of talking about The Offensive, it makes more sense to say The Initiative. Second, the equivalent to Mobility for the individual fighter or an army, in business is Flexibility – the ability to move resources from one application to another. Third, Mass in war finds its business counterpart in Scale. And, finally, in this age of individual autonomy and mobility of employment, Leadership is a more appropriate concept than Command. With these small changes we now have the nine Principles of Competition to use as a guide and test as we develop business strategies.

Let's look at each of them in turn. In each case we will state the principle and then discuss it. In Appendix 3 there is a section which turns each of the nine principles into a list of questions that we can derive from them, to act as a guide to the manager seeking to add strategy to operations, and a tool to use them as a screen for the evaluation of strategic proposals.

The Objective

> Every business endeavor must be directed toward a clearly defined, decisive and attainable objective. The ultimate objective is the achievement of sufficient, sustainable competitive advantage to allow the enterprise to fulfill its purposes. The objective of each endeavor must contribute to this ultimate objective. Each intermediate objective must be such that its attainment will most directly, quickly and economically contribute to the purpose of each endeavor.
>
> The selection of an objective is based upon the means available, competition, and the market-place. Every manager must understand and clearly define his or her objective and consider each contemplated action in light thereof.

Just as grand strategy starts with clarity of purposes, so must every business endeavor begin with a clear understanding of the objectives it is trying to achieve. Coca-Cola aimed at winning The Pepsi Challenge mistakenly believing that would lead to its purpose of reversing its decline in market share. Later both Pepsi and Coke aimed to win the battle for Cola bragging rights, which was only part of a much wider war for market share between suppliers of non-alcoholic beverages. Business objectives tend to get set hurriedly, with little debate about their attainability and based on hidden assumptions about the nature of competition and the market-place. The result is strategies which simply don't fit with reality, and plans which mismatch ends and means. Like the argument that stems from a false premise, the strategy that is built to achieve a faulty objective is doomed from the very outset.

The Initiative

Taking the initiative is necessary to achieve positions of advantage and maintain freedom of action. It permits the manager to impose his or her will on competition; to set the pace and determine the course of development of opportunities; to exploit competitive weakness and rapidly changing situations; and to meet unexpected developments.

A posture of reacting to competitive moves may be forced on the manager but should be deliberately adopted only as a temporary expedient while awaiting an opportunity to return to the initiative; or for the purpose of avoiding the expenditure of resources in an area where a position of advantage is not sought. Even when reacting, the manager should seek every opportunity to seize the initiative and achieve positions of advantage.

In the military this principle is known as The Offensive. Its importance is that victory, unless the enemy simply adopts suicidal actions and thereby destroys itself, cannot be achieved without at some stage taking the offensive in some form. With its translation in business into the Initiative it becomes even more important in an era of unprecedented competitive intensity and accelerating change. Both these conditions make it certain that the worst strategy of all is to do nothing, since there can be no doubt that there will be someone using change as an opportunity to break the competitive equilibrium, if only by mistake! It is indeed in the definition of how the initiative is to be exercised that lies the very substance of winning strategy.

Scale

Superior resources must be concentrated at the critical time and place to achieve advantage. Superiority results from the proper combinations of the resource elements. Proper application of the

principle of scale, in conjunction with the other principles of
strategy may permit an organization with overall, inferior
resources to achieve decisive superiority at the point of competition.

The first two principles embody the direction and substance of
strategy. The next three deal with how concentration, or focus, is to
be achieved to bring superior resources to bear at the decisive points.
The first of the three corresponds to the principle of mass in war and
ensures we take account of the simple arithmetic of conflict that
dictates that, other things being equal, "God is on the side of the big
battalions". Those big battalions therefore like direct battles of
attrition which are certain to go their way if they can afford the
resources. The United States lost in Vietnam in large part because the
nation eventually refused to go on supplying the key resources –
young men. Minnetonka was temporarily able to "achieve decisive
superiority at the point of competition" – a tested, attractive liquid
soap and the manufacturing capacity to make it – but lost it the
moment P&G followed. The British motorcycle makers misunderstood that manufacturing scale was the decisive weapon, not famous
superbike brand names. These are simple examples. It is usually much
more complex, requiring combinations of resource elements, as it did
with Pepsi's attack on Coca-Cola through supermarkets, with cans,
aggressive pricing and an advertising campaign focused on the young.

Economy

Skillful and prudent use of resources will enable the manager to
accomplish his or her mission with minimum expenditure thereof.
This principle is the corollary of the principle of scale. It does not
imply withholding resources but rather their measured allocation
to the primary task, as well as secondary tasks that can lead
competition to over-allocate their resources elsewhere, and thus
ensure sufficient superiority at the point of competition.

The purpose of this principle is to ensure that superior resources are
available where they are needed. Deceit, trickery and craftiness are
the skills needed to get competitors to allocate resources to areas that
are not decisive to your strategy. While Napoleon's maxim – it is
impossible to be too strong at the decisive point – may have been a
sophisticated application of prudence by that most daring of

generals, it should not be taken alone. Napoleon was at his best in economically posing the threats which led his adversaries to tie up forces away from where he would then strike. In a world of scarce and expensive resources, we need to bring exquisite judgment to the balancing of resource allocation between primary and secondary tasks. Remember the Duke of Wellington and Lord Combermere.

Flexibility

Flexibility is an essential ingredient in the allocation of resources. It contributes materially in exploiting successes and in preserving freedom of action and reducing vulnerability. The object is to be able to bring to bear resources in such a manner as to place competition at a relative disadvantage and thus achieve results which otherwise would be more costly to attain.

Maintaining flexibility involves organization, the attitude of leadership and adaptability of control as well as the technical ability to redeploy assets. It is the antithesis of permanent allocation of resources and implies avoidance of stereotyped patterns of operation.

The third "focus" principle is aimed at ensuring the ability to exploit change and reducing the vulnerability to it, in particular unexpected change. Capacity tied up in inflexible technology, made obsolete either by process innovation (steel: the mini mills), or product substitution (paper: plastic grocery bags), will perhaps provide the most evident examples, as the drivers of the fourth wave give way to a whole new set of industries.

Flexibility is as much a psychological as well as a physical characteristic. It is the inability of senior managers to face the need to change the way they manage that poses the biggest threat of all to the giants of the dying wave. Remember that Rosabeth Moss Kanter said that flexibility will be *the* distinguishing characteristic of the companies that are successful in the emerging, new economy.

Unity of Leadership

The decisive application of available resources requires unity of leadership. Unity of leadership obtains unity of effort by the coordinated action of all parties toward a common goal. While coordination may be attained by cooperation, it is best achieved by vesting a single manager with the requisite authority.

The final four principles deal with questions relating to the implementation of the proposed strategy. As we saw with the "disaster" that began Chapter 5, the consequences of disunity among an organization's leadership can be devastating. As the complexity of business increasingly demands collaboration between parties with allegiance to different organizational entities, clarity of responsibility, accountability and authority become more not less important. The increasing use of teams does not change the reality that to compete in a dynamic world often requires the decisiveness and speed of action that only the vesting of authority in a single individual can provide. What has changed, as we will explore in the next chapter, is the way that authority is legitimized in the modern society of organizations.

Security

Security is essential to the preservation of resources. Security is achieved by measures taken to prevent surprise, preserve freedom of action and deny competition information of proposed plans. Since risk is inherent in business, application of the principle of security does not imply undue caution and the avoidance of calculated risk. Security frequently is enhanced by bold seizure and retention of the initiative, which denies competition the opportunity to interfere.

Clausewitz once commented when dealing with the subject of prudence that "no one in his right mind tries to cross a broad ditch in two steps". So, security is not a simple, monolithic idea demanding caution, the keeping of resources conservatively concentrated and the uniform maintenance of a defensive posture. These may enhance tactical security, but only at the potential expense of its strategic counterpart.

Security can even be enhanced by giving competitors information about proposed plans – remember IBM's and GE's advance notice of, respectively, the introduction of new computers and additions to manufacturing capacity. In each case the publicity increased the security of their plans by freezing out competitive action that might hurt them.

Surprise

Surprise can decisively shift the balance of competitive advantage. By surprise, success out of proportion to the effort expended may be obtained. Surprise results from taking a competitive initiative at a time, place, and in a manner for which competition is not prepared. It is not essential that competition be taken unaware but only that it becomes aware too late to react effectively. Factors contributing to surprise include speed, deception, application of unexpected resources, effective information gathering and variations in methods of operation.

Surprise is itself a form of indirection, and is pretty much mandatory if the full effect of an indirect strategy is to be achieved. It works best when it exploits areas of competitive inflexibility, both psychological and physical. Small, cheap cars did both admirably because of the US industry's conviction that they were inherently unprofitable, and the inability of its manufacturing capacity to be adapted readily. Minnetonka's huge, initial success came because it caught its huge competitors completely unawares.

For surprise to be important it must be in an element that is significant to the outcome of competition. American industry is paranoid about confidentiality, to keep its plans secrets, in order to achieve surprise. Yet most of the time what it keeps secret is not strategically very important, and merely handicaps itself, because it is also kept from its own people and *is* operationally vital information. So, as with all the other principles, judgment is needed in the way the principle is applied.

Simplicity

Simplicity contributes to successful operations. Direct, simple plans and clear, concise directives minimize misunderstanding and confusion. If other factors are equal, the simplest plan is preferred.

It is almost impossible to overemphasize the importance of that last sentence, "if other factors are equal, the simplest plan is preferred". Murphy's Law applies with great force in anything to do with competition between organizations because of the uncertainty of who is doing, or will do what, and the number of variables. Wellington once said, "Napoleon's battle plans are like the harness of a racehorse, the perfect article to do the job. But, break one strand, and it won't work. Mine, on the other hand, are like an old fisherman's net – clumsy, patched holes all over the place, but you can cut strand after strand and it will still catch fish".

Simple, robust plans building in redundancy wherever possible are to be preferred. But of course, this can conflict with at least the principles of scale, economy and security. So once again there are trade-offs, and the art of strategy is contained in the way every element is used to provide the best overall combination.

The above is a brief exploration of the nine principles of competition. In Appendix 3 there is a set of thirty-eight questions derived from them, which enables strategy to be added to every aspect of operations, and a tool to use them as a formal screen for strategic proposals. Here we will conclude with a brief reminder of the essence of each of them (see Table 6.4).

Table 6.4   The principles of competition

Direction	
The Objective:	*Clear, achievable goals*
The Initiative:	*Quicker and more effective exploitation of emerging trends*
Focus	
Scale:	*Superior scale in critical resource areas*
Economy:	*Only the necessary resources needed*
Flexibility:	*Ability to move resources around*
Implementation	
Unity of Leadership:	*Shared commitment of key people*
Security:	*Protection from competitive countermeasures*
Surprise:	*Amount of unexpected originality involved*
Simplicity:	*Simplicity of the plan*

In this chapter we have so far examined the arts of strategy as they need to be brought to bear in grand strategy's pursuit of the creation and maintenance of competitive advantage in the way every decision is made. We have seen how The Dimensions of Value enable advantage to be gained from the choice of what industries and what parts of them to participate in, what positions to be sought in those industries and what patterns of resource utilization to be adopted. We have learned a philosophy of competition – the strategy of the indirect approach – to provide a foundation for thinking through how we go about trying to achieve the profile of industry participation, competitive position and resource utilization that using the Dimensions of Value shows will result in the best profitability. Finally we have explored The Principles of Competition that guide the development and evaluation of specific strategic proposals.

Mastering these three concepts and the tools they give rise to is what we mean by learning to think strategically, and then bringing that strategic thinking to bear on the decision-making that determines how strategic intent is turned into operational action.

We said at the beginning of the chapter that there was another skill that management teams have found they needed to learn – strategic planning. So we will turn briefly to that now to complete this chapter's exploration of how to cope with the challenge of competition.

STRATEGIC PLANNING

During the Seventies, strategic planning was tried and found wanting. Or was it? Corporate leadership's response to the tremendous increase in competitive intensity in the Seventies was, appropriately, to elevate strategy to its number one priority. It is interesting that, despite the widespread perception that strategic planning failed to deliver in the Seventies, in the mid-Eighties research showed that strategy was still American CEOs' number one priority. And it still is today. It wasn't the concepts of strategy that failed, but the way we tackled the planning. Let's see what happened.

Over the years, as business has become increasingly complex, we have responded by establishing specialized resources focused on each new challenge. The result has been the burgeoning of staff departments at each organizational level, with one of the most recent, significant additions being strategic planning. That in itself was not a problem. The difficulty arose from the failure to understand and define the responsibility of the new department properly. For planning is a *skill*, not a *function*. It is a skill that the Chief Executive Officer, Chief Operating Officer, and every other operating manager need to do their jobs. It is not a set of specialized activities to be carried out by a new staff department (which is what most of us created). This failure in role definition made the planner inherently threatening to line managers. To most people, the implication was that the new departments were designed to make up for a lack of skill on the executive's, or line managers' part.

And we made it worse for ourselves. We staffed all those planning departments by placing greater emphasis on their intellectual caliber than their institutional credibility. Then, because of their inherent role problem, the planners tried to establish a power base by creating a process – things people had to do – that might give them legitimacy. This was followed by more elaborate processes, demands for mountains of data and, of course, the ultimate test of legitimacy, tangible output – plans.

But those plans all too often ended up gathering dust on remote shelves. What went wrong?

Fig. 6.2 shows an adaptation of Noel Tichy's model of the nine elements that need to be addressed to bring about strategic change.

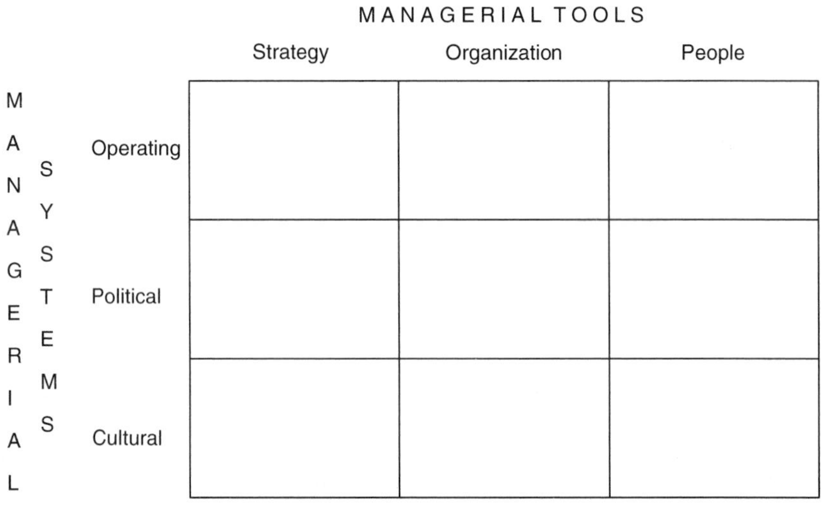

MANAGERIAL TOOLS

	Strategy	Organization	People
MANAGERIAL SYSTEMS — Operating			
Political			
Cultural			

Fig. 6.2 *Strategic change matrix*

Source: Adapted from Tichy (1983).

Practically all the planners operated, and continue to operate, only in the top left hand corner box – developing concepts of Strategy to direct the Operating System of the company. Every time they venture over one of the boundaries to try to tackle issues associated with organization, people, or the realities of power and behavior within their organizations, they very quickly find those are "beyond their scope". Meaning that, most of the time, in most strategic plans, within most organizations, eight of the nine boxes on the chart are left unaddressed. No wonder plans fail!

Many a planning career, and many a consultant's reputation, has foundered on the entirely well meant, but equally badly misunderstood attempt to correct the problem. And yet, the solution is so simple: *The doers must be the planners.*

If the planners cannot effectively address what is needed to create a winning strategy, then the people who do control those things (which are in the other eight boxes) must develop the plans. That it is difficult, time consuming, foreign to their training and all those other familiar excuses is irrelevant. It is, quite simply, necessary – that is, if you want a practical plan that will actually be implemented.

That does not make the planners redundant. Their new role, and that of their consulting counterparts, is to manage the process and be able to give expert input on competitive dynamics. They must be facilitators, strategic thinkers, and "expert" members of the team, preferably with a strong aversion to pages of words and tables of numbers! They and their line-manager clients must be prepared for hard work, much frustration, a heavy time commitment, and the most intellectually and psychologically demanding experience of their lives. Not surprisingly, not many have completed the course.

In the Seventies, many very good plans may well have been written, but most of us didn't really try strategic planning at all. In the Eighties, a small number of managers began facing up to the severe problems inherent in putting planning back where it belongs – in the line. But, in doing so, they surprised even themselves with the dramatic, positive impact it had on the way they ran their organizations. In the Nineties, we should all be ready to take advantage of what has been proved to work.

As I said earlier the first thing that has been proved to work is *team* planning to ensure that the whole complex, interactive system that is the modern corporation is properly addressed in any strategy that is developed. A piece of that team planning, the front end, is team learning – the process whereby the team charged with strategy development, working together, reaches a common understanding of the facts of the situation with which it is faced.

This is not to say that many of the tasks of information gathering and analysis cannot be delegated beyond the team responsible for strategy development, or that every member must have the same depth of understanding of every piece of information. Clausewitz wrote, "It is not necessary for a general to understand how a gun works, but only what effect it has". What matters about information to the strategist is what it says about competition. It is vital that the whole team share the same understanding of the strategic import of information or, if it can't agree on that, on its possible imports and their colleagues' views of them, *before* it tries to develop its strategy. At the root of the vast majority of disagreements I have seen in management teams have been unexposed disagreements about the basic facts of the situation and/or their potential implications for strategy. When it comes to strategies for the longer term it is virtually never the *how* that divides them, but always the *what* – different views as to which scenario is most likely to occur. Once a common position on the "what" is achieved, it is rare to find great difficulty in agreeing on the "how".

However, to create that common position the leader has to lead. It is the lonely burden of the leader to have to stake his or her future, and that of the organization, on judgments about how the world is going to evolve, and about the best strategy to cope with the possible scenarios that have been painted. Consensus is achieved, not by an attempt at a compromise between positions, but by everyone on the team first having had the chance to be heard and, more importantly at this stage, having the opportunity to "get on board" in the privacy of the team process. This, not democratic decision-making, is the true use to which the Japanese have put consensus as a management tool. They have also then had the discipline to implement the other, and absolutely mandatory feature – never break ranks after the decision is made.

7 Performance: The Techniques of Integration

"Everything in war is simple, but even the simplest thing is difficult to accomplish." (Clausewitz)

"In order to be saved you must know what you believe, know why you believe it and know how to act upon it." (St. Thomas Aquinas)

PARADIGM

"A constellation of concepts, values, perceptions and practices shared by a community which forms a particular vision of reality that is the basis of the way a community organizes itself."
(Thomas Kuhn, *The Structure of Scientific Revolutions*)

Having set a mission, and developed a strategy to achieve its goals, we come to the third challenge of grand strategy: Performance – how do we deliver the results? Or, putting it in the language of grand strategy, how do we ensure higher quality implementation than competitive organizations? In the early Eighties the "Excellence" movement sprang up as a response to this challenge following the widespread perception that strategy, at least in the way it had been practiced in the Seventies, had failed to deliver on its promises of better financial results.

As we learned more about the challenges of seeking a superior method of strategy implementation, we found that "Excellence", as it was being practiced, was only part of the answer in an age where only total competition – the business equivalent of total war – would suffice to ensure survival, let alone success. The real need was to integrate every aspect of the organization's activities into the effort to create the distinctive capabilities which is how vision is turned into reality. Change in the market-place, change in technology, change in the characteristics of the driving industries and change in the nature of the workforce meant that the management paradigm that had worked so well in the growth phase of the fourth wave too had to be changed. The interest in corporate culture, rising in the mid-Eighties, gave evidence of this need for a more fundamental change than simply trying to add new techniques to the old paradigm. By the

167

Nineties it was evident that nothing short of a radical transformation in the way businesses were run would meet the need. Let us trace the demise of the old management paradigm, and the emergence of the new one which will form the basis for the integration of organizations that successfully meet the challenge of performance in the new economy.

As we have seen, the business world we left behind as the recessionary phase of the fourth wave began in the Seventies was characterized externally by a stable environment, predictable change and what we've now come to recognize was only moderate competition. Internally it enjoyed a workforce with an enormous pent-up desire for material goods put off for a decade-and-a-half by depression and war. This was as close to the "rational economic man" of the behavioural textbooks as we are ever likely to see.

Our underlying model for managing him (!) was the army, a world of specialized roles, clear hierarchies and following orders. Much of what we knew about organizational behaviour at that time had its foundation in work done in the US Army during the Second World War, and a large proportion of both the management cadre and workforce all around the world had come from a military training. Management theory viewed the management task as one of planning and control – planning how to allocate resources, and then controlling how they were actually used – in an exact match with the two concerns of operational management (risk, and efficiency), whose roots we explored in Chapter 3. As a result there developed a management paradigm, now widely referred to as "Command and Control", which very naturally married the way of managing that a generation had learned in the military, with the executive concerns created by the economic environment of the decade after the end of the Second World War.

There were four roles within this old management paradigm, corresponding to each level of the hierarchy, and modeled very much on the way the military operates:

1.	Top management determined what needed doing	The generals
2.	Middle management figured out how to do it	Officer corps
3.	Lower management made sure it happened	Non-commissioned officers
4.	Everybody else did as they were told	Rank and file

These roles were based on three underlying managerial assumptions: (1) the management prerogative, i.e. everyone accepted the right of management to tell them what to do; (2) an ample supply of adequate management, i.e., there was enough talent available to fill the broad and deep hierarchies needed to figure out how to get things done, and make sure they then got done; and, (3) that top management knew what needed doing, so we could rely on their commands to be appropriate to the needs of the situation. For a long time these assumptions held very well as the environment was relatively stable, the workforce had been trained for this hierarchy by its military experience and, in the US, the GI Bill was providing a tremendous new supply of university-educated, potential managers.

As we have seen, as the situation grew more complex, new managerial tools evolved to deal with new challenges but, until recently, it was always possible to add these tools onto the foundation of assumptions that underpinned the "Command and Control" management paradigm of the fourth wave. Gradually, though, it became apparent that it would no longer work to pile new tool after new tool onto the old base. The foundation itself had become the problem. The assumptions on which the old paradigm rested no longer held.

THE DEATH OF THE MANAGEMENT PREROGATIVE

Like it or not, in most organizations, at least in the West, people don't obey orders any more. The most fundamental of all the assumptions on which "Command and Control" rests no longer holds. The unions first challenged management's absolute rights in a formal way. Then, far more devastatingly, once the basic economic needs of the workforce had been met, the individualism and healthy disrespect for authority that underpins the whole history of the American republic reasserted itself. The Vietnam experience reinforced the trend. People simply stopped taking for granted that what they were told to do was the best thing to do, either for themselves or their organizations. Because of the nature of the new world of unprecedented competitive intensity and accelerating change this would eventually prove to be a source of great strength, but in the short-term it dealt a death blow to existing methods of management.

Next, unquestioning loyalty to organizations began to ebb away, as career mobility became the rule and not the exception. When I told my father in 1966, half jokingly, that one of the reasons I was joining Ford Motor Company was because it was a good company to leave, he practically threw me out of the house! The idea of joining a company because it would be a good preparation for a wider, more self-driven career did not even occur to most of my parents' generation. A generation later many, if not most young people felt they were training for a career in a profession, not a company. This trend was accelerated by the breaking of the previous, unwritten contract of a long-term job in return for loyal service, by company after company as intensifying competition forced them to take drastic actions to trim their costs.

Finally, as Larry Wilson, founder of The Pecos River Learning Center put it, today everybody has a "share of the gun". Willy Sutton, a bank robber of the Thirties, had been made famous in American folk lore for his answer to the question: "Why do you rob banks?" – "Because that's where the money is!" he replied. He had done his information analysis very well. But it was his answer to the next question, "Why do you carry a gun?" that, showing he was also a good strategist, is what is relevant here. "Because," he said, "it is easier to get what you want with a gun and a smile, than with just a smile by itself."

Today everyone has a share of that gun. Everyone in your organization has the power to stop you making happen what you want to make happen. We all have enormous negative power, and the way we run our organizations needs to reflect that. Put this together with the reduction in organizational loyalty, and the unwillingness to follow orders and we can see that the management prerogative is well and truly dead.

THE OVERSTRETCHING OF THE MANAGEMENT CADRE

The second assumption was that there is an ample supply of management talent. Today this too is gone. For some time now the changing shape of the economy has meant that "knowledge" jobs have been growing faster than the talent pool available to fill them. Whereas we may have an excess of people for low skill jobs, there is already a shortage of people truly capable of filling the management cadres of companies organized and managed in the traditional, hierarchical way. Secondly, rapidly increasing complexity and our response to it, specialization, is leaving us with fewer and fewer people who can take a broad view of the needs of our organizations, and thus relate their piece of the action to the whole puzzle. Finally the education crisis is threatening the supply of even what talent we're getting today. The result again is the end of an underlying assumption of the old management paradigm. We need a new way of managing our organizations that does not depend on a huge number of middle and lower managers to interpret, implement and report back the effects of top management's orders. Fortunately we have the foundation for it in information technology, and the reawakening of belief in shared values as a way of ensuring the behaviours we desire. But again, this means a very different way of running a business to "Command and Control".

THE END OF TOP MANAGEMENT INFALLIBILITY

The third assumption was that top management knows what needs doing. And, again, three forces make that simply no longer the case. First, the size and diversification of the modern corporation make it literally impossible for its leadership to know enough to be able to exercise the detailed command of the old paradigm. Secondly, decentralization and divisionalization, our perfectly appropriate responses to size and diversification, have added enormously to the distance of corporate leadership from the point of action. And finally what Peter Drucker called The Age of Discontinuity, i.e. change itself in unpredictable and discontinuous forms, rapidly makes obsolete the knowledge of even the most well informed of corporate leaders. Top management infallibility, as an assumption on which to build a way of managing, if it ever was a good idea certainly isn't one any longer. We need a new way of running the corporation.

The change problem has been summarized with great elegance by Rosabeth Moss Kanter in the inequality: MTBD > MTBS. The Mean Time Between Decisions is greater than the Mean Time Between Surprises! In other words it takes so long to get a decision made, approved by all those layers and centres of negative (disapproving) power, that by the time it's made, approved and that approval has been communicated to the person with the original idea, the assumptions on which the idea were based have changed! Most decisions are obsolete before they can be implemented.

It is very easy to stop this. Simply decentralize all decision-making authority to radically lower levels of the organization. (I used the term "lower" levels instinctively because that is the conventional language. But it doesn't sit well with the new world. We should really be saying, "radically nearer the point of action".) The challenge is how to decentralize radically, without losing control – which is where the shared values comes in, as we have seen.

THE NEW MANAGEMENT PARADIGM

The new management reality then is the opposite of the old one:

- *Leadership* is earned, membership is voluntary
- *Leadership* is in short supply
- The *leadership* doesn't know what needs doing, and can't find out in time.

First, we can't "manage" the complex, modern organization in any traditional sense of the word from the era of "Command and Control". "Manage" comes from an Italian word that means, literally, to train or handle horses. Today's workforce simply won't be treated that way. We will have to learn how to lead it. Moreover that leadership will have to recognize that at least its most talented members have options, and don't regard organizational loyalty in the same light as earlier generations. In effect they are volunteers – and anyone who has ever played a role in a voluntary effort or organization knows what that means! Second we need to spread the leadership task throughout the organization. It is not leaders that are in short supply, it is our ability to tap into them. I remember overhearing two managers debating whether they should let a maintenance lady have a key to the supplies area, and organize her own work schedule. What they didn't know was that, in her non-paid work hours (I nearly said "spare time!"), she led a very successful volunteer agency with an annual budget of over $10 million! How many more leaders are going to waste?

What we do have to manage is change, since the alternative is to let it manage us which means abandoning our fate to the forces of evolution. As I have said earlier, the whole purpose of strategy is to beat evolution, and thereby take control of our own destinies. The new management paradigm will take many varied forms in the hugely diverse, intensely competitive market-place that we now face. But all its forms will share one central feature, the name that is being given to this new paradigm – managing change.

Just as the new management reality is dramatically different from the old one, so are the characteristics of the new workforce. There is now much more to motivation than just money. People want to feel they are appreciated, that they have some control over their own lives and that they are contributing to something worthwhile. Pay is for know-how not effort, the age of the "hired-hands" is long gone. And talent, at least for the new, knowledge jobs, is scarce not ample. Putting the new reality together with these new characteristics of work and the workforce, we find that the new management paradigm is very different from the old one:

Table 7.1   The old and new management paradigms

"Command and Control"	"Managing Change"
• Top management determines what needs doing	• Everybody does what they think is right, guided by the organization's mission
↓	↑
• Middle and lower management figure out how to do it, and make sure it gets done	• Their managers are there to help them in figuring that out, and remove any obstacles in their way
↓	↑
• Everybody else does as they're told	• The organization's leaders ensure alignment of everyone's efforts through focus on shared purposes, shared values and the distinctive capabilities that turn vision into reality

This entails a fundamental shift in thinking about how to deal with people at all levels of the old hierarchy – from command to align, from control to enable, and from manage to lead. Pascale's claim, that less than two percent of American managers have the skills to cope, is beginning to make more and more sense. Their skills are not up to the task not because of some inherent deficiency in American managers, but because the new paradigm involves new tasks and new roles that they have not been educated or trained to undertake, or in many cases even take seriously.

NEW TASKS, NEW ROLES

As we learn more about "Managing Change" we find that it contains three major task areas, and our current cadre of managers is well prepared to undertake only one of them – and that the one that should least involve management! These tasks are Vision and Strategy, Change and Improvement, and everyday, On-going Activities.

Vision and Strategy

As I mentioned earlier the first part of this task was once described to me by a senior British manager as "semi-religious claptrap". The second, I was once told by an even more senior, American executive, is "not real work". Both are often regarded, if taken seriously, as once-in-a-generation activities; and, if not, as luxuries to be addressed ritually at an expensive, resort location and then ignored in the way the organization is actually run. Today leaders are recognizing that they involve hard, serious and never-ending work if their organizations are to keep up with, let alone get an edge on their competition.

Change and Improvement

Much concern has been expressed about the shrinking role of middle management in the modern organization. Trapped between inspiring leaders with modern communications capabilities at their fingertips, and a workforce eager to exercise initiative and manage its own work, the theory is that middle management will wither away and organizations will take on an hour-glass shape. If, after some kind of cataclysmic disruption we were to return to a world of no, or slow, change this might be true. However that is not what we face, or are going to face for the foreseeable future. The new, and vital role of middle management is to deal with a new necessity – the need to be continuously adapting and improving the distinctive capabilities that turn vision into reality, and enable the organization to keep a step ahead of its competition in a dynamic environment.

On-going Activities

The third set of tasks comprises the designing, developing, making, selling, hiring, training, planning, counting, reporting, monitoring activities and everything else that enables the organization to achieve its purposes, and fulfill the functions for which it exists on an everyday basis. Until recently, because we didn't regard Vision and Strategy as serious work, and we didn't see the need for a lot of change, nearly everyone was trying to carry out these everyday tasks. It is no wonder that middle management became frustrated, and everyone else felt that only a tiny proportion of what they could contribute was being utilized. There was a terrible overcrowding in, and over-supervision of the on-going activities of organizations, misusing senior and middle management time, leaving everyone else with no room for initiative, and overburdening the whole system with the demand for reports on what was going on to the detriment of getting on with it.

If we go back to the three bullets I used to describe the "Managing Change" paradigm we find they in fact define three different roles – leadership, management and membership – which when we match them up with the three task areas we have just discussed make clear what people *should* be doing within an organization under the new management paradigm (see Fig. 7.1).

As we might expect, Vision and Strategy are the province of Leadership. The primary Management Role, as described above, is to

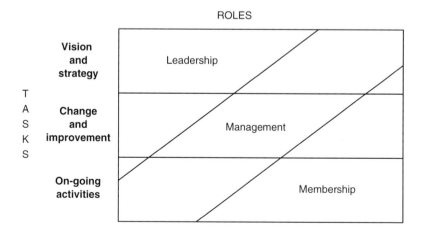

Fig. 7.1 *Tasks and roles*

ensure that the Change and Improvement, needed to implement Vision and Strategy in a turbulent world, take place without direction from above. It is only secondarily to supervise On-going Activities. (Note the difference from the old role under "Command and Control", which was to ensure top management's orders were being carried out, and that there was *no* change to the pattern that had brought success.) And all the people in the organization, its Membership, run the everyday activities of the company. I have used the term "roles", not positions or jobs, deliberately. Of course there is still a hierarchical correlation between the roles and levels in an organization. But in a very real sense under "Managing Change" *everyone* has a bit of each task as the diagram shows, and each role has to be played if they are to fulfil their responsibilities. But the diagram is just as important for what it shows we don't want the three primary groups of role players to be involved in, as well as what we do. Top management simply must get out of the way of the people trying to run the company. Middle management must get right how it relates "upwards" – participating in the setting of Vision and Strategy, as the experts on what it is possible to achieve; and "downwards" – coaching, helping figure out the right things to do, and removing the obstacles in the way of its people as they try to get them done. The rest of the organization does not need to spend a lot of time worrying about Vision and Strategy. It does need to make creative input to the tasks of Change and Improvement, since it will have the job of carrying out the resulting plans. And it does need to be taking the tactical initiatives necessary to run the company on an everyday basis in pursuit of its shared purposes, within the guidelines of its shared values.

The newest and least well understood (though perhaps most talked about) role in the new management paradigm is leadership. And remember, although for a whole corporation this is primarily the province of top management, there is a piece of this role for everyone. Not just because we want everyone to share in the task of leading the whole organization, but because there is a leadership element, however informal, in every job in every organization.

THE LEADERSHIP ROLE

The job of the CEO is not so much to run the company as to manage the way the company is run. But don't misunderstand, this does not imply detachment from the everyday operations of the organization. It implies focus on how he or she adds value to those operations. The job has three primary components – setting a Shared Vision, making Strategic Choices, and ensuring Communication throughout the organization.

Shared Vision

Task number one is to set clearly the Vision that will drive everything else. In Chapter 5 we described how a vision is a word picture of an organization successfully fulfiling its mission. Let us remind ourselves of the components of that mission.

1. *Shared Purposes*, which provide *focus* by driving strategy. Without them decentralization is positively dangerous. It leads to everyone going off in different directions. An organization's Shared Purposes are usually found in an organization's statement of Mission and/or Vision, in the way it describes its relationships with its key stakeholders (Customers, Employees, Shareholders, Suppliers and Communities), and in its Participation Strategy.

2 *Shared Values,* which provide *control* by guiding behavior. In a chaotic world it is impossible either to foresee the dilemmas the individual decision-maker will face, or to come to the top for rulings on every one of the exponentially increasing number of exceptions. Consistency with the organization's intent is ensured by a shared set of underlying guiding principles, or values. These enable people, in the presence of uncertainty, to make vision supporting decisions when they can't get input from a "higher" decision-maker.

There is a third component that needs to be added to bring the vision down from an albeit inspiring set of words, to a practical set of quantified outcomes that are specific enough to enable the rigorous development of strategy to achieve them.

3. *Shared Results* which, by identifying the gap between where we are and where we desire to be, provides the tangible challenge the organization needs to galvanize itself into action. Peter Senge describes this gap as the producer of a tension, as if there were an elastic band stretched between where we are and where we want to be, pulling us toward our goal. Most Quality

programs don't work because they fail to quantify the desired results; they are *activity* (let's hold a meeting to see what we can do to improve quality), not *results* (we need to get from here to there, Quality Management is our process to do it) driven. The tension between the vision of success and the status quo is absent.

Shared Results add the quantification to Shared Purposes needed to bring rigor to planning. Shared Values need Shared Results to bring the same to implementation, to inspire effort and measure progress toward the goals that quantify the vision.

Strategic Choices

The second task of leaders is to make the strategic choices that determine where resources will, and will not, be allocated. People in organizations expect their leaders to make the difficult choices, and they have a right to – the leaders get paid a whole lot more to do so! There are four big ones:

1. *In which parts of the market shall we participate?* These are the fundamental focus and segmentation decisions, from which all else in strategy stems.
2. *On what bases will we compete?* Quality, Price, Features, Time, Service, Partnership. . . What distinctive combination of capabilities are we going to be the best at, to serve our targeted part of the market-place?

The reasons for these first two choices and the assumptions on which they are based must be made explicit so that they can be monitored over time. Most rigidities of management belief come about because the assumptions on which they rest have become unquestioned, hidden dogma. In a world of accelerating change even these two most basic of choices must constantly be held up to question by its leaders if an organization is to keep pace with its competitive environment. The third question begins the process of operationalizing the answers to the first two.

3. *Where is the money to be spent?* It is not until we begin to specify the way resources are to be allocated that we move beyond mere intent to real, implementable strategy. If we don't line up expenditures – of expense as well as of capital – squarely

behind our stated strategies they simply aren't going to be implemented.

Finally, most neglected and, because of the pace and pervasiveness of change (remember less than 2 percent of American managers have the skills to meet the new challenge), maybe the single most important:

4. *Who will do what on the team?* The matching of people with roles, including determining who simply doesn't have the skills to play the new game.

The fourth choice would not make a lot of lists even today. Yet it is absolutely the determinant of success much of the time. Real strategy is not in plans, but in what people do. And people do what they know how to do, particularly senior people who got to where they are because what they knew how to do worked for them! We are not all interchangeable and in a world of increasing specialization less so than ever. The punch-your-ticket, tour of duty, short duration assignment way of moving people around is gone forever.

The success or failure of strategy depends, rather obviously, on the ability of management to develop and implement it. Yet, the development of people with the right skills to do that is frequently excluded from the practice of strategic management.

Strategy allocates resources in the pursuit of competitive advantage. To manage strategically is to bring a strategic orientation to all decision-making, at all organizational levels, and across all functional lines. It is consequently ludicrous, but all too often true, that the ability of an organization's key resource, its management, to manage in the required way should be taken for granted when strategy is being formulated. This fundamental oversight is especially dangerous when a new strategic course is being charted. Changes in objectives, in the environment and in the activities of competition *require* changes in resources to re-establish the balance between means and ends.

Management development ensures that the key players have the right skills to achieve corporate and business unit objectives within the foreseeable environment, allowing for competitive action. It ensures the existence of the management capabilities required by a strategy and its implementation. It must, therefore, be part of strategic planning. Otherwise, management development loses its requisite lead time, and strategy loses the managerial resources necessary to achieve its objectives.

Far too many corporate executives believe an edict laying out newly desired behavior is sufficient to harness old management to a new course. That is akin, in American football, to leaving the defensive team on the field after getting the ball back, and sending out an exhortation to play offense. Managers are not infinitely flexible in their skills and attitudes. They need, at least, to reorient themselves and acquire new skills so as to be able to implement new strategy. Some may not be able to do this at all.

If major strategic or cultural change is desired, it is mandatory either for people to change, or to change the people. Educate and train them, or replace them. There is simply no other alternative.

As the leaders of an organization, what managers communicate simply by being who they are is as important as the other capabilities they possess. The current managers personify the old culture and strategy to everyone in the organization. Many hold their positions as the result of having successfully promoted old values. A majority of an organization's people are not going to be convinced of its adoption of a new strategy and supporting culture if the old regime remains unchanged. It doesn't matter how many courses management attends, nor how many changes they profess will take place, people will wait for action to make up their minds.

Only when the great majority of the members of an organization are convinced that old ways are no longer rewarded and that new ways are required for personal success, will the new strategy be truly adopted. This is crucial, as it is the behavior of lower and middle organizational levels of a company that ultimately executes strategy and defines culture. New role models, new heroes and new myths are needed. It is not enough to put a fresh coat of paint on an old management team. A genuinely new article is required.

In fact, it is often better literally to pay a senior manager to stay at home than to put him or her into a position that requires a style or skill radically different from what he or she personifies. Otherwise, at best, there will be a long delay, first while he or she acquires and practices new skills, and second while his or her people satisfy themselves that there has been a real change. At worst, they will never believe the change is real, and the new strategy and culture will not be implemented at all.

New strategies and any other significant changes in the course of an organization will fail if insufficient attention is paid to people and cultural issues. Until discerning, rigorous attention is paid to the way human resources are allocated, as an integral part of strategy formulation and implementation, many strategic ventures will continue to be doomed to failure before they are even begun.

COMMUNICATION

The third part of the Leadership Role is to communicate, and ensure that proper communication is going on throughout the organization.

Communication is a hot topic. Effective relationships with our people require it. Many of our current organizational woes are attributed to its absence. And a great deal of management time is spent on it. Nothing is wrong with any of that. The problem is that most of the time what we actually do is just inform, not communicate.

Inform, v., to tell of, about
Communicate, v., to impart, to share with

As the above definitions suggest, there is quite a difference between the two. The act of informing is complete simply with the telling, i.e., sending the message. Communicating, on the other hand, is defined as imparting, i.e., the message must also be received. The second definition of communicate goes even further, implying a common view of the message's import, and, at its strongest, a common intent to act upon it. How do we bridge the gap between informing and communicating?

We must start with the reason why we communicate. The ultimate purpose of communication within an organization is to bring about behavioral change. Whether we want an instruction followed, a plan implemented, an idea given appropriate consideration, or even an activity avoided, we are looking for a different behavior pattern to result. The desire for the new behavior is implied by the act of communicating. So communication, if it has any useful meaning for an organization, has not occurred unless the desired action results, or the undesired action is avoided. The test is not the quality or frequency of the message, or the number of people told, but whether the desired behavior occurs.

Not long ago, information was enough. The design of most organizations stemmed, as we have seen, from the World War II army model with its central assumption that people would do as they were told. That model worked fairly well while most people's agenda was economic, that is providing for their financial security and improving their standard of living by purchasing material goods. Today it simply will not suffice. We can no longer give a simple instruction and expect it to be acted upon. New forces are at play – for example, the end of the compulsory military service, an affluent society, new values in the workforce, two-income families, and the acceptance of career mobility. People now want to know the reasons and reserve the right to make up their own minds about how they will act. Clearly, we must go much farther to move from information to communication. Specifically, we must do three things:

Education

The first step is to recognize that we must achieve understanding, and that requires education. We must reach agreement on the underlying facts of the situation and then, and only then, carefully trace the path from that to the conclusion we want to convey. We will have to be prepared to take great pains and be very patient, for neither the situation nor our logic will be as clear to our people as it is to us. Ideally, we would like our people to reach the desired conclusion by themselves. At least we must make sure everyone understands why we reached it.

Authentication

We must also authenticate our message. It is unfortunately the case that, in many if not most organizations, people have learned to be wary about the pronouncements they hear from their leaders. Consider the following, all too typical, examples of why that is so:

- "Quality is our number one priority! Then how come the biggest bonus always seems to go to the plant manager who everyone knows ships rejects at the end of the period to meet his volume targets?"
- "Our most important asset is our people! Then why is it that the first option we always consider to make up for a profit shortfall is laying off employees?"

The gap between words and actions has grown so wide in so many organizations that only sustained, consistent implementation will serve to authenticate the message. People are no longer ready to be convinced by slogans; we must substantiate our messages through our actions.

Motivation

Last, we must motivate each of our people as individuals. After successful education and authentication, they are likely to be saying to themselves something like the following:

"Okay, so I understand what they're trying to tell us, and this time I believe they're serious. But, what's the implication for me? Do I buy the idea? Do I want to be part of the organization they're describing? Will I be able to achieve my goals as well as they theirs?"

These are not the questions of a newly selfish workforce. Nor are they evidence that the work ethic has disappeared. Rather, they are the signs of a generation that wants to believe in and identify itself with the goals of the organizations to which it belongs. The new workforce wants more than simply to earn a living. It also wants to make a real contribution and, moreover, to enjoy doing so. Surely we should be glad that our society has reached the point where that is so, not resentful that the goad of economic necessity has lost its power.

Only when we have helped our people to understand our message, to believe it, and to see that they will find it rewarding to be part of making it happen can we say we have truly communicated. However, if we do achieve real communication, we will also have achieved the most powerful competitive weapon of all – a self-motivated workforce that shares a common vision.

The above has begun the task of describing the new management paradigm, "Managing Change", whose features will eventually become the conventional managerial wisdom of the emerging new order, like those of "Command and Control" were during the fourth wave. I say "begun" because we are at an even earlier point in the cycle than when "Annual Budgets: State-of-the-Art Tool to Help the CEO Run the Organization" was published in 1952. That was thirteen years after the start of the fourth wave. Take out six years of wartime disruption, and it was still some seven years after the start of that wave, whereas we are just at the beginning of a new economic era. We have explored some of the aspects of the new paradigm – its underlying assumptions, its new tasks and new roles, and the central part that leadership will play in it. If the fourth wave was the age of the manager, the new era will surely be that of the leader, because the complexity of the task and the nature of the workforce demand the skills that the latter can bring to bear. This is not to say the need for management just disappeared, but it is to say that the old way of managing people did. "Command and Control" is gone forever. Integration, what the leader/manager has to bring about to address this third challenge of grand strategy, will have to be accomplished by new means. Much of the managerial experimentation of the last decade, for example the tremendous interest in the concept of corporate culture, has been a search for new means of integration. Shared Purposes, Shared Values and Distinctive Capabilities are the beginning of grand strategy's response to the challenge. Beginning in the mid-Eighties these formed the foundation for a new methodology of integration which combines leadership and management, the qualitative and the quantitative, strategy and operations to create a framework through which grand strategy can achieve its goal of higher quality implementation than competitive organizations.

STRATEGIC FRAMEWORK

The purpose of the final section of this chapter is to bring together all the elements that are needed to translate strategy into action under the umbrella of the integrating device that has come to be known as the Strategic Framework. I will address two questions: "What are Strategic Frameworks?" and "Why do we need them?" The third rather obvious question, "How does one go about using them?" is very situation-specific. But I'll be delighted to introduce you to someone who can help!

WHAT ARE STRATEGIC FRAMEWORKS?

In 1984 I set out to help organizations develop and implement winning strategy. The problem I very rapidly found myself working on was how to bring about significant change in the way they were managed. Of course strategy was vitally important and would have to be addressed during the process, since it was usually one of the major elements needing to be changed. But it was my early observation that large amounts of the change that was needed in the way companies were run in the mid-Eighties was going to be quite consistent with *any* of the directions realistic, new strategies might define. Most organizations were much more broken in their approach to Integration, than in their ability to develop Strategy.

In the early Eighties John Dyment, partner of Arthur Young (Big Eight Accounting Firm) in charge of planning had faced a similar problem. He was collecting strategic plans from all over the firm packed with laudable intent, but nothing much seemed to be changing. The firm's overall plan was symptomatic of the whole problem. It began with aspirations that were inspiring, followed by goals behind whose achievement the partnership would have no difficulty to align. But by the time it got to the plans to achieve these goals, there seemed to be an awful gap between ends and means. To "be the most innovative accounting firm in the world" was one of the goals. But a hunt through the many pages of very detailed plans revealed *none* that were specifically aimed at achieving it. He needed a way to demonstrate the problem irresistibly to his fellow partners.

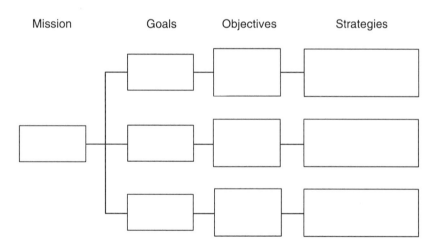

Fig. 7.2 *Strategic planning diagnostic*

Dyment's solution was a simple, four-column display that connected all of the elements of the firm's plan, shown in Fig. 7.2. It progressed from the general – the aspirational Mission on the left – to the particular – the specific, activity-oriented strategies on the right. It connected the details of plans for action to the specific sets of objectives at which they were aimed, the goals that would be achieved if those objectives were met, and the mission that achievement of the goals was presumably going to fulfil. It was a marvelous diagnostic device, or, more cruelly, hot air deflator, as the expanses of white paper in many of its boxes vividly displayed the inadequacy of the firm's plan. If the firm was serious in its intent the mandatory next step was to fill in those gaps.

Then, what had started as a diagnostic tool turned quickly into one for planning and implementation as we realized that its elements could also be used prospectively, to develop a fully fledged operating strategy. Immediately we discovered that through its structure, the Strategic Framework, as it came to be called, facilitated a quantum leap in rigor compared to anything we'd seen before. With the addition of a fifth step, Action Plans, laying out the Who, What and When of implementing each Strategy we also found we had a tool that very nicely fitted the five great challenges of strategic management that Chapter 3, The Evolution of Executive Concerns, has revealed, as Fig. 7.3 shows.

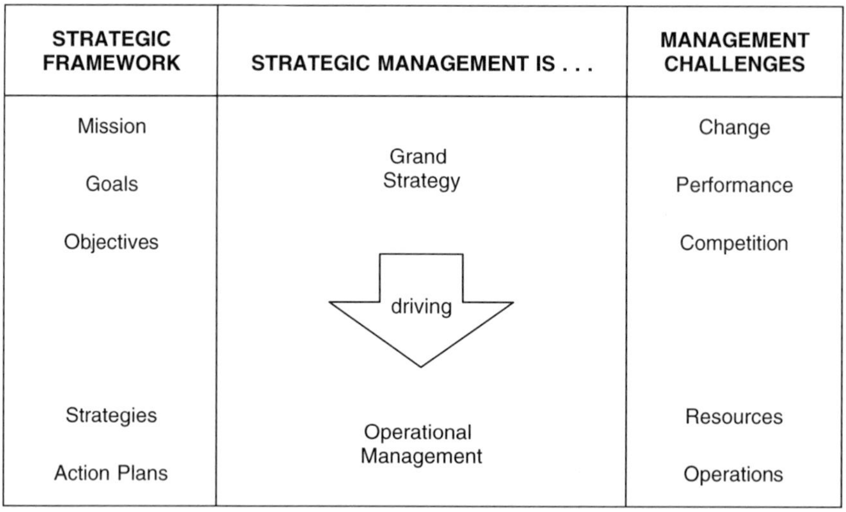

STRATEGIC FRAMEWORK	STRATEGIC MANAGEMENT IS . . .	MANAGEMENT CHALLENGES
Mission	Grand Strategy	Change
Goals		Performance
Objectives		Competition
	driving	
Strategies	Operational Management	Resources
Action Plans		Operations

Fig. 7.3 *The operationalization of grand strategy*

- *Mission* defines the broad purposes of *Change*, and the values that are to guide its achievement
- *Goals* define the distinctive capabilities that will result in the *Performance* necessary to fulfil the mission being achieved

- *Objectives* define the quantification of those goals, i.e., the specific levels of performance in each of them needed to beat the *Competition*
- *Strategies* define the levels of *Resources* allocated to specific projects, programs and activities which together will result in achievement of the objectives
- *Action Plans* define who will do what, by when – in other words provide the guide to the actual *Operations* that have to be carried out to implement the strategies.

Grand strategy, translated from the concept of a superior way of dealing with the challenges of competition, performance and change into a practical guide to action, comprises the three elements: Mission, Goals and Objectives. Using grand strategy as a management technique simply means the rigorous use of these three elements as the driver of the development of specific strategies (i.e., the resource commitments to achieve them), and their associated action plans (i.e., the individual operational activities to implement them). The "purposes" element of mission would drive the development of strategy, and the "values" element would guide its implementation in operation. In short we found we had a practical tool that could ensure a coherent addressing of all aspects of operational management, through the elements of grand strategy.

It is not usually possible to share a real Strategic Framework publicly, since by its very nature it is an internal document with some competitive significance. However, the very first framework, used as a planning and implementation tool rather than a diagnostic device, was prepared by a team of citizens for Bay County, Michigan, facilitated in their efforts by Arthur Young partner Dan Malachuk. The team comprised over sixty representatives of every constituency of Bay County. It is small wonder that Dan later became famous in our circle of change agents for one of the most useful pieces of advice any of us ever received. Known as Malachuk's Maxim, it was: "if in doubt, break them into small groups!" The framework that resulted from their efforts was published in the form that was to become the standard – a folded 11″ × 17″ piece of paper with the Mission on the front, the framework inside and some messages (often the organization's statement of Values or guiding principles) on the back – as an insert to the local newspaper in January 1986. It is thus in the public domain, and Fig. 7.4 illustrates it. The accompanying article that led the newspaper that day was entitled "Sound on the

188

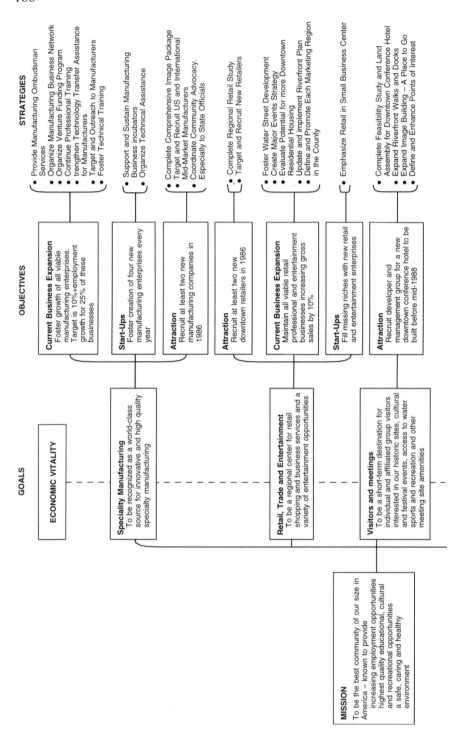

STRATEGIES

- Provide Manufacturing Ombudsman Services
- Organize Manufacturing Business Network
- Organize Venture Funding Program
- Continue Professional Training
- Strengthen Technology Transfer Assistance for Manufacturers
- Target and Outreach to Manufacturers
- Foster Technical Training

- Support and Sustain Manufacturing
- Business incubators
- Organize Technical Assistance

- Complete Comprehensive Image Package
- Target and Recruit US and International Mid-Market Manufacturers
- Coordinate Community Advocacy. Especially to State Officials

- Complete Regional Retail Study
- Target and Recruit New Retailers

- Foster Water Street Development
- Create Major Events Strategy
- Evaluate Potential for more Downtown Residential Housing
- Update and implement Riverfront Plan
- Define and Promote Each Marketing Region in the County

- Emphasize Retail in Small Business Center

- Complete Feasibility Study and Land Assembly for Downtown Conference Hotel
- Expand Riverfront Walks and Docks
- Expand Image Building – A Place to Go
- Define and Enhance Points of Interest

OBJECTIVES

Current Business Expansion
Foster growth of all viable manufacturing enterprises. Target is 10%+employment growth for 25% of these businesses

Start-Ups
Foster creation of four new manufacturing enterprises every year

Attraction
Recruit at least two new manufacturing companies in 1986

Attraction
Recruit at least two new downtown retailers in 1986

Current Business Expansion
Maintain all viable retail professional and entertainment businesses increasing gross sales by 10%

Start-Ups
Fill missing niches with new retail and entertainment enterprises

Attraction
Recruit developer and management group for a new downtown conference hotel to be built before mid-1988

GOALS

ECONOMIC VITALITY

Speciality Manufacturing
To be recognized as a world-class source for innovative and high quality specialty manufacturing

Retail, Trade and Entertainment
To be a regional center for retail shopping and business services and a variety of entertainment opportunities

Visitors and meetings
To be a short-term destination for individual and affiliated group visitors interested in our historic sites, cultural and festival events, access to water sports and recreation and other meeting site amenities

MISSION
To be the best community of our size in America – known to provide increasing employment opportunities highest quality educational, cultural and recreational opportunities a safe, caring and healthy environment

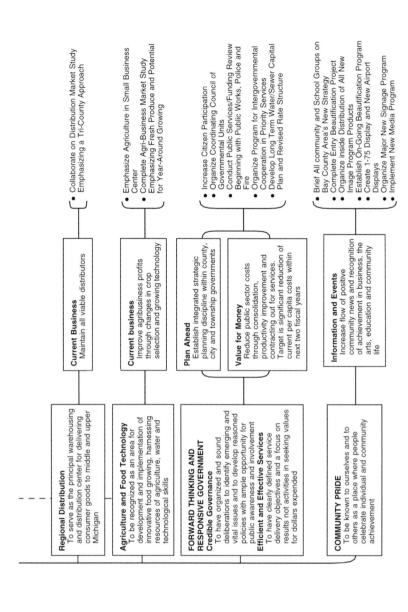

Fig. 7.4 *Bay County Strategic Framework*

ground, not pie in the sky". Would that every strategic plan received such an accolade; it summarized just what we had in mind for this new management technique.

In the years following that first application literally hundreds of frameworks have been produced, in industrial companies such as The Coca-Cola Bottling Company of New York, Loctite, AMR Services, Sterling Winthrop, Eastman Kodak and Alliant Technologies, to name just a few I have personally been involved in creating. And it has been used by teams in organizations as diverse as a bank in Florida, a law firm in Baltimore, a church in Alaska, a school district in New Jersey, a charity in Toronto, a hospital in Tennessee and a town in Alabama. It has also found its way around the world, not just through American multinationals but, for example, also to the World Wildlife Fund in the United Kingdom.

In all cases the users faced the quadruple challenges of grand strategy: mission, both to renew their purposes, and to revitalize their values (what happens to your goals and culture when another company acquires you . . . or spins you off?); strategy, to deal with their competition (what do you do when you're the only church in town, and someone opens another one?); integration, to improve their performance (how do you get all the different constituencies of a small, southern American community to pull together?); and the need to change much of what they were doing as the emergence of a new economy began to make all the old assumptions obsolete.

The tool evolved as we used it. Definitions became tighter. And an additional element was added – Measures of Success of the Mission – to provide the third element of setting a shared vision I described earlier in this chapter, Shared Results. Sometimes there was just one framework, serving as a guide to the whole organization. In other cases, every unit and every person in the organization had their own, individual framework, showing how their objectives, and their planned actions, contributed to the common goals.

State-of-the-art in 1994, based on Sterling Winthrop, Kodak Imaging Group and some generic definitions as illustrations, looked as in the next two figures. First, Fig. 7.5 shows how it became common to put the issues, summarizing shared purposes and shared values on the front; and then an expansion of the latter on the back.

STERLING WINTHROP

OUR VALUES

We are a winning team
We believe that we will succeed only as a team and that the full participation of all is essential to the fulfilment of our mission. It is imperative that we create an environment of mutual respect, candor and trust; where all can reach their highest potential; where individual initiative and performance are recognized and rewarded; where all identify with the success of the company; and where a winning attitude prevails.

We are customer driven
We believe that the success of our business depends on understanding and satisfying the needs of the consumer. Market needs must drive our choice of products and services and the way we deliver them. At the same time, success in delivering those products and services requires that the recipients of internal services and staff work deserve the same consideration so that all our activities create value.

We are dedicated to continuous improvement
We believe that sustained success depends on the maintenance of superior quality, which we will only achieve through continuous improvement in everything we do. In a dynamic, competitive world to stand still is to be left behind. We encourage a healthy dissatisfaction with the status quo and the creativity and initiative to do something about it. Openness to change, to experimentation and to the search for a better way characterizes our attitude to every aspect of our work.

We have a sense of urgency
We believe that being first, speed of action, hard work and an aggressive determination to get things done are characteristics of every winning team. In our business they are a condition for survival. The first to market has an often insurmountable advantage. The quickest to move keeps everyone else off balance. The will to succeed very often wins the day through sheer determination.

We act responsibly
We believe that integrity is an essential asset. Our success is worth having, and ultimately will occur only if our every action is characterized by staying true to our values, and the best of each of the societies in which we live and work. We will always do the right thing.

STERLING WINTHROP

MISSION

OUR PURPOSES

We are a worldwide team committed to creating distinctive solutions for the needs of mankind in pharmaceutical and consumer health products.

We measure our success by the achievement of market leadership, superior financial returns and an environment of trust and personal growth.

We accomplish this through the dedication of all of us and all of our resources to continuous improvement in all that we do.

OUR VALUES

We are a winning team

We are customer driven

We are dedicated to continuous improvement

We have a sense of urgency

We act responsibly

Fig. 7.5 *The Strategic Framework – I*

Inside pages

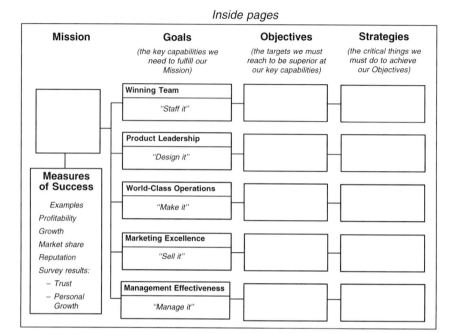

Fig. 7.6 *The Strategic Framework – II*

The fifth and final element of the Strategic Framework, Action Plans, is eloquently summarized by a quote from Bruce Wray, quality process leader in Kodak's Health Sciences Division. It is a fitting place to end this section.

ACTION – THE REAL DELIVERABLE

The purpose of Action Planning is not to end up with a set of plans that *would* implement our Strategy, *if* we did them, over the next ninety *weeks*; but rather to end up with a set of Actions that *will* implement our Strategy, *when* we do them, during the next ninety *days*.

WHY STRATEGIC FRAMEWORKS?

Strategic Framework came to mean the process by which it was developed, as well as the document that was its symbolic output.

I say 'symbolic' output because the purpose of all this effort – the development of the organization's Strategic Framework, by the team comprising the critical mass of leaders who would determine whether it was actually implemented – was not simply to create a better plan. This inefficient, time-consuming, even scary at times, team process was aimed at more effective implementation, not more elegant planning. The required result, as Jack Thomas endlessly told his Kodak Imaging Group managers was not better plans, but

An Aligned Team . . .

. . . Effectively Implementing . . .

. . . An Agreed Strategy.

We defined what this meant by describing the shifts of behavior it implied.

An Aligned Team meant moving individuals from telling to learning; groups from conflict to collaboration; resource commitments from waste to leverage; and the whole organization from a world of Win/Lose, Lose/Win to one of Win/Win, Lose/Lose.

Effectively Implementing meant a similar set of shifts in activity; from Writing Plans to Delivering Results; from Intent to Action; from "Why we can't" to "When we will"; and from Defense to Offense. And,

An Agreed Strategy meant a parallel change in attitude; from Terminal Politeness to Honest Agreement; from "They should" to "We Will"; from Ritual Obedience to Passionate Involvement; and, from Individual Reservation to Personal Commitment.

Time after time we observed that organizations were full of people who not only agreed how things needed to change but even came very close to describing the same set of actions to make it happen. Somehow knowing what needed to be done and doing it had become disconnected. Strategic Framework, the process, is simply an opportunity to reconnect them; that is, for an organization working as a team to establish a common vision for its future, develop a strategy to achieve it and manage the change that it implies.

I make no special claims for this particular tool. Many such processes can achieve the desired result, if that is what the leadership regards as its job, its real work. And no process will do it if the leadership does not accept this responsibility. It is not the process that brings about change, it is the leadership. Conversely, it is not the process that fails, it is the leadership. Process is a tool of leadership. Leadership is not a component of process.

All the Strategic Framework – the tool and the process – does is to provide some degree of structure and some evidence of genuine commitment, and, with that, the confidence to those who participate that, this time, they won't get into trouble for breaking the old and obsolete rules so as to do the right thing. The bottom line, the end result of a successful effort, is the most exciting experience anyone who has ever been part of a winning team has known:

The right people . . . working together . . . to build commitment . . . to achieve a worthy cause.

Ultimately, for anyone involved, it comes down to a personal decision: obligation or opportunity? The choice is yours.

8 Change: The Challenge of Transformation

"If it ain't broke, fix it."   (Donald Petersen)

"It is impossible to be too strong at the decisive point."
(Napoleon Bonaparte)

"The small reform may become the enemy of the large one."
(John Morley)

"Managing Change" is the name I have given, in common with many others, to the generalized version of the management paradigm that is taking the place of "Command and Control" as the new era begins. In a world of increasing uncertainty, change is a journey without a tangible destination. We know little more about where it will take us than that, at its end, we will have to be able to go on managing change better than any of our competitors if we are to survive and prosper over the long haul. Like a nomadic tribe, the modern corporation maintains its competitive health internally by the endless renewal of its capabilities, and externally by continual migration to markets where its capabilities, old and new, can sustain it. The organization, its competitors and its markets are in constant flux. The winners are those *dynamically* able to develop distinctive capabilities, with special value, to particular parts of the market-place. Financial performance is the measure of success at doing this at a particular point in time. Sustained financial performance is the measure of success at doing it over time, i.e., of the superior ability to change in a competitive world. Where the old management paradigm, "Command and Control", was eminently suited to a static world, the new management paradigm, "Managing Change", is the *destination* as well as the *transition* process of the transformation project all of the world's business enterprises need to undertake, and only a few have really begun.

The last sentence and the title of this chapter introduced a new term – transformation. Why do we need it, and why is it the right subject for the final chapter of this book?

195

Grand strategy is the overarching discipline that deals with defining and refining the way an organization is managed so as not just to succeed in the current period, but to maintain its competitive health into the indefinite future. When faced with massive change in multiple aspects of the competitive environment the steady, continuous refinement of an organization's management paradigm, that typifies the leadership task in stable times, will no longer suffice. Now the very assumptions on which the paradigm rests are changing. Now something more dramatic, more discontinuous, more far-reaching is needed. This "something" is transformation – of the way the organization is managed, of its business processes, of the behaviors of its people, of its use of information technology, of the way it treats all its stakeholders and of the way it competes; in other words the development and adoption of a whole, new, grand strategy suited to a whole, new, economic order.

The shift from one economic long wave to the next is *the* definitional time of transformation for business. Thus the particular form that grand strategy takes in such a period is business transformation. This book began with a description of the massive economic shift that is taking place as we approach the fifth, distinguishable, economic era since the industrial revolution. We saw how, each of the previous times this has happened, there have been equally fundamental changes, first in the industries that drove the economy, and then in the business enterprise itself and the way it was managed. One more time a generation of business leaders faces the same challenge – to transform the way their organizations are managed, to make them the winners in a new, this time global, economy.

Here, in the final chapter, we will explore some of the aspects of this transformation project that have proved to be important in bringing about success. The first, and perhaps the most important aspect of transformational change given our highly individualistic society, is that it is above all a challenge that demands a team process. Let us see why.

THE PROCESS OF TRANSFORMATION

We start by taking the first two dimensions of competitive health – strategy and integration – and use them to define the axes of a two-dimensional chart. Then we imagine ourselves as an organization in trouble, without a winning strategy, and in need of a process for bringing about internal integration. In other words, we are in the bottom, left-hand corner of the chart, wanting to get to the top right – which is reached by having a well defined, fully detailed set of strategies and a well aligned, smoothly operating organization (see Fig. 8.1).

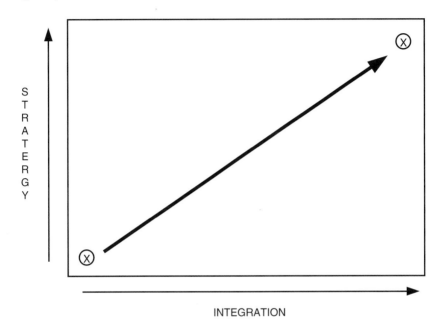

INTEGRATION

Fig. 8.1 *The goal of transformation*

The first step up the Strategy axis is to define a business concept, or Participation Strategy. This comprises a basic definition of the business and where in the industry we will participate, i.e., *where* we're going to compete. The second step is to develop an Operating Strategy, or *how* we're going to compete, down to the level of detailed, product/market, functional and geographic plans. These are not discrete, sequential steps, since *what* we are practically capable of doing, or becoming able to do, and *where* these capabilities have value, are directly connected. However we have to start somewhere. So, in practice, we undertake an iterative process, hypothesizing first a desired, participation strategy based on our aspirations and understanding of the competition, technology and marketplace. Next we attempt to develop an operating strategy that can be demonstrated to be value-creating. Then, on the basis of this learning, including early experience of product development and market participation, we adjust both participation and operating strategies until we have a feasible whole.

Similarly, now looking at the Integration axis, there are two steps to the desired, fully integrated organization. First we must build a Top Team to exercise leadership and personify the behaviour we are going to demand of the whole organization. This team may simply be comprised of the direct reports to the organization's leader. More usually it is larger than that, including the key managers from the next level of the organization. It is rare that it numbers less than twelve, and impractical that at least its core much exceeds forty. The goal in composing it is to include the critical mass of power wielders and opinion leaders needed – first to ensure the credibility of the team's pronouncements, and second to bring along the rest of the organization.

The second step along the Integration axis is to expand the core team to cover the whole organization and everything that goes on within it, with particular emphasis on all the aspects of the way people relate to each other and are managed. As with strategy, in practice this must be an iterative process since the ideas of the leadership need ultimately to be owned by everyone if true alignment throughout the organization is to be achieved. Now we can fill in the

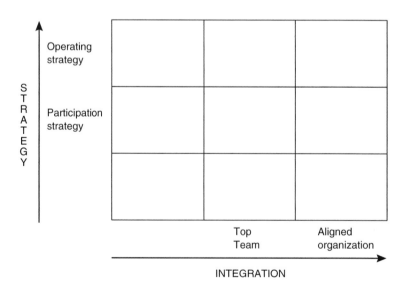

Fig. 8.2   *The Transformation Matrix – I*

lines and define the nine boxes of what has come to be called the Transformation Matrix (see Fig. 8.2).

The first thing to recognize about this matrix is that every surviving organization was at some time in the top right hand corner having achieved Strategic Integration – a well aligned organization, with a fully detailed, operating strategy being implemented to deliver strategic success. This is a very important insight for two reasons. The first is externally focused. Every single one of our surviving competitors was once also in that top right box. Moreover if we are in trouble there is a very good chance that one of the reasons is that at least one of those competitors is still there! A healthy respect for one's competitors is mandatory to maintaining competitive health.

The second is internally focused, and has two, rather paradoxical parts. It reminds those of us who are in trouble that, just because we've got problems it doesn't mean we're failures. We did it right once, we ought to be able to do it again. But it also requires us to recognize that the biggest barrier to getting it right again is the institutionalized character of the way we got it right before. We are probably in trouble because our success locked us into "the way we do things around here", and when the assumptions on which we'd built that paradigm ceased to be valid, because of shifts in the external and internal environment, we failed to change with them.

In the language of the Transformation Matrix, what this means is that the axes move! And if they move far enough, and fast enough even, or perhaps in particular, the most successful organizations – if they don't change with them – will find themselves in the bottom, left-hand corner as Fig. 8.3 illustrates. This is what happened to many of the "excellent" companies – the axes moved and what they were excellent at meant they were no longer in the top right-hand corner of the old matrix, but in the bottom left-hand corner of a new one. They had to start all over again.

Changed requirements in the elements of strategy, and the means of integration is a natural phenomenon moving the ground under all organizations, all the time. People who have been in earthquakes describe how disorienting it was to have the ground move under them. The bewilderment of senior managers faced with the problems of the giants of yesteryear shows a very similar kind of disorientation. That is what unpredictable, rapid change does to organizations and their management, and what they must cope with if they are to maintain their competitive health. It is not that those managers lack competence, or character, but that they often simply cannot accept

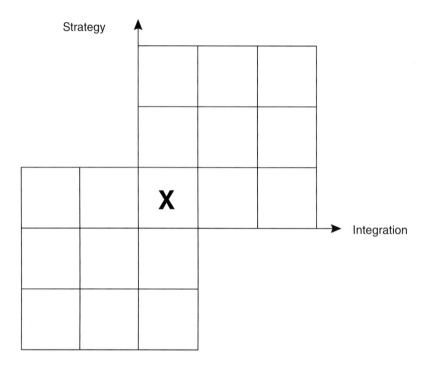

Fig. 8.3 *The impact of change*

that an earthquake has literally destroyed the foundations of the way they run their businesses, and that they therefore *have to* start anew.

In times of gradual change, a stable workforce, and a level of success less complete than, for example, Kodak's, it should be possible for organizations continuously to adjust the way they run their businesses to keep up with, and even gain advantage from the environment's evolution without the need for extraordinary, transformational leadership. However in today's business environ-ment when one era is ending, and another beginning it would be a very foolish, and even more arrogant management team that assumed that some rather fundamental change was not necessary. The prudent leader's assumption in these times is that we start from the bottom left box, needing a new strategy, and a new way of integrating our organization. If it ain't broke now, it's about to be, and in some ways no-one can predict.

ACHIEVING STRATEGIC INTEGRATION ANEW

For the last ten years I and a few colleagues have been helping organizations which, for all practical purposes, found themselves in the bottom left box, and had leaders who understood they needed to get to the top right. Our first observation was that the further we went up the Strategy axis, without also dealing with the Integration axis, the bigger the wall we built in the way of getting the organization to align behind our plans. And the further along the Integration axis we went, without also dealing with the Strategy axis, the bigger the wall we built in the way of getting the organization to rigorously address its need for a new strategy.

At one extreme one would find, in the top left box, a chief executive officer, using an outside consultant or internal planning team secretly to produce the complete blueprint of success. However good the plan there was no chance anyone was going to implement it. In the "command and control" world we inherited from the management generation with military experience in the Second World and Korean Wars, this was extraordinarily common, probably at one time including the executive suite of every major corporation in America. In that world it worked seductively well. But it doesn't have a hope in a world where no-one obeys orders.

At the other extreme, in the bottom right box, we found a wonderfully self-contented, compatible group with no idea of what to do to win. The leadership of a Savings & Loan, a Mutual Life Insurance company, or maybe even an Airline, at the point deregulation arrived might be good examples.

This told us that some routes through the matrix didn't work. Practice eventually showed that in fact there was only one way out of the bottom left box into the centre – through the very narrow, corner gap between the walls of resistance rising along the vertical axis to alignment behind the plans of an autocratic leadership, and along the horizontal axis to taking a hard-nosed look at the need for a new strategy by an inward-looking management team (see Fig. 8.4).

In organizations that successfully tackled transformation, the top team created the new business concept, or participation strategy, and developing the concept created the team. The reasons were two-fold.

First we discovered that "integration", for business purposes, only happens in real time. Sending management teams down the Colorado

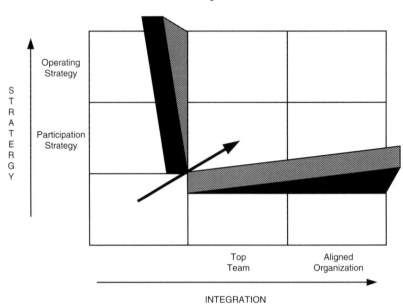

Fig. 8.4 *The Transformation Matrix – II*

Rapids together creates teams quite good at going down the rapids together. But the half-life of that kind of teamwork is until the first, real, business crisis hits when they get back home. The best way to create a business team is to get it to work on a business issue of great importance to everyone in the group. And there is no more important task than the organization's new strategy to deal with the threat to its very survival posed by accelerating change. The problem, in our current world, is how to get them to take the task seriously when they have been used to strategy being dictated to them under the old paradigm – and, combined with what's coming next, this is often the biggest challenge their leader faces when undertaking transformation.

Second, we discovered that the two axes are interrelated. Not all strategies are consistent with all ways of integrating an organization. For example, a strategy demanding intensive teamwork (e.g., creating a breakthrough computer) cannot be effectively implemented with a reward system that emphasizes only the individual (e.g., high, personal, performance based bonuses). Consequently the fundamental rules for governing behaviour, and the basic strategy of the organization have to be developed together, by the top team. The problem again is to get this usually hard-nosed group to take this "soft" subject seriously.

The art of organizational leadership is at its finest in this shepherding, and leading of a group of tough, competitive and, at least in their personal careers, successful managers through a task most of them often don't want to engage in, but to which they also won't accept a dictated answer. The key is finding the right balance between exercising the leader's duty to decide, and facilitating the participative processes of the team. The amount of debate to allow, how far to go to keep everybody on board and the timing for making the ultimate decisions, are delicate judgments the leader has to make in lonely isolation.

Remember also, this team is a function of the size and complexity of the organization, and probably numbers between twelve and fifty. At the higher number the processes for carrying out the first move, i.e. from the bottom left-hand box into the centre, will be complex and time-consuming. With *very* large organizations even the larger number will not contain a critical mass of leadership to change the direction of the whole organization. Extensive communication, feedback and strategy refinement activities will be required as part of the immediate follow-through to the first, strategic decisions if the rest of the organization is to be brought on board.

Complicating matters, in particular in this time of huge transition, is the fact that the matrix won't stay still. The ground keeps moving, probably in unpredictable directions and in a jerky fashion even as the team keeps trying to move up the diagonal. This places even more onus on utilizing open, two-way communications and a process that anticipates and welcomes iteration. Not only is team-building possible only in real time, but strategy too can only evolve in real time, even as it is being implemented. The old way where, like a Soviet Five-Year Plan, it was set and then implemented for a given period no longer works, if it ever did. Now we need a more flexible, and more robust concept of strategy which recognizes that all plans are obsolete the moment they are written, so serves not as a rigid blueprint but as a guide to spontaneous action in a moving marketplace – another reason why we found the term, and the tool 'strategic framework' worked better than the conventional 'strategic' plan as a guide for implementation.

Once in the middle box the same principle – of progressing along the diagonal – applies to the myriad other teams now needed to turn the basic strategic and integrational concepts into detailed processes and procedures. It is a very fundamental, and maybe *the* insight about successful transformation that it requires teams up, down and

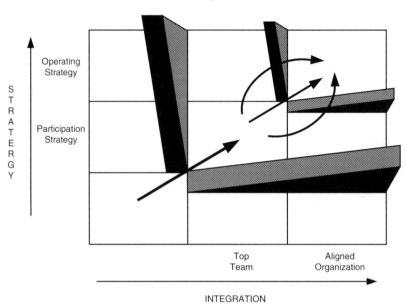

Fig. 8.5   *The Transformation Matrix – III*

across the organization, building plans for new ways of doing things and the requisite alignment behind them at one and the same time. Experience however shows that, once firmly in the middle box (see Fig. 8.5), it is both necessary, and fortunately possible to be a little more flexible about moving on one dimension, and then catching up with the other (e.g., buy-in, if it was operating strategy first; or planning, if it was organizational change first).

It seems that the existence of the basic elements of external and internal strategy, *as long as it is accompanied by the demonstrated commitment of the top team*, buys the trust needed for progress off the diagonal. But, ultimately, whichever route is taken the destination is the same. For sustained, competitive health, at every point in the organization there *must* be tightly knit teams built around totally shared concepts for their areas of responsibility. These strong words are not chosen lightly because this is what the winners are doing, in a small number of companies and industries already, but everywhere eventually. There isn't an alternative, unless you're satisfied with coming second, or worse.

So organizational transformation is an intensively team-driven process, where the strategy needed to deal with the external world, and the alignment needed to execute it in the internal world are developed at one and the same time in myriad places, to deal with the myriad changes that have to be made in the way the organization is run. The single biggest change that has to be made is to the existing management paradigm, the philosophy of competing and managing that has been institutionalized by previous success into the fabric of the organization. We turn now to this, the greatest challenge of transformation.

THE STRATEGY OF RENEWAL

Transformation implies massive change – in its literal meaning from one physical form to a quite different one. When we talk about people being transformed, we mean that some or all of their behavior, appearance and character have undergone a rather complete change from the way they were before. So it is with organizations. The word *renewal* maybe suggests a more gradual process and that is indeed what we should be aiming for, since the alternative, revolution, is the most destructive and expensive form of change there is. But make no mistake, we are talking about very complete change, and with the urgency many organizations face it may not be possible to achieve it very far short of revolutionary means.

What is more, and let us be quite blunt about it, transformation has a very clear "enemy" – the existing management paradigm, that is the way we are doing things now, which got us in the mess we're in (despite the fact that, probably before some sort of corruption of it set in, it is also what gave us the success we previously enjoyed). And an enemy implies a war. So let's see what war can tell us about a strategy for renewal.

In the late Summer of 1992, while I was struggling with determining what to advise a client to do next about a very powerful, enemy paradigm indeed, I was reading a book, *The Age of Battles* (Weigley, Indiana University Press) that describes the almost two-hundred-year period from 1631 (when Sweden won the Thirty Years War) to 1815 (Napoleon's final downfall at Waterloo), when nations attempted to use the decisive battle as a means to victory in the implementation of national policy. Invariably all the battles seemed to start in the same way. An initial reconnaissance was conducted to find out the enemy's position and the nature of the battlefield. A concept for the battle would be formed and the troops drawn up in appropriate array. Then some sort of head-on, general engagement of the enemy would start the battle. This puzzled me as I had always been taught, as we explored in an earlier chapter, that direct assaults were the most likely way to fail, and the most expensive in victory. Yet here were all the great, not just the lesser generals apparently always engaging in direct assaults along wide fronts. Then I began to understand what was really going on. Despite welcoming and exploiting any initial, isolated successes the real purpose of those broad and direct engagements was to be only a first step, intended to "fix" the enemy in position, by forcing him to stand and fight. This allowed a probing of his defenses, and an assaying of his strong and weak points so that at the critical moment, and in the critical place, resources could be massed, and strength could be applied against weakness. The breakthrough would then be exploited by cutting off bodies of troops still standing and threatening them in the rear, usually causing them to surrender or flee, piecemeal, in rout.

It suddenly dawned on me that the renewal process as it was playing out in my client's organization bore many of the same features. Table 8.1 illustrates that process as I had drawn it up for a meeting only a month before.

In Phase I, we had started with an interview process (reconnaissance) which had identified the client's critical management challenges (the enemy's position, and the nature of the battlefield). Then we had helped the client's leadership team develop a Vision for its future (concept for the battle) and put in place an organizational Superstructure (troops drawn up in appropriate array).

In Phase II, the parallels continued. Our Immediate Operating Improvements corresponded to "initial, isolated successes"; our Broad Change Process to "head-on, general engagement", and the client's Integrated Group Strategy to "resources could be massed and strength applied against weakness". This not only gave me a degree of confidence that there was some conceptual sense to the strategy we had evolved, but also provided a fertile field of analogy for understanding the transformation process as a subject for more general study.

The typical organization attempts transformation only when things have got so bad that fundamental change appears likely to be less painful than maintaining the status quo. So it is in war. Battles are the last, not the first resort of the general. To get an enemy to give up

Table 8.1 The strategy of renewal, July 1992

Phase I:	Order	Aug. 1991 – Nov. 1991

- Critical Challenges
- Vision
- Superstructure

Phase II:	Foundation	Dec. 1991 – Jul. 1992

- Immediate Operating Improvements
  - Business Performance
  - Inter-unit collaboration
- Broad Change Process
  - Make a start
  - Diagnose the problem
- Integrated Group Strategy
  - Participation Strategy
  - Operating Strategy: Strategic Framework

Phase III:	Change	Aug. 1992 – Jul. 1994

- Strategic Changes
- Organizational Changes
- People Changes

Phase IV:	Institutionalization	Aug. 1994 –

- Embedding the new way
- Evolving the strategy
- Developing the organization

his purpose without fighting is a far greater victory than to defeat him in the open field. To change the way an organization is managed without wholesale restructuring and restaffing is vastly the preferable course. Things are therefore widely agreed to be bad when you start (and when they're not, as Jack Welch found out, the task of the leader intent on pre-emptive change is overwhelmingly more difficult). The more normal situation was a Ford in dire straits led by Donald Petersen, not a currently well performing GE led by Jack Welch.

So, usually the organization is in trouble and the first steps are to understand the main features of the problem, and put in place a top team, often under a new leader, to tackle it. Planning theory says Mission before Strategy before Structure. In the real world there is a step between Mission and Strategy – Grand Strategy and Super-structure – which begins the mandatory first move along the diagonal of the business transformation matrix. The "Barons" won't even engage in the subject of Strategy until their own, personal uncertainty has been reduced by giving them positions in the new structure. So at the end of Phase I, which needs to be very rapid, we have a top team in place and an initial consensus on the grand strategy to be adopted. Phase II now has three priorities – Immediate Operating Improvements both to improve financial results and to develop the momentum of early successes behind a new way of running the business; Broad Change Process to make a start at least on educating people about the situation and hopefully on the easier changes, but more importantly to allow diagnosis of the problem; and Integrated Group Strategy, getting the top team to work together to define the overall Participation Strategy and lead their own teams to develop the Operating Strategy to carry it out.

We now come to Phase III. The Participation Strategy developed in Phase II is the transformation process's parallel to the choices of where to launch the breakthrough attacks in battle. The Operating Strategy is the allocation of resources to put it into practice. They *must* both be very different from the past. They *must* be over-whelmingly concentrated on the critical areas. And they *must* involve significant Strategic, Organizational and People Changes. If they don't, to return to the battle analogy, we will have bogged down in the trench warfare of widefront, head-to-head conflict between the old and the new. At best this is a slow war of attrition, at worst it is never-ending stalemate with the champions of both the old and the new paradigms eventually exhausted and discredited. In this case the result will be a bemused, demoralized organization aghast at the internal conflict it has watched between its leaders, and desperate for someone to clean house, and return the organization to an external focus on its real competition, outside the company. But this is what happens much of the time.

To stop it, Phase II has to be accomplished with ruthless, intellectual honesty, and Phase III undertaken with a matching degree of toughness. Compromises on strategy during transformation are akin to the failure to concentrate in war, or half measures in a revolution. Avoiding the disruption of organizational change is like leaving an army drawn up in an inadequate posture to defend itself. And providing second chances, i.e. hoping people can change, or putting up with weak players, is like leaving inadequate generals in command. It may be all too understandably human for a top executive to be reluctant when faced with having to take action on a senior manager who has been a colleague for many years, but it's not humane to all the people who report to him or her. Ultimately the problems will have to be solved but by then at more pain to the individuals, and at the cost of much greater misery to the organization at large. Too many leaders interpret compassion to mean the way they treat the people who report directly to them, ignoring the tens, hundreds and maybe even thousands who are out of sight, so all too often out of mind.

Inevitably many of the actions and most of the casualties relate to people, initially mostly senior. "Changing the way we run the business" means more than anything else changing the way people relate to each other in the way they work. As I have emphasized earlier in this book, people get to where they are because of their success in implementing the existing management paradigm. Senior management personifies it. The whole Finance, Human Resources and Communications functions exist to ensure it is respectively adhered to, staffed, and its needs and successes are communicated. The existing Information Systems have been set up to provide them with the information to do that. It is folly to attempt major change without leading the way with changes of key people in management, and the way these four functions operate. Such steps are the equivalent to the breakthroughs in battle. They allow new leaders who personify the new paradigm to make changes in practice and procedure in these critical areas, and thereby remove the underpinnings of the old way of running the business.

The final phase is Institutionalization of the new way. This is akin to putting in place the arrangements for a better peace, having won the war. We know very little about this phase at this time since there are hardly any, and maybe no examples of organizations that have truly got there! What we do know, though, is some of the characteristics that successful companies will need to maintain when they do get there. And it is fitting that as good a summary as I have seen should come from a manager at Eastman Kodak, who not only was one of those who understood what was going on during its decline, but had a clear vision for the characteristics it needed in the future (see Fig. 8.6). It is not an understanding of the destination that is the problem. It is the difficulty of the journey to get there. But I guess that's always been true of anything worth undertaking.

The Well-run Companies of the Future will be:

Focused
- Resources are applied where they add greatest value
- Individual decisions are guided by an understanding of how they support corporate directions
- The customer – not the technology – is the focal point of activity
- Management time, attention and information is driven by the 20% of the situations which yield 80% of the value

Fast
- Time to market from idea to launch is less than 18 months
- Completion of business process cycles like billing and collection is becoming instantaneous
- Delivery of product and services – both external and internal to the company – is speedy enough to meet or exceed customer needs
- People – especially high potential people – move quickly and easily through assignments that cross organizational and geographic boundaries

Flexible
- Organizational lines are not a barrier to progress
- Decisions are made on the front lines with latitude to make mistakes
- Products and services are provided in ways that allow global customer customization and flexible use of people, plant and equipment worldwide
- Cross-organizational teams are readily formed to address product development, customer service, key business issues, etc.
- Compensation and reward approaches vary by unit and over time as situations warrant

Friendly
- The company is easy to do business with
- Suppliers are considered partners in the business enterprise
- Employees have open communication and easy access to each other and to the four levels of supervision and management between them and the "top"
- The company operates in harmony with the environment
- Bureaucratic barriers to employee success are virtually non-existent

Fun
- It's a great place to work
- Celebration of success is a regular occurrence
- The employees are proud to be part of the company
- All corporate stakeholders identify the company with a "greater good" for the betterment of our world

---

Source: Kathy Hudson, Eastman Kodak (1989).

Fig. 8.6 *Characteristics of the Well-run Companies of the Future*

One of the principal reasons for this difficulty is the resistance to change that tends to be built into an organization's culture along with the institutionalization of the management paradigm that creates its success. Edgar Schein describes, in *Organizational Culture and Leadership*, how a culture is formed by the way a group tackles the challenges of survival in the external environment, and integration in the internal environment that are at the heart of this book.

> The process of culture formation is, in a sense, identical with the process of group formation in that the very essence of "groupness" or group identity – the shared patterns of thought, belief, feelings, and values that result from shared experience and common learning – is what we ultimately end up calling the "culture" of that group. Without a group there can be no culture, and without some degree of culture we are really talking only about an aggregate of people, not a "group". So group growth and culture formation can be seen as two sides of the same coin, and both are the result of leadership activities.
>
> What we need to understand, then, is how the *individual* intentions of the founders, leaders, or conveners of a new group or organization, their own definitions of the situation, their assumptions and values, come to be a *shared, consensually validated* set of definitions that are passed on to new members as "the correct way to define the situation". These intentions and definitions, as they exist consciously or not in the leader's mind, can always be analyzed into an *external* and an *internal* set of issues. The external issues have to do with the leader's and the group's definition of the environment and how to survive in it; the internal issues have to do with the leader's and the group's definition of how to organize relationships among the members of the group to permit survival in the defined environment through effective performance and the creation of internal comfort.

The power of those words "the correct way to define the situation" by themselves indicate why it should be that a resistance to change should go along with them. If the leaders responses to the group's earliest issues do not work the organization will cease to exist. When they do work their effectiveness validates them to the other members of the group as the basic assumptions on which the organization is founded. As success follows survival the patterns of strategies and behaviors that create that success – what I earlier referred to as the "replicable pattern" – then enrich the developing culture and define its conventional wisdom. Growth will depend on implementing "what works" as rapidly as possible wherever the opportunity may arise, before a competitor can get to it first. The greater the success of that replicable pattern, and the fewer the failures or false starts that the blossoming organization experiences, the greater will be the resistance to tampering with it.

The longer success is sustained, and the greater it is, the harder it will be to change, as the early struggles get shrouded in the mists of time and only the accepted behaviours, but not the reasons for them, get passed on to new recruits. When the need for renewal comes a formidable obstacle to change has been built into the very heart of what the transformation process has to address – the organization's culture, the rules it has built into itself for guiding the way its people tackle the challenges of strategy, and integration.

Consequently understanding the dynamics of cultural change is a key building block of the strategy for renewal. Fortunately we can find some help from an old friend, Isaac Newton.

NEWTON'S LAWS OF CULTURAL CHANGE

Remember Newton's Laws of Motion?

1. A body will remain at rest or keep moving in a straight line at constant speed unless acted upon by a force.
2. The rate of change of velocity of a body is directly proportional to the force acting upon it.
3. The action and reaction of two bodies on each other are always equal and opposite.

It requires a very small adjustment of language, and absolutely no leap of intuition to make them apply to the phenomenon of cultural change in organizations.

Law 1 An organization's behavior will not change unless acted on by an outside force
For a long time I used to write this as "An organization's behavior will not change unless *an abnormal effort is put into it*." Then I

realized that I knew of *no* examples of organizations that have successfully faced up to the need for significant, internal change without some, substantial degree of outside force being applied to them. (American GE is as near to an example as I know. The primary impetus, Jack Welch himself, was certainly internal. But there has been a considerable amount of external talent added without which maybe the change would not have occurred. And his own number one regret, that he didn't do everything more quickly, maybe speaks to the value that more outside force might have had to him.) New owners, new managers, and consultants are three typical, direct forms of applying such force. Bankers, stock analysts, raiders and the media are indirect forms that make life so uncomfortable for the insiders that they begin to take action. Normally both are needed, the latter preceding the former. And the larger and more historically successful the company the more of the latter will be needed to get any action, and the more of the former will be needed for success. All too often we see attempts at organizational change peter out in failure because the means never matched the end. The impetus for change nearly always comes from the outside, and it seems a significant amount of the means must too. When the outside world takes the pressure off, and when there has not been a significant infusion of new blood the probability is that the originally desired change will not be achieved, and the organization may even lapse back into its earlier state.

It is worth adding a note about the use of consultants, who have elements of both direct and indirect force attached to them. In fact I think a term like facilitators, or change agents might be better than consultants, since the last thing a transformation process needs is the classical consulting approach of an outside team independently studying the situation for six months and then providing top management with a confidential report on its findings and recommendations. That takes us straight into the top left box of The Transformation Matrix with no hope that wholehearted implementation will follow. Outsiders can fill several valuable, and maybe even mandatory roles, when they work genuinely as part of the internal teams that the transformation process demands Some of these are: understanding of the nature of the issues, provision of a rigorous framework for change, a hearing for the unpalatable, devil's advocacy, a truly independent point of view, and finally disposability. One of the few things I remember about school chemistry is what happens to a catalyst in a chemical reaction – it gets left behind. That can be very painful for the insider! It's the job of the outsider.

*Law 2   The amount of behavioral change will be directly proportional
to the amount of effort put into it*
The "amount of effort" begs the question of the effectiveness of
different kinds of effort. Whereas it is clear that major strategic
change requires major changes in resource commitments, doing this is
not automatically accompanied by the required behavioral change.
The results of a European study of decision-making in medium-sized
companies gives us a clue why this is so (see Fig. 8.7). The problem is

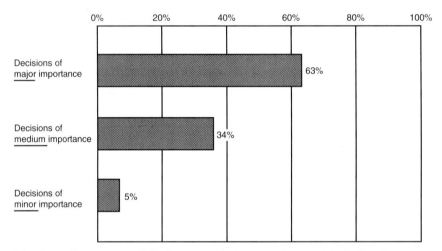

Fig. 8.7   *Percentage of decisions made in accordance with declared strategy*

that the taking of the few, major decisions that shift big amounts of
resources occurs in private, with a small number of people present.
Moreover these decisions, virtually by definition, are infrequent,
probably no more than five or six a year; and they are often kept
confidential, along with the accompanying reasoning, for perfectly
legitimate, strategic reasons. In contrast there are many, many minor
decisions taken by an organization's leaders and they are usually
quite visible to large numbers of people. Since "do what I say, not
what I do" works no better with mature adults than it does with little
children, people *infer* from the behaviors they observe in their leaders
what their "*real*" priorities are, and act accordingly. Unless the
leaders' observed behavior is ruthlessly consistent with the outcomes
they desire there is little chance that an organization's behavior will
shift in that direction. We end up with the strange paradox that it
may be that the minor decisions are more important in bringing
about significant, strategic change than the major ones!

I experienced this paradox personally just before I left Continental Group in 1984. In my last position I worked directly for the Chairman's Office and was present when most of those major, strategic decisions were made. And, despite the many, many leadership problems that company had, there was no question that, in those major decisions of how to spend large amounts of money, its leaders were consistent with their declared strategy. But when I told people that, I was constantly challenged on my integrity. I have never forgotten what one middle manager said to me: "Mike, I thought you'd be the last person to sell out. I've watched Bruce Smart take decision after decision, and I haven't yet seen him take one that was consistent with where he said he was taking this company." I'd seen many of the private decisions, he'd seen the public ones.

One of the last things I did at Continental before leaving was to attend a very good workshop on leadership styles and skills. At the end of it, the unanimous commitment of the group (comprising every senior corporate manager below the level of corporate officer) was that we would implement what we had learned in the way we managed our people, and interacted with each other. There was also unanimous agreement that this would damage our careers.

Eventually, when there is a perceived gap between words and actions, more words about intentions, however worthy, will have a net, negative impact; even if "this time" they really are going to be followed by the promised actions.

Law 3   The resistance of an organization to change will be equal and opposite to the amount of effort put into changing it
This is the law that keeps the change agent awake at night. The more homogeneous, the more historically successful, and the more inbred in its ways the organization is, the less sleep the change agent can expect. The stronger the culture the stronger the pushback. If no way can be found to channel the resistance outside the result is stalemate. If the change agents are small in number and the only source of external force (see Law 1), the odds on them bringing about significant change are very low. Resistance takes many forms – badmouthing (the process, the last meeting, the leaders, the change agents, each other); withholding involvement (watch out for the silent ones, and for the participant with his chair perpetually drawn back from the table); applauding cynics (when you should be putting them down); protecting turf (instead of seeking the good of the whole); delegating to staff (the attendance at meetings and follow-through

work); focusing on the documents not the behaviors ("send the plan in, that'll get them off our backs"); deliberately misunderstanding (sticking to the letter of the request/rule/instruction and ignoring its intent).

In practice this resistance *must* be channeled outside, or removed, since this is the only way to avoid protracted internal conflict. The classic way of channeling resistance outside is to find an external enemy to blame for the pain, and whose defeat it can be claimed will make things better. The United States has done this for just about the whole of its existence. With a diverse, immigrant population and no centuries-long, shared, cultural history to act as a bond, it probably had no better strategy for avoiding internal strife. When the Soviet Union collapsed it was left with a very real, very large and very new challenge: to define its national purposes and values without having recourse to comparison with an obvious enemy. In an organization there is another solution – the removal of the sources of the resistance from the organization releasing the forces for change from combating them, and thus channeling their energy into the transformation. Ultimately this will be necessary anyway since the new management paradigm will demand the same degree of consistency of behavior as the old one did. This brings us back to the systems and processes in which the work of the organization is embodied and the behavior of its people. What has come to be called business process reengineering is aimed at removing the obstacles that outdated, uncompetitive systems and processes create. Training people in and recruiting people with the new skills, inculcating new cultural norms, changing the way performance is evaluated and rewarded and adopting new leadership and managerial behaviors are the complementary tasks for transforming the nature of work relationships. In particular, since the visible actions of senior managers are perceived as the embodiment of the organization's management paradigm, change will, at best, be very slow if there are not significant changes in their ranks. Even the most trusting believe you can't teach *many* old dogs *many* new tricks! Consequently who goes, and who replaces them, is the single most significant set of "events" in determining the amount, direction and speed of cultural change.

Even with all the right internal events, the path of change is not a smooth, upward progress from the moment of decision until transformation is complete. Like any other "war", the tide of battle between the old and the new ebbs and flows. Mistakes are made, resources squandered in ill-advised ventures and plans knocked off course by unanticipated external events. The path is rockiest of all in this critical area of cultural change because it is so tied up with people's emotions, and so impacted by the actions of key individuals. On top of that it is hostage to the way human beings cope with major change. So in this last section of our exploration of the challenge of transformation we will explore the trajectory that change is likely to take, and how its leaders can affect it (see Fig. 8.8).

A Attitudinal response to positively perceived change

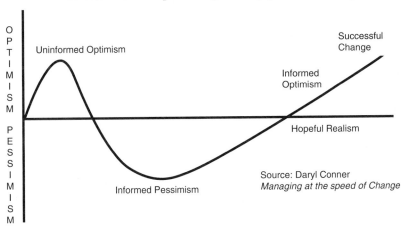

B Attitudinal response to negatively perceived change

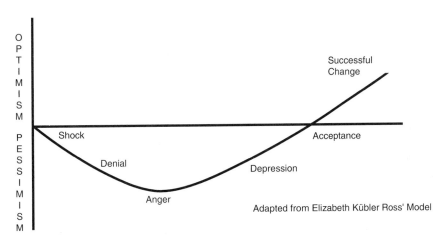

Fig. 8.8 *Attitudinal responses to change*

THE CHANGE TRAJECTORY

Figs 8.8A and 8.8B show the trajectory of attitudes towards an ultimately *successful* change initiative within a typical organization. Fig. 8.8A shows how those starting with a positive view of the declared intentions react; Fig. 8.8B those with an initially negative view. It seems to be an unavoidable Law of Change that, even for the most positively inclined, Uninformed Optimism is always followed by Informed Pessimism. Attitudinally things get worse before they get better. The graph in Fig. 8.8B is similar to the classical stages experienced by people informed of a life-threatening illness to themselves or to someone dear to them. The first steps toward recovery from alcohol or drug dependency show the same pattern.

At about the stage that the positively inclined are getting pessimistic, and the negatively inclined are getting angry, several things are typically going on. . .

- The promise of participation is turning into the burden of involvement
- Management's personal exposure in having to lead the transformation process, which they don't yet either know a great deal about or have a lot of confidence in, is becoming very apparent
- There is perceived to be a huge gap between what is being invested and what is being accomplished
- The sheer size of the task is becoming horrifyingly clear
- There are more people on the "Resistance" and "Denial" teams than the "Do it" team.

People in the organization are saying things like. . .

"Not another **?#*! meeting on this *!@**! process!"
"I'm not sure your/their/his/her process is working."
"This is just another process of the month. They're not serious."
"The last workshop didn't go well. I can't ask my people to waste any more time."
"This isn't going fast enough – we haven't the time."
"This is going too fast – we're not thinking deeply enough."
"If I don't see results soon, we're going to can it."
"*When* will it be over?"

Those trying to facilitate the process are saying things like. . .

"Boy, did I/you/he/she screw up that meeting."
"Were we ever arrogant to think we could make a difference."
"They don't like us, want us, respect us or what we're trying to do for them."
"X, Y and certainly Z ought to be shot."
"They're spending too much time on this – they need to decide something."
"They're spending too little time on this – they need to take this stuff more seriously."
"If I don't see results soon I'm going to give up."
"Flight attendant, I need another drink."

For the leader intent upon change, or the change agent intent on helping him or her, it is sobering to add the two graphs together, as in Fig. 8.9 (the break at the bottom is intentional).

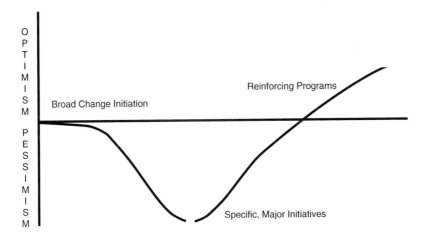

Fig. 8.9 *The change trajectory: positive and negative responses*

Fig. 8.9 is drawn assuming the sentiments pro- and against change are evenly weighted at the start. In my experience at the outset positive opinion often outweighs negative, because many people have known for a long time that change was needed. In this case the attitude at Broad Change Initiation will begin with a balance toward optimism, but it will still dip to a deep, negative low in *all* cases because both those who started with positive and negative attitudes experience a pessimistic low at about the same time. All this is quite normal (which doesn't stop it being terribly depressing every time, for even the most experienced of change agents!). But it does define the critical moment in the change process. The trajectory doesn't automatically turn upward. It has to be made to do so. At the lowest point of the curve, ultimate success is in the balance. It depends, just like the use of a general's strategic reserve at the critical moment in a battle, on the launching of specific, major initiatives reinforcing the commitment to change. These may build on any earlier successes but, more likely, they will be the kinds of steps we have already explored, removing major strategic, organizational and people underpinnings of the old paradigm, and clearly committing significant resources, of money and people, to the new paradigm.

What happens at this point will determine the success of the transformation.

Conclusion

"Of course one can 'go too far' and except in directions in which we can go too far there is no interest in going at all; and only those who will risk going too far can possibly find out how far one can go."   (T. S. Eliot)

"This is a story about four people named Everybody, Somebody, Anybody and Nobody. There was an important job to be done and Everybody was sure that Somebody would do it. Anybody could have done it, but Nobody did it. Somebody got angry about that, because it was Everybody's job. Everybody thought Anybody could do it, but Nobody realized that Everybody wouldn't do it. It ended up that Everybody blamed Somebody when Nobody did what Anybody could have done!"

(Anon)

Hopefully this book has given you some ideas about how to lead, manage and participate as your organization battles its way through the turbulent maze of competition, performance and change. Its lessons come from the school of hard knocks – what has actually happened to some of us who have tried to use the concept and tools of grand strategy during the two and a half decades in which the fourth economic wave of the American economy was slowing, maturing and giving way to a new economic order. In the Seventies we developed ideas of strategy in response to the new challenge of competition. In the Eighties we tackled the challenge of performance, and learned again the lessons of integration. By their end, and into the Nineties the monumental challenge of change had been added to our plates as the economy's very foundations began to shift, ultimately bringing into question the legitimacy of all of our most treasured institutions. We finally put all these things together into a comprehensive discipline called grand strategy which we are using, in the Nineties, to find the new ways of running our organizations that we will need to survive and succeed in the emerging new era. Let us remind ourselves briefly of some of the important things we have learned, and that this book has covered.

1. *The doers must be the planners.* Strategic planning is a line task to be undertaken by those responsible for the plan's implementation. The planner's and consultant's role is to manage the process, provide expertise on strategic thinking,

221

generate novel ideas, and act as devil's advocate. If there is no inside person who can do all those tasks *and* survive, outside assistance is a necessity.

2. *The "soft" issues are more important than the "hard" ones.* In the Seventies, managers did not talk about "soft" issues – e.g., mission, vision, purposes, beliefs, and values. They focused on "hard" issues – e.g., profits, costs, prices, market shares, and growth projections. In a world of accelerating change and unprecedented competition, however, issues that once were considered "hard" are now "soft", i.e., erratic, unreliable, and subject to unpredictable change. So to create a foundation for planning and for adjusting to change, we must make the so-called "soft" issues "hard", i.e., predictable, consistent, and stable. The key to effective strategy, therefore, is first to develop a clearly understood, broadly agreed-upon and qualitatively stated mission stipulating the organization's shared purposes and values, and the distinctive capabilities that must be developed to fulfil it.

3. *Measurement is essential to recognizable achievement.* Mission and the definition of distinctive capabilities *must* be qualitative if they are to survive in a rapidly changing world. However, they only become practical to implement if they have *quantified* measures, and objectives that define their accomplishment in any given time period. These objectives are unlikely to be reached unless they have equally specific strategies (i.e., resource commitments) focused on their achievement. Most failures in strategic planning can be attributed to lack of rigor in one or both of these steps. This is because such rigor both tests the viability of the grand strategy, represented by mission and distinctive capabilities, or goal statements, and provides the framework for monitoring and controlling implementation.

4. *If the effort does not result in action plans, it is probably wasted.* An action plan consists of a task, the responsibility for undertaking it, and a timeframe for accomplishing it. Even the greatest strategy with the most precise quantification is generally futile if it does not specify the steps, accountabilities, and timing to implement it. Without these steps, the plan is merely an aspiration or intent left to individual discretion.

5. *Strategy development is more about choice than analysis.* While information must be gathered and analyzed to reduce the need for intuition, the determination of strategy is ultimately a question of

choice in the face of uncertainty. This will always be the case since, even in a more certain age, there will be competitors whose actions will still be, at least to some extent, unpredictable.

6. *Strategy implementation is more about commitment than correctness.* An excellent strategy with adequate implementation will always lose to an adequate strategy with excellent implementation. However, the adequate plan must have deep personal and organizational commitment if its implementation is to be truly excellent. When a plan has that commitment, minor imperfections in strategy will easily be overcome by the sheer momentum of the organization.

7. *Change will occur, either by chance or design.* It is never the case that everything is running smoothly. Only a manager who is leaving change to chance would explain, as I have heard more than one do, that the planning effort is useful "even if it only confirms that the right things are being done already". Strategy is the deliberate attempt to beat evolution, i.e. to ensure the survival of the organization as one of the fittest, through strategic management. In a dynamic environment, the management of change is, therefore, the central purpose of strategic planning.

8. *Strategic change is about managing people, not money.* If the behavior of the people in an organization, especially that of the middle managers, does not change, then neither will its strategy. In fact, if the way financial resources are allocated changes, but the way human resources operate does not, the organization will probably be worse off than before. Strategy implementation must focus on the day-to-day decision-making behavior of the people in the organization. The right investment decisions will then follow naturally.

9. *Practice works, preaching does not.* "Do as I say, not as I do" does not work with children, so we should not expect it to work with adults. The organization's people must be shown that there is no gap between words and actions. It is a sad observation that in many organizations more people are penalized for adhering strictly to stated values than for not doing so. Only ruthless consistency of actions and statements, beginning at the highest organizational levels and applied for a long time, will result in fundamental change.

10. *There is no one, right dogma for anything.* With the exception of this rule, of course.

Not all these lessons have been accepted yet. Some of them are still controversial. Professors will no doubt develop theories to validate and refine them in due time. But we do not have to wait for that to take advantage of them. They have already been proved the hard way – by trial and error, in practice. Hopefully this book has given you enough confidence to try them yourself, to create the superior way of running your business that is the only competitive advantage on which you can rely in this turbulent era of unprecedented competitive intensity and accelerating change.

Now, finally, what lies ahead? What should you bear in mind, even as you begin to use the insights grand strategy will hopefully give you, so that you don't get caught unawares by the next advances in management technique that are surely just around the corner? I think the first thing to remember is that grand strategy is a comprehensive discipline, so that anything new that comes up should fit somewhere within its boundaries. Thus it is not so much a new, overarching methodology you should be looking for as advances in specific techniques within each of the areas of mission, competition, performance and change.

Having said that, I personally expect that the area of mission will become less urgent, at least at the level of the whole enterprise, insofar as far as it is satisfactorily dealt with in the next few years. Mission is not something that should need resetting very frequently for a whole organization, and only major change – which is the reason it is temporarily so universally important – should require revisiting it. I agree with Thomas Watson, Jr, that the values should never change (which is not to say they should not be reinterpreted in the light of new circumstances, which you will remember is what IBM failed to do). The task most organizations face is to codify them if they are just starting, and to rediscover and revitalize them if they are in need of transformation. Once that is done it is their purposes, the bases for the mutually beneficial relationships with each stakeholder group, that will have to be most carefully watched and managed, both at the level of the whole enterprise and for each venture within it, to make them the vital driver of strategy in the face of ever-changing needs.

Next, I also agree with Kenichi Ohmae that, in the area of strategy "what we need today, perhaps, is not a new theory, concept, or framework but people who can think strategically". So I would be wary of adopting yet another new technique of strategy, and much more inclined to put my organization's effort into teaching people to think strategically. We know how to do that (well, some of us do!) up to a really quite sophisticated level of understanding. The problem up to now is that both the importance and difficulty of strategic thinking have been seriously underestimated by the decision-makers on where consulting/educating/developing money will be spent.

However I do think there will be some very significant additions to the art of thinking strategically in the not too distant future, coming from our rapidly increasing understanding of the new sciences of chaos and complexity. Strategy has by and large developed in a world driven by traditional ideas of diminishing returns leading, for example, to economic equilibrium between competing technologies. Coal versus water power for generating electricity is a good example. As the best sites for hydro-electric power stations are used up, the marginal cost of electricity so produced goes up making coal power more attractive. Then as the most easily mined coal is used to capacity the reverse happens. The result is an equilibrium between the amount of electricity produced the two different ways set by the point where the cost of the next unit is the same from either source.

In the new world of, for example, software the investment in producing the first unit is huge and the cost thereafter is tiny. The result is that instead of "negative feedback" loops that bring about competitive equilibrium, there are "positive feedback" loops that can lead one competitor to drive others out completely. The victory of VHS videotape players over Betamax is a case in point. The greater adoption of the former than the latter at some critical point led to a mutually reinforcing cycle of people buying VHS players and the availability of VHS tapes that eventually drove Betamax out of the market. Yet Sony was apparently the more powerful company, with all the advantages under the previous rules (including, many would say, the better technology). So, how did it happen? What were the critical events that decisively shifted the market to VHS? And, how do you devise a deliberate strategy to make it happen in your favour? New ideas about strategy will soon emerge to try to deal with these kinds of situations.

In the area of performance, the new management paradigm – managing change – is in its infancy today. Consequently we can expect a lot of offerings and experimentation with techniques to implement it. New organizational forms will also be proposed to match the new kinds of work that are emerging in the new economy. The problem is going to be sorting the wheat from the chaff, to find the ideas that have staying power, and so will be incorporated into the new paradigm. One thing we can certainly expect is attempts to organize around business processes rather than the traditional functions. This will add to the already fierce debate about the dimensions through which to manage, and in particular the use of matrix structures.

The resistance of the old paradigm is seen at its very strongest whenever the matrix is raised. The most cherished notion of "command and control" is the one boss/single person accountability it inherited from the military. A *lot* of work is needed to develop concepts of shared accountability and multiple reporting relationships into practical operating procedures; and no less effort will be needed to help managers from the old paradigm learn to use them. One aspect of shared accountability that is already receiving considerable attention is cross-functional collaboration in pursuit of more effective business processes. We will increasingly see this emphasis on co-operating-to-compete move beyond the boundaries of traditional structures as strategic alliances between more focused, and specialized firms, joined together into "virtual corporations", become a common feature of the organizational landscape.

Finally, bringing about change will for a time be the hottest subject of all. What lies ahead here is clear – movement away from today's partial, deal-with-the-pieces-separately, individual problem-solving approach to a holistic, total system view of the challenge. Business process reengineering, *the* hot idea of the first half of the nineties, is already being reassessed as it has become apparent that a lot of the improvements it promised have not been realized, and even when there have been initial successes they have not been sustainable. Just before I sat down to finish this final chapter I read a review of *Reengineering Management* under the headline "Reengineering II – The sequel to an influential book (*Reengineering the Corporation,* Hammer and Champy, 1993) takes a softer approach to management." The new book recognizes, as its title suggests, that new processes were only part of the answer. Champy now focuses mostly on the need for change in the management of people if those new processes are to fulfil their promise. But there is more to it than even that as we have seen as we have built up the overarching discipline of grand strategy. What is needed is a truly holistic approach, addressing the totality of the organization, and so leading to a genuine transformation of management.

Perhaps the first book to be consistent with such an approach is *Transforming The Organization* by James Kelly and Francis Gouillart, published in April 1995. Their 4R model (Reframing, Restructuring, Revitalizing and Renewing) for business transformation is a one-to-one fit with the elements of grand strategy. It recognizes the systemic nature of relationships between these elements, and shows how only comprehensive change will suffice to give us the sustainable, long-term results the new economic order demands. As more and more academics, consultants and managers recognize that it is indeed a 'total system' change that is needed we will see a convergence of attention on this way of tackling the challenge, very similar to the convergence on a common body of strategic thinking in the Seventies. For the sake of everyone working in the organizations in desperate need of transformation today, let us hope that, this time, it doesn't take their leaders a whole decade to accept the new synthesis.

Most of this book has been about what groups and teams need to do, and what needs to be done to make them effective. So I would like to conclude with three thoughts – on courage, initiative and skill – for you, the reader, as an individual and leader who wants to put into practice some of what you've read.

As T. S. Eliot says above, of course one can "go too far". And you may have been tempted to conclude that I have at times done so in the starkness of my conclusions and recommendations, maybe for dramatic effect. Actually, I have tried very hard not to, and have double-checked my perceptions wherever I could with others familiar with what I have described. The fact is that these are simple truths and, as I said on the first page, there *are* some rules which the winners obey, and the losers don't. Wars and revolutions are painful affairs, and transformational change is about as close to them as you get, short of the loss of life, in peace. I cannot think of a situation involving a major change initiative where the danger from going too far was greater than the danger from not going far enough. Lou Mattis, Chairman of Sterling, looking back at the change process he and Jack Thomas had led once said to me, "Let's face it, Mike, what we did was turn the whole of Sterling into one gigantic laboratory". That was a leap of faith, taken because there were only two things they were certain of: that everything they knew when they started would not suffice, and that the one thing they knew wouldn't work was to do nothing. Strategy, integration, change – these are not areas where half-measures, caution, or going slow succeed. Remember that Clausewitz was in fact talking about prudence when he said, "No one in his right mind tries to cross a broad ditch in two steps". I have seen, and tried to rescue from drowning, oh so many people and organizations who have tried to do in two steps what could only be done in one. So the first characteristic required of those who would lead change is courage.

My second thought is taken from the second quote at the beginning of the Conclusion, a sad little tale, but probably as good an epitaph on most organization's attempts at change as has been written, "It ended up that Everybody blamed Somebody when Nobody did what Anybody could have done." Before Lou Mattis and Jack Thomas initiated the Sterling change process, Herb McKenzie, one of the all-time, great, tribal leaders, had begun experimenting with some of these ideas in a division of the pre-Kodak-takeover Sterling Drug called JCAP (Japan, Canada, Australasia, Pacific Rim), a hodge-podge of units with low prestige and little importance to the leaders of the company. He pointed out to me, when I made my initial proposal, that I was talking about things that should start at the top, with the Chairman and President of the company. He was right, but was he going to wait to see if that would happen? No way. He began the initiative that first created a team out of JCAP, then made Sterling International the fastest improving part of Sterling, and finally helped Sterling meet its commitments to its new owner for twenty-five successive quarters. Nobody got mad at Anybody because Somebody did what Everybody eventually had to do!

So, don't wait, most breakthroughs come from the wrong people, in the wrong place, at the wrong time. Take the initiative, now.

Thirdly there are some intellectual skills you will need along the way. They have been called the skills of leaders, or "conceptual" skills or the third career skill – to distinguish them from the "technical" skills that are the basis for our first jobs, and the "human" skills that we need as we progress to the job of managing others and interacting with other areas of our organizations. There are five of them:

1. To be able to ask and answer the question, "Why?"
2. To see beyond the pieces of the problem to the whole puzzle
3. To understand interactions between elements of systems, and the nature of feedback effects
4. To recognize the long-run consequences of short-run actions
5. To see the generic, or general truth behind the specific, or particular example.

These are the skills that distinguish great leaders, not charisma, or speaking skills, or empathy with others. The latter characteristics can be useful when placed at the service of those with high conceptual ability, and the initative and courage to use it. They are downright dangerous when not guided by conceptual rigor. And, as Lucius Annaeus Seneca wrote long ago, "No man ever got wise by chance." It takes practice, which means errors, and failure, and pain. But developing conceptual skill is the foundation for exercising leadership.

I'll end as I began, with Thomas Watson, Jr. Whatever happened to IBM, whatever will happen to IBM, he gave us a glimpse, or more accurately a long look at what it means to conceive, and implement a grand strategy, and thus create the foundation for the long-term competitive health of a business:

> One may speculate at length as to the cause of the decline or fall of a corporation. Technology, changing tastes, changing fashions, all play a part. But the fact remains that some companies manage to flourish while others in the very same industry may falter or fail. Normally we ascribe these differences to such things as business competence, market judgment, and the quality of leadership in a corporation. Each one of these is a vital factor. No one can dispute their importance. But I question whether they in themselves are decisive.

> I believe the real difference between success and failure in a corporation can very often be traced to the question of how well the organization brings out the great energies and talents of its people. What does it do to help these people find common cause with each other? How does it keep them pointed in the right direction despite the many rivalries and differences which may exist among them? And how can it sustain this common cause and sense of direction through the many changes which take place from one generation to another?

Appendix 1:
The Dimensions of Value

Value is created by *choosing* attractive industries (or, more commonly, segments) within which to compete, by *achieving* positions of competitive advantage within them and by *utilizing* resources efficiently and effectively to turn the vision of strategic success into the reality of financial returns (see Fig. A1.1).

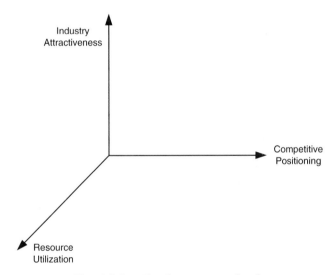

Fig. A1.1   *The dimensions of value*

- *Industry Attractiveness* provides the basis for predicting the average returns available in an industry and their risk. It looks at the forces which determine the general pressures on the profitability available to all players in an industry (or business, or market segment depending on the level of analysis) to assess how high that is likely to be, and how much it can be expected to vary over time.
- *Competitive Positioning* provides the basis for predicting how a given company will perform relative to its industry peers. It looks at the strategic (i.e., relative) characteristics of companies that have been shown to correlate with profitability to assess how high that is likely to be for each player.

- *Resource Utilization* then provides the basis for predicting how well a given company will translate the potential for profit defined by the first two dimensions into an actual return on investment. It looks at the way resources are actually utilized and assesses how this will turn into future cashflows.

INDUSTRY ATTRACTIVENESS

We will now consider each dimension in turn, exploring the variables that make it up (see Table A1.1).

Table A1.1 Industry attractiveness variables

---

1. Growth Rate
2. Number of Competitors
3. Number of Customers
4. Product Significance to buyer *(i.e. its criticality vs. how much it costs)*
5. Number of Suppliers
6. Regulation
7. R&D Intensity *(i.e. R&D as a percentage of Sales)*
8. Cyclicality *(not seasonality)*
9. Experience Curve effect *(ability to turn learning into lower costs)*
10. Marketing Intensity *(i.e. Marketing Costs as a percentage of Sales)*

Some thought about each of the above variables before you read on will greatly enhance the value of what follows. To assist that thought, ask yourself: "If this variable is high, does that make for an attractive industry?" If yes, put an H (for High) next to it; if no, put an L (for Low). Remember attractiveness is defined here as meaning good returns available to players already in the industry.

Growth Rate

You almost certainly put an H. But why? We all think of high growth making for an attractive industry, but why specifically is this the case with our definition of attractiveness – that there are high returns available to all current players?

The answer can be seen from the illustration of prices and relative costs we used in an earlier chapter (see Fig. A1.2). Let's say Competitor B is the "marginal competitor", that is the competitor with the highest costs. When growth is high Competitor B needs as big a profit margin as it can get to fund that growth. In the illustration let's say there is a 12% growth rate in the industry and Competitor B's margin of 10% gives it just enough cash to

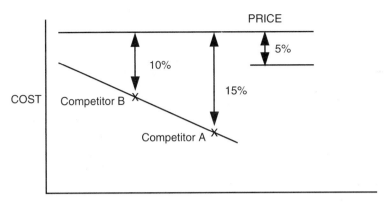

Fig. A1.2 *The importance of relative cost*

grow at that rate and not lose market share. Now what happens if growth slows, say to 6%. Competitor B now has a significant "surplus" cash flow it doesn't need to plow back into investment to provide it with the capacity to grow. The most likely use for those surplus funds in this competitive world is to try to continue to grow as before by gaining market share. Almost always this means bringing down the price level and hence the return of all the players. So the higher the growth the higher margins needed to fund that growth, and hence the higher the profitability of all players in the industry.

Number of Competitors

The answer here is Low. The smaller the number of competitors the more their behavior can be expected to be oligopolistic in nature and hence the more competitively stable the industry is likely to be. Profitability is highest when all players feel that there is more to be lost than gained from disturbing the competitive equilibrium. The smaller the number of players, and the bigger the gaps between them, the more likely they are to conclude that this is the case.

Number of Customers

Those who have studied Michael Porter's Competitive Intensity matrix will have answered High. Reason – the more customers there are the lower their individual buyer power (i.e., ability to dictate price). Interestingly though it turns out there is a limit: the companies with the highest number of customers in a given industry are usually not the most profitable. It appears that there are real economies of scale in serving customers so that as their number goes up costs rise, eventually offsetting the gains in prices from decreasing purchasing power. What that means for practical strategy is that the number of customers should be constantly monitored, and experimented with, to keep as close to the optimal point as possible. Here "customers" means those to whom our product is immediately sold but, in many cases, there is the added complication of trade customers and end consumers. The same thinking applies to both groups who can equally properly be thought of as "customers". However there is only one "king" (as in "the customer is king") – the end consumer!

Product Significance

The answer is High. The more important a product is to a customer, and lower its cost relative to other things that must be bought, the less price sensitive that customer will be. Some examples – cholesterol-lowering drugs, radial tires (Michelin: "So much is resting on your tires"), and sadly perhaps the ultimate, "O" rings for Space Shuttles.

Number of Suppliers

High, and exactly the same logic applies as with customers. There is an optimal point, which is much lower than most of us have thought as the motor industry finally found out in the Eighties, because of the value of strategic partnerships with suppliers as the world becomes a more and more complex place to compete in.

Regulation

This is an interesting one. Most American business people instinctively put Low because we have been taught since grade school that government interference in business is a "bad thing". But what would an Airline or Savings & Loan (Building Society) say? The impact of deregulation may have been hugely in the consumers' interest but, by making competition broader and freer, it has also reduced the profitability of many industries. So the answer is mixed. From the viewpoint of industry attractiveness there is "good" and there is "bad" regulation. The strategist needs to be careful not to take a monolithic view, and to see how regulation can be used to advantage to build entry barriers against potential and existing competitors.

R&D Intensity

As a general rule high R&D intensity makes for higher industry-wide profitability, because it creates the potential for (often patented) differentiation, and barriers to entry against those without the know-how it can provide. Where R&D can lead to lower profitability is when it is unproductive, but this is really a company- not industry-specific problem.

Cyclicality

For whole industries cyclicality leads to lower profitability. When coupled with high fixed cost, (e.g., Paper mills), or low entry barriers (e.g., property and casualty insurance), the result is usually that the scramble for profits in good times means they never get high enough for long enough to make up for the terrible returns of bad times.

Experience Curve Effect

The answer is emphatically High. The Experience Curve is the phenomenon discovered by the Boston Consulting Group as the "B" phase of the fourth wave began, that the cost of producing something can be made to drop by a constant percentage each time the *accumulated* volume (i.e., experience) of producing it doubles. Given the importance of relative cost as a determinant of profitability, the more experience translates into lower costs the greater the entry barrier to those not already in the industry.

Marketing Intensity

High – and this may be the most important characteristic of the lot. Earlier in this book there have been quotes about the number of companies that have disappeared from the *Fortune* 100 and 500. The same is not true of brands. A US study of the twenty-five strongest consumer brands in 1925 and 1985 revealed that twenty-one of the original list were still there sixty years later! The consumer's need for a surrogate for trust in product efficacy and quality, in an age of increasing information overload, plus the inertia of habit, make the importance of brand a tremendous force for higher profitability. The huge figures companies have been prepared to pay for portfolios of established brands during the Nineties attest to the value consumer goods strategists put on them, particularly when compared to the cost and risk of trying to establish a new one.

Component	Trend ← ? →					What to do about it
	– –	–	0	+	+ +	
Growth rate	Negative				High	
Competitive concentration	Many Cos				Few Cos	
Customer concentration	Few cust				Many cust	
Product significance	Low				High	
Supplier concentration	Few suppliers			Many suppliers		
Regulation	"Bad"				"Good"	
R&D intensity	Low				High	
Cyclicality	Very cyclical			Not cyclical		
Experience curve	Flat				Steep	
Marketing intensity	Low				High	

Fig. A1.3 *Industry attractiveness work form*

COMPETITIVE POSITIONING

We will consider seven variables. I suggest you again think about each before reading what follows, putting an H (for *H*igher) this time, and an L (for *L*ower) depending on which you think means a stronger, competitive position. Remember that stronger position is defined as the potential for achieving higher profitability than competitors in the industry (see Table A1.2).

Table A1.2 Competitive positioning variables

1.	Market Share
2.	Market Rank
3.	Quality Image
4.	New Product Intensity
5.	Product Line Breadth
6.	Cost Position
7.	Selling & Distribution Integration

Market Share

Higher, yes. But why? And what is a high market share? As we will discuss in a moment it is really *relative* market share that matters, but studies usually show that higher market share by itself correlates positively with higher profitability. The reason is probably that it often cross-correlates with some other positive factors such as higher relative market share and smaller number of competitors. In general it is relative market share that indicates strength of competitive position – so 30% is strong if the next competitor has 20%, and weak if it has 40%.

Market Rank

It follows from the above that market rank, i.e., place in the industry in terms of size, is of vital importance in the assessing of the potential for superior profitability. Let us return to the Experience Curve for a moment to see why. Relative accumulated experience (which dictates relative cost position) is the same as relative market share if the latter stays stable for any length of time. If I have higher market share in a given year, I add more to my experience than my competitor that year. If our shares stay stable my greater experience, hence potential for lower cost, is accurately measured by my greater market share, i.e., higher market rank. Moreover the strongest brand, the competitor with the highest market share, usually also enjoys the highest price realization because of its greater power in the market-place. So share wins at both ends – cost and price. Jack Welch says he will only stay in a business if it has the potential to be number 1 or 2 in its industry. This certainly supports his view.

The critical question is market rank in *what* industry? Or, market share of *what*? i.e., What is the segment in which we are measuring share? Let's use the US motor industry again to illustrate, and let's take a time (say, the early Sixties) before the impact of the Japanese outside their own market (see Fig. A1.4). There were two routes to profitability – low cost and differentiation, which at its extreme is what Michael Porter called "niche". It clearly makes no sense to measure the market share of Rolls Royce or Mercedes against General Motors. They weren't and aren't selling in the same market-place. Thus the segmentation decision becomes crucial both in terms of understanding what is driving profitability, and in terms of strategic focus to improve it.

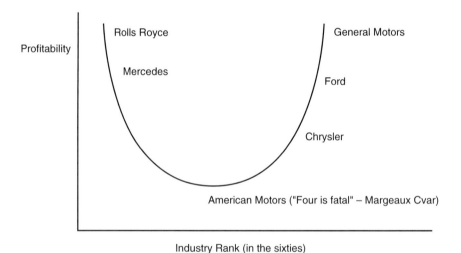

Fig. A1.4 *Industry rank and profitability*

Quality Image

The higher the customer perceives quality relative to other offerings the higher will be profitability. Customers reward suppliers in many ways for higher quality – higher prices, less hassle, loyalty and recommendations, to mention but a few. Why do the very poor Nigerians buy expensive Mercedes trucks? Because they don't break down in remote places. As mentioned above, for a long time much of western manufacturing seemed to believe that high quality and low cost were mutually exclusive characteristics. Partly this was a confusion between features and quality, but it was mostly because for too long we aimed, inefficiently and inexactly, to maximize quantity (out of the volume maximizing habit, created by the demand-exceeding-supply characteristics of the immediate post-war period), and inspected quality in after the event. The Japanese have taught us two very important and painful lessons about quality. First, high quality is the route to low cost, not its enemy. And second, the only satisfactory definition of quality is Total Customer Satisfaction.

New Product Intensity

Higher, if they are truly new and not last year's products warmed over, with the label "new and improved" affixed to them. A stream of new products keeps competitors, in particular those pursuing a "follower" strategy, off balance. It gives the salesforce an extra weapon, and enables the company to keep up with the ever-evolving nature of demand.

Product Line Breadth

Typically the people from sales and marketing people answer Higher, those from finance and manufacturing, Lower. The data suggest that the former are more right in theory, but the latter have a good point in practice. A broad product line is a potent weapon in the market-place, but can be a fierce adder of cost internally. Here we face a crucial, focus decision in a form that impacts every function in the organization. Yet it is amazing how many companies try to take this decision without recognizing that it requires all of the functions to be present, since it involves one of the most basic of trade-offs. However it is resolved, subsequent action also requires the contribution of all the functions, since it involves the orchestrated combination of activities and resource deployments which is the essence of strategy.

Cost Position

Facing the evidence of the last few years, it would be a true (and probably confused) contrarian who did not answer, Lower. Low cost is the condition to enter the competition at all. Now that every competitor has absorbed the lesson of quality, so that it is rapidly ceasing to be a source of significant differentiation anymore, to be anything other than truly cost competitive is to commit corporate suicide. The Nineties has been called the "value" decade where the customer looks with great suspicion at anything beyond the basic product, at high quality and a low cost. The campaign for higher productivity and lower cost that has swept through US industry, and now *has* to have its same devastating impact in Europe if there are to be any decent jobs left there at all, is not a one-time corrective action but a management focus that must last forever. The good news is that, if it does, jobs of the future will prove inherently more secure than they have in so many of the great companies during the latter part of the fourth wave.

Selling and Distribution Integration

Here is another characteristic that causes debate, because the answer is affected by the particular circumstances of each company, each segment and each industry. Yet the bias must be in favour of Higher, since the alternative is to risk someone else having control over the most crucial relationships for any organization – those with its customers or clients. It is a weakness that companies entering new markets are particularly prone to. They need the distribution scale and savvy of the local player, but too often end up hostage to that capability by not building it for themselves. The all-time champion has to be Heineken, the number 1 imported beer in America, which many years ago gave Van Munching of New York the sole right to import its beer *in perpetuity*! The only way out – to buy Van Munching at a very high price, to gain control of what had become a very important part of its business.

Component	Trend ← ? → − − − 0 + + +					What to do about it
Market share	Low				High	
Market rank	Low				High	
Quality image	Low				High	
New product intensity	Few				Many	
Product line breadth	Narrow				Broad	
Cost position	High				Low	
Selling & distribution integration	Low				High	

Fig. A1.5 *Competitive positioning work form*

RESOURCE UTILIZATION

The third dimension of value determines how well the potential of the first two are turned into realized returns. Ask yourself the same High/Low question on each of the eight variables in Table A1.3 before reading on.

Table A1.3   Resource utilization variables

1.   Value-Added per Employee
2.   Unionization (*or labour rigidity*)
3.   Capacity Utilization
4.   Value-Added per Overhead Dollar
5.   Vertical Integration
6.   Working Capital
7.   Fixed Investment
8.   Long-Term Liabilities

Value-added per Employee

It is easy to answer High; how could it be anything else? And in general that is true, but it turns out that the companies with the very highest value-added per employee do not have the highest profitability. There comes a point where employees get over-stretched, burnout sets in and there are no spare resources to take advantage of the unexpected opportunity.

Unionization (or labor rigidity)

Most readers will answer Lower, and they will be right most of the time, at least in the Anglo-Saxon countries. It is a sad, sad thing that history has resulted in one set of employees, management, being at odds with another, the unionized. Now that management and owners are almost universally separate groups of people it is an absurd and unnecessary conflict. Yet it exists and the statistics reflect it – unionization tends to mean lower profitability, again, at least in the Anglo-Saxon countries. An exception to the rule is the company which strongly expects to be unionized at some time. Here voluntary, upfront creation of a mutually beneficial relationship with a single union can avert more conflict-bound unionization, quite possibly by several unions, at a later date. This strategy has proved very successful for new entrants in the United Kingdom in the last two decades.

Capacity Utilization

Clearly high capacity utilization leads to better profitability than low. However, similarly to value-added per employee, the companies with the highest capacity utilization are not the most profitable, and for similar reasons. There is no spare capacity for unexpected opportunities, maintenance gets deferred, quality suffers and overhead costs rise. High, but not to the limit seems to be the optimal target.

Value-added per Overhead Dollar

Much of the recent efforts at cost-cutting have been aimed at overhead. No one is against low overhead costs, hence high value-added per overhead dollar. In theory we should reach a limit here too, since overhead is never (at least in theory!) added for a bad reason. So, at some point, something must be sacrificed by cutting it back. In practice that point is a long way off in even the leanest organizations I have seen.

Vertical Integration

This is a trade-off – between control, which is enhanced by increasing vertical integration (i.e., ownership of the steps in the value-adding chain from raw materials through to after-sales service), and flexibility which is higher with outside sourcing. The critical issues in the decision are: (1) who can perform a given step most effectively and efficiently? and (2) is it of strategic importance to have proprietary control of a particular capability?

One of the signature characteristics of the new economy is going to be a huge swing away from vertical integration. We will more and more recognize the value of focus, and develop strategies based on collaborative relationships of strategic partnering between highly specialized firms, in particular supplier/customer alliances, to replace the costly, turf-ridden, bureaucracy-intensive, inward-looking structures of ownership and control.

Working Capital

On Receivables, the Vice-President of Finance answers Low, and the Vice-President of Sales answers High. Again it's a trade-off. No one wants excess working capital, but the value of the marginal, additional sale can be very high. On Inventory it's the same; we don't want capital tied up in excess, maybe aging inventory, but there are real sales opportunities, and economies of production-run length that are sacrificed if the nature of the trade-offs is not properly recognized. It is shocking how few companies reflect the importance of finding the optimal point in the way they take working capital decisions. They are usually taken by edict in the name of improving short-term cash flow, by freeing up capital; they should be seen for what they are – strategic decisions requiring the proper attention of all the functions involved.

Fixed Investment

The lower you can make fixed investment the better. The higher it is, the more it increases the capital base on which a return must be made and reduces flexibility to respond to the changing environment. The nature of the business determines the level of general capital intensity relative to other businesses. Within that constraint the competitors who keep their fixed investments down are the most profitable.

Long-term Liabilities

It is surprising how many people say Low when, given that the simple criterion we are using is what leads to higher profitability, the economic answer is clearly High. Debt is a cheaper way of financing assets than equity (and its cost – interest – is tax-deductible making it cheaper still), so its use enhances point-in-time profitability. The real issue is one of risk. Again we have a trade-off. Financial risk is increased by adding debt, since the interest must be paid and the higher it is the more the company risks insolvency. However, *business* risk is decreased by adding debt, because it reduces the price that needs to be charged to make the same return on equity. This is why we use the terms leverage or gearing when referring to the debt/equity ratio. With a fixed profit margin, return on equity is a function of how much debt is used – the debt levers the margin into a higher return. So, contrary to conventional wisdom, business and financial decisions are not independent. They must be taken together in the full knowledge of competitors' attitudes to them, so that the optimal balance between the two kinds of risk is achieved.

Component	Trend ← ? →					What to do about it
	− −	−	0	+	+ +	
Value-added per employee	Low				High	
Unionization	Highly unionized		No unions			
Capacity utilization	Low				High	
Overhead value-added	Low				High	
Vertical integration	Low flexibility		High flexibility			
	Low control		High control			
Working capital	High				Low	
Fixed investment	High				Low	
Long-term liabilities	Low D/E			High D/E		

Fig. A1.6 *Resource utilization work form*

Appendix 2: The Dimensions of Functional Value

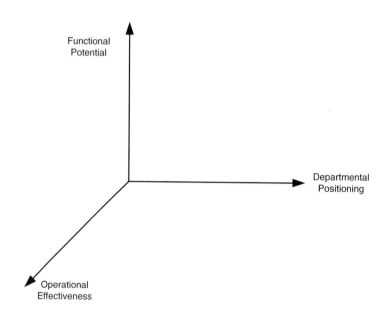

Fig. A2.1 *The dimensions of functional value*

- *Functional Potential* provides the basis for assessing the contribution this function could make to the business. It looks at the need for the function, how important are its inputs and how available are its skills to assess what contribution it could make to the organization.
- *Departmental Positioning* provides the basis for assessing how well the function is positioned to deliver on its potential. It looks at how much it is being used and what its reputation is to assess what contribution it is likely to be able to make, relative to what it could.
- *Operational Effectiveness* provides the basis for determining how well the functional will actually perform. It considers the function's operational characteristics to assess how it is turning its potential and positioning into value-added for the enterprise.

There are respectively ten, seven and six variables making up these dimensions, as Table A2.1 shows.

Table A2.1 The variables of functional value

Functional potential	Departmental positioning	Operational effectiveness
Expenditure Growth	"Customer" Penetration – Absolute	Employee Productivity
Sources of Service	"Customer" Penetration – Relative to Potential	Unionization (or labor rigidity)
Breadth of Application		Capacity Utilization
Service Significance (cost vs. criticality)	Quality Image	Supervisory/ Administrative Productivity
Availability of Skills	New Service Intensity	
Legal/Regulatory Requirement	Number of Services	Internal Self-Sufficiency
	Cost Position	Capital Investment
Technological Change	Centralization/ Decentralization	
Stability of Need		
Experience Curve Effect		
User Understanding		

Figs A2.2–A2.4 illustrate each dimension to facilitate their application as a diagnostic and strategy development device.

Component	Trend ← ? →					What to do about it
	− −	−	0	+	++	
Expenditure growth	Negative				High	
Sources of service	Many				Few	
Breadth of application	Narrow				Wide	
Service significance	Low				High	
Availability of skills	High				Low	
Legal/ regulatory requirement	"Bad"				"Good"	
Technological change	Low				High	
Stability of need	Very unstable			Very stable		
Experience Curve Effect	Flat				Steep	
User understanding	High				Low	

Fig. A2.2 *Functional potential work form*

Component	Trend ← ? →					What to do about it
	− −	−	0	+	+ +	
"Customer" penetration – absolute	Low				High	
"Customer" penetration – relative to potential	Low				High	
Quality image	Low				High	
New service intensity	Few				Many	
Number of services	Few				Many	
Cost position	High				Low	
Centralization/ decentralization	Highly centralized				Highly decentralized	

Fig. A2.3 *Departmental positioning work form*

Component	Trend ← ? →					What to do about it
	− −	−	0	+	+ +	
Employee productivity	Low				High	
Unionization (or labor rigidity)	Highly unionized			No unions		
Capacity utilization	Low				High	
Supervisory/ administrative productivity	Low				High	
Internal self-sufficiency	Low				High	
Capital investment	High				Low	

Fig. A2.4   *Operational effectiveness work form*

Appendix 3: The Principles of Competition

DIRECTION

The Objective

Every business endeavor must be directed toward a clearly defined, decisive and attainable objective. The ultimate objective is the achievement of sufficient, sustainable competitive advantage to allow the enterprise to fulfill its purposes. The objective of each endeavor must contribute to this ultimate objective. Each intermediate objective must be such that its attainment will most directly, quickly and economically contribute to the purpose of each endeavor.

The selection of an objective is based upon the means available, competition and the marketplace. Every manager must understand and clearly define his or her objective and consider each contemplated action in light thereof.

1. Can we achieve sufficient competitive advantage to fulfill our purposes?
2. What is the objective of this proposal?
3. In what way does it contribute to the ultimate objective?
4. How will the outcome be determined?
5. Is it attainable with the resources available?
6. Does it take proper account of possible competitive actions?
7. Is it based on a realistic view of the marketplace?
8. Are intermediate objectives clear steps toward the main objective?

The Initiative

Taking the initiative is necessary to achieve positions of advantage and maintain freedom of action. It permits the manager to impose his or her will on competition; to set the pace and determine the course of development of opportunities; to exploit competitive weakness and rapidly changing situations; and to meet unexpected developments.

251

A posture of reacting to competitive moves may be forced on the manager but should be deliberately adopted only as a temporary expedient while awaiting an opportunity to return to the initiative; or for the purpose of avoiding the expenditure of resources in an area where a position of advantage is not sought. Even when reacting, the manager should seek every opportunity to seize the initiative and achieve positions of advantage.

1. In what way are we being leaders in implementing this proposal?
2. What positions of advantage will successful implementation bring?
3. How will our freedom of action be sustained or enhanced?
4. How will we be controlling the development of the business?
5. What competitive weaknesses are we exploiting?
6. What occurring or anticipated change are we exploiting?

FOCUS

Scale

Superior resources must be concentrated at the critical time and place to achieve advantage. Superiority results from the proper combinations of the resource elements. Proper application of the principle of scale, in conjunction with the other principles of strategy may permit an organization with overall, inferior resources to achieve decisive superiority at the point of competition.

1. What are the points of critical competitive interaction?
2. What will determine the outcome of conflict at those points?
3. What are the nature and amount of our competition's resources focused on those points?

Economy

Skilful and prudent use of resources will enable the manager to accomplish his or her mission with minimum expenditure thereof. This principle is the corollary of the principle of scale. It does not imply withholding resources but rather their measured allocation to the primary task, as well as secondary tasks that can lead competition to over-allocate their resources elsewhere, and thus ensure sufficient superiority at the point of competition.

1. How does the amount of allocated resources measure up to the task?
2. Have resources been allocated to cause competition to over-allocate elsewhere?

Flexibility

Flexibility is an essential ingredient in the allocation of resources. It contributes materially in exploiting successes and in preserving freedom of action and reducing vulnerability. The object is to be able to bring to bear resources in such a manner as to place competition at a relative disadvantage and thus achieve results which otherwise would be more costly to attain.

Maintaining flexibility involves organization, the attitude of leadership and adaptability of control as well as the technical ability to redeploy assets. It is the antithesis of permanent allocation of resources and implies avoidance of stereotyped patterns of operation.

1. How easily will we be able to re-allocate different resources?
2. Do we have any spare resources of the potentially critical kinds?
3. How easily can we change organization, and then achieve new effectiveness?
4. Do we have leaders with the right abilities to adapt in the right places?
5. Can our information and control systems cope with change?

IMPLEMENTATION

Unity of Leadership

The decisive application of available resources requires unity of leadership. Unity of leadership obtains unity of effort by the co-ordinated action of all parties toward a common goal. While co-ordination may be attained by co-operation, it is best achieved by vesting a single manager with the requisite authority.

1. Do we have responsibility, authority and accountability clearly and consistently assigned?
2. How will achievement/failure be treated?
3. What kinds of co-ordination will be needed between which parties?
4. In what ways have we ensured the required co-operation will occur?

Security

Security is essential to the preservation of resources. Security is achieved by measures taken to prevent surprise, preserve freedom of action and deny competition information of proposed plans. Since risk is inherent in business, application of the principle of security does not imply undue caution and the avoidance of calculated risk. Security frequently is enhanced by bold seizure and retention of the initiative, which denies competition the opportunity to interfere.

1. What measures have been taken to avoid surprise?
2. What information must be kept secure, and how will that be achieved without handicapping the operation?
3. What opportunities exist to take a lesser risk to guard against a greater one?
4. What actions are we taking to reduce competitions' ability to interfere?

Surprise

Surprise can decisively shift the balance of competitive advantage. By surprise, success out of proportion to the effort expended may be obtained. Surprise results from taking a competitive initiative at a time, place, and in a manner for which competition is not prepared. It is not essential that competition be taken unaware but only that it becomes aware too late to react effectively. Factors contributing to surprise include speed, deception, application of unexpected resources, effective information gathering and variations in methods of operation.

1. In which ways will surprise be achieved?
2. What competitive advantage will accrue from those surprises?
3. How will surprise lead to competitive inability to react effectively?

Simplicity

Simplicity contributes to successful operations. Direct, simple plans and clear, concise directives minimize misunderstanding and confusion. If other factors are equal, the simplest plan is preferred.

1. Are there simpler options for achieving specific objectives?
2. How have we ensured the potential for misunderstanding has been minimized?
3. What mechanisms have we established for eliminating confusion when it arises?

	STRATEGIC OPTIONS		
PRINCIPLES	A	B	C
The Objective			
The Initiative			
Scale			
Economy			
Flexibility			
Unity of Leadership			
Security			
Surprise			
Simplicity			
TOTAL			

Evaluating Questions:

1. What does intuition say about the results?
2. Should any of the principles receive special weighting?
3. Does a very low score anywhere constitute a veto?
4. Is there a combination of options which is better still?

Fig. A3.1 *Evaluating strategic options*

Bibliography

Ackerman, Carl W. *George Eastman* (Boston: Houghton Miflin Company, 1930).

Albrecht, Karl. *The Northbound Train: Finding the Purpose, Setting the Direction, Shaping the Destiny of Your Organization* (New York: AMACOM, 1994).

Alexander, Bevin. *How Great Generals Win* (New York: W.W. Norton, 1993).

Andrews, K.R. *The Concept of Corporate Strategy* (Homewood, IL: Irwin, 1980).

Ansoff, Igor. *Corporate Strategy* (New York: John Wiley, 1988).

Ansoff, Igor. *Implanting Strategic Management* (New York: John Wiley, 1979).

Argyris, Chris. *Overcoming Organizational Defenses* (Boston: Allyn and Bacon, 1990).

Ayres, Robert U. *Technological Forecasting and Social Change* (New York: McGraw-Hill and Elserio Science Publishing Co., 1969).

Bennis, Warren G., and Nanus, Bert. *Leaders: The Strategies for Taking Charge* (New York: Harper & Row, 1985).

Birch, David. *Job Creation in America: How Our Smallest Companies Put the Most People to Work* (New York: Free Press, 1987).

Boston Consulting Group. *Perspectives on Experience* (Boston: BCG, 1972).

Bradford, David L. *Managing for Excellence: The Guide to Developing High Performance in Contemporary Organizations* (New York: John Wiley, 1984).

Brandt, Steven C. *Entrepreneuring in Established Companies: Managing Toward the Year 2000* (Homewood, IL: Dow Jones-Irwin, 1986).

Burns, James M. *Leadership* (New York: Harper & Row, 1978).

"Business New Link: Ethics and the Bottom Line", *Industry Week* (October 1984).

Carkhuff, Robert R. *The Age of the New Capitalism* (Amherst, MA: Human Resource Development Press, 1988).

Carlzon, Jan. *Moments of Truth* (Cambridge, MA: Ballinger Publishing Co., 1987).

Champy, James. *Reengineering Management; The Mandate for New Leadership: Managing the Change to the Reengineered Corporation* (New York: Harper Business, 1995).

Chandler, Alfred D., Jr. *Scale and Scope: The Dynamics of Industrial Capitalism* (Cambridge, MA: The Belknap Press of Harvard University Press, 1990).

257

Chandler, Alfred D., Jr. *The Visible Hand: The Managerial Revolution in American Business* (Cambridge, MA: The Belknap Press of Harvard University Press, 1977).

Chandler, Alfred D., Jr. *Strategy and Structure: Chapters in the History of the American Industrial Enterprise* (Cambridge, MA: MIT Press, 1962).

Clausewitz, C. von. *On War* (New York: Dutton, 1918).

Cohen, Allan R., and Bradford, David F. *Influence without Authority* (New York: John Wiley, 1991).

Conner, Daryl R. *Managing at the Speed of Change: How Resilient Managers Succeed and Prosper When Others Fail* (New York: Villard Books, 1993).

Davis, Stan M. *Managing Corporate Culture in the 1990s* (New York: Harper Business, 1991).

de Geus, A. P. "Planning as Learning." *Harvard Business Review* (March/April 1988) 70–74.

Dent, Harry S., Jr. *The Great Boom Ahead: Your Comprehensive Guide to Personal and Business Profit in the New Era of Prosperity* (New York: Hyperion, 1993).

DePree, Max. *Leadership is an Art* (New York: Doubleday, 1989).

Donaldson, Gordon A., and Lorsch, Jay W. *Decision Making at the Top: The Shaping of Strategic Direction* (New York: Basic Books, 1983).

Drucker, Peter F. *Post-Capitalist Society* (New York: Harper Business, 1993).

Drucker, Peter F. *Managing for the Future: The Nineteen Nineties and Beyond* (New York: Dutton-Truman Talley, 1992).

Drucker, Peter F. *The New Realities: In Government & Politics – In Economics & Business – In Society & World View* (New York: Harper & Row, 1990).

Enrico, Roger, and Kornbluth, Jesse. *The Other Guy Blinked: How Pepsi Won the Cola Wars* (New York: Bantam Books, 1986).

Fuller, J.F.C. *The Conduct of War: 1789–1961* (New York: DaCapo Press, 1992).

Gardner, John W. *On Leadership* (New York: Free Press, 1989).

Gardner, John W. *Excellence* (New York: Norton, 1987).

Gardner, John. *Self Renewal: The Individual & The Innovative Society* (New York: W.W. Norton, 1981).

Halberstam, David. *The Next Century* (New York: William Morrow Co., 1991).

Hallett, Jeffrey J. *Worklife Visions: Redefining Work for the Information Economy* (Alexandria, VA: Am Soc for Personnel Admin., 1987).

Hamel, G., and Prahalad, C.K. *Competing for the Future* (Boston: Harvard Business School Press, 1994).

Hammer, Michael and Champy, James. *Reengineering the Corporation* (New York: Harper Business, 1993).

Handy, Charles. *The Age of Paradox* (Boston: Harvard Business School Press, 1994).

Handy, Charles. *The Age of Unreason* (London: Arrow Books, 1989).

Hart, Basil Liddell. *Strategy* (2nd rev. ed., New York: Meridian [1991], c.1967).

Henderson, Bruce D. *The Logic of Business Strategy* (Cambridge, MA: Ballinger Publishing Company, 1984).

Henderson, Bruce D. *Henderson on Corporate Strategy* (Cambridge, MA: AH Books, 1979).

Hickman, Craig R., and Silva, Michael A. *Creating Excellence* (New York: NAL Books, 1986).

Hopwood, B. *Whatever Happened to the British Motor Cycle Industry?* (San Leandro, CA: Haynes Publishing Co., 1981).

Johnston, William B. and Packer, Arnold H. *Workforce 2000* (Indianapolis, IN: Hudson Institute, 1987).

Kanter, Rosabeth Moss. *The Changemasters: Innovation for Productivity in the American Corporation* (New York: Simon & Schuster, 1983).

Kaplan, Robert S. and Norton, David P. "The Balanced Scorecard – Measures that Drive Performance", *The Harvard Business Review* (January/February 1992) 71–79.

Katzenbach, Jon R. and Smith, Douglas K. *The Wisdom of Teams: Creating the High-Performance Organization* (Boston: Harvard Business School Press, 1993).

Kelly, James N. and Gouillart, Francis J. *Transforming the Organization* (New York: McGraw-Hill, 1995).

Kennedy, Paul M. *Grand Strategies in War & Peace* (New Haven, CT: Yale University Press, 1991).

Kotter, John P. *The Leadership Factor* (New York: Free Press, 1988).

Lodge, George Cabot. *The New American Ideology* (New York: Knopf, 1975).

Ludeman, Kate. *The Worth Ethic: How to Profit from the Changing Values of the New Work Force* (New York: Dutton, 1984).

Luttwak, Edward N. *Strategy: The Logic of War & Peace* (Cambridge, MA: Belknap Press of Harvard University Press, 1987).

Luttwak, Edward N. *The Grand Strategy of the Roman Empire: From the First Century A.D. to the Third* (Baltimore: Johns Hopkins University Press, 1976).

Luttwak, Edward N. *The Grand Strategy of the Soviet Union* (New York: St. Martin's Press, 1983).

Machiavelli. *The Prince* (New York: Bantam Classic, 1966).

Marakon Associates. *The Dangers of Strategic Intent*.

Michael, Donald N. *On Learning to Plan, and Planning to Learn* (San Francisco: Jossey-Bass, 1973).

Mills, D. Quinn. *The New Competitors: A Report on American Managers from D. Quinn Mills of the Harvard Business School* (New York: John Wiley, 1985).

Mintzberg, Henry. *The Rise and Fall of Strategic Planning* (New York: Macmillan, 1994).

Mobley, Lou, and McKeown, Kate. *Beyond IBM* (New York: McGraw-Hill, 1989).

Naisbitt, John, and Aburdene, Patricia. *Reinventing the Corporation: Transforming Your Job and Your Company for the New Information Society* (New York: Warner Books, 1992).

Ohmae, Kenichi. *The Mind of the Strategist: The Art of Japanese Business* (New York: McGraw-Hill, 1982).

Ouchi, William. "Made in America under Japanese Management" *Harvard Business Review* (September–October 1974) 61–69.

Pascale, Richard Tanner. *Managing on the Edge: How the Smartest Companies Use Conflict to Stay Ahead* (New York: Simon & Schuster, 1991).

Pascarella, Perry. *The New Achievers: Creating a Modern Work Ethic* (New York: Free Press, 1984).

Peters, Tom. *Liberation Management: Necessary Disorganization for the Nanosecond Nineties* (New York: Alfred A. Knopf, 1992).

Peters, Tom, and Austin, Nancy K. *A Passion for Excellence* (New York: Warner Books, 1989).

Peters, T. H., and Waterman, R. H., Jr. *In Search of Excellence* (New York: Harper & Row, 1982).

Porter, Michael E. *Competitive Advantage: Creating and Sustaining Superior Performance* (New York: Free Press, 1985).

Porter, Michael E. *Competitive Strategy: Techniques for Analyzing Industries and Competitors* (New York: Free Press, 1980).

Prahalad, C.K., and Hamel, Gary. "Strategic Intent" *Harvard Business Review* (May/June 1989) 63–76.

Pumpin, Cuno. *The Essence of Corporate Strategy* (Aldershot: Gower, 1987).

Quinn, J.B. *Strategies for Change: Logical Incrementalism* (Homewood, IL: Irwin, 1980).

Reich, Robert B. *The Work of Nations: Preparing Ourselves for 21st Century Capitalism* (New York: A.A. Knopf, 1991).

Ries, Al, and Trout, Jack. *Positioning: The Battle for Your Mind* (New York: McGraw-Hill, 1985).

Ries, Al, and Trout, Jack. *Marketing Warfare* (New York: McGraw-Hill, 1986).

Rodgers, F.G. *The IBM Way* (New York: Harper & Row, 1986).

Rogers, David J. *Waging Business Warfare: Lessons from the Military Masters in Achieving Corporate Superiority* (New York: Charles Scribner's Sons, 1987).

Ross, Gerald and Kay, Michael. *Toppling the Pyramids* (New York: Times Books, 1994).

Rothschild, W.E. *Strategic Alternatives: Selection, Development and Implementation* (New York: AMACOM, 1979).

Rothschild, W.E. "Putting It All Together: A Guide to Strategic Thinking" (New York: AMACOM, 1976).

Sargeunt, H.R., and West, Geoffrey. *Grand Strategy* (New York: Thomas Y. Crowell, 1941).

Sayles, Leonard R.The Working Leader: The Triumph of High Performance over Conventional Management Principles (New York: Free Press, 1993).

Schein, H. Edgar. *Organizational Culture and Leadership* (San Francisco: Jossey-Bass, 1985).

Schein, Edgar G. *Organizational Psychology* (Englewood Cliffs, NJ: Prentice-Hall, 1980).

Schwartz, Peter. *The Art of the Long View* (New York: Doubleday/ Currency, 1991).

Stalk, George, Jr. "Time-Based Competition and Beyond: Competing on Capabilities", *Planning Review* (September/October 1992).

Steiner, G.A. *Strategic Planning: What Every Manager Must Know* (New York: Free Press, 1979).

Summers, Harry, Jr. *On Strategy – A Critical Analysis of the Vietnam War* (Novato, CA: Presidio, 1982).

Summers, Harry, Jr., *On Strategy II – A Critical Analysis of the Gulf War* (New York: Dell, 1992).

Sun Tzu. *The Art of War* (New York: Delacorte Press, 1983).

Thurow, Lester. *Head to Head: The Coming Economic Battle Among Japan, Europe, & America* (New York: Morrow, 1992).

Tichy, Noel M. *Managing Strategic Change: Technical, Political & Cultural Dynamics* (New York: John Wiley, 1983).

Tichy, Noel M., and Sherman, Stratford. *Control Your Own Destiny or Someone Else Will: How Jack Welch is Turning General Electric into the World's Most Competitive Corporation* (New York: Doubleday, 1993).

Toffler, Alvin. *The Third Wave* (New York: William Morrow, 1980).

Toffler, Alvin. *Future Shock* (New York: Random House, 1970).

Tomasko, Robert M. *Rethinking the Corporation: The Architecture of Change* (New York: AMACOM, 1993).

Waddell, William C. *The Outline of Strategy* (Oxford, Ohio: Planning Forum, 1986).

Watson, Thomas, J. *A Business and its Beliefs: The Ideas that Helped Build IBM* (New York: McGraw-Hill, McKinsey Foundation Lecture Series, 1963).

Watzlawich, Paul *et al. Change: Principles of Problem Formation and Problem Resolution* (New York: W.W. Norton, 1974).

Weigley, Russell F. *The Age of Battles: The Quest for Decisive Warfare from Breitenfeld to Waterloo* (Bloomington, IN: Indiana University Press, 1991).

Wheatley, Margaret J. *Leadership and The New Science: Learning about Organization from an Orderly Universe* (San Francisco: Berrett-Koehler, 1992).

Wilkins, Alan L. *Developing Corporate Character: How to Successfully Change an Organization without Destroying It* (San Francisco: Jossey-Bass, 1989).

Wolf, William B (ed.). *Management, Readings towards a general theory* (Belmont, CA:Wadsworth Publishing Company, 1964).

Wright, J. Patrick and DeLorean, John D. *On a Clear Day You Can See General Motors* (Grosse Pointe, MI: Wright Enterprises, 1979).

Zaleznik, Abraham. *The Managerial Mystique: Restoring Leadership in Business* (New York: Harper & Row, 1989).

Zuboff, Shoshana. *In the Age of the Smart Machine: The Future of Work & Power* (New York: Basic Books, 1989).

Index